'Big questions are asked by good scholarly books, and this book helps comparative scholars think more deeply about modernity, justice and democracy through the prism of police development in Taiwan. Well-written and honest in its assessment of policing in contemporary Taiwan, the book is the first detailed treatment of this subject in English; it will remain a landmark publication for many years to come.'

Bill Hebenton, *Centre for Criminology and Criminal Justice, University of Manchester, UK*

'The book is substantial, solidly located in historical and political processes in Taiwan and across the region. It reveals the extraordinary difficulties of developing a democratic police force, not only in organizational structures that enhance democratic traditions, but in the development of policies and practices that actually act democratic toward citizens.

In the world today, we are discovering that democracy itself is neither as strong nor as inevitable as we once thought. This book gives some insights into the enormous historical roadblocks that impede (and sometimes that facilitate) democratic development, and how the move to democratization is tied to larger societal and regional international forces. This book is helpful, not only for those who are interested in Taiwan, but in the broad topic of democratic development itself: It provides insight and detail into the processes that sustain and threaten democratic policing, the ways it can be fortified, and the constant pressures to relent and let democracy fail.'

John Crank, *Professor, School of Criminology and Criminal Justice, University of Nebraska, Omaha, USA*

Policing in Taiwan

The police in Taiwan played a critical role in the largely peaceful transition from an authoritarian regime to a democracy. While the temptation to intervene in domestic politics was great, the top-down pressure to maintain a neutral standing facilitated an orderly regime change. This is the first monograph to examine the role of the police as a linkage between the state and civil society during the democratic transition and the role of the police in contemporary Taiwan.

Starting with a brief history of Taiwan, this book examines the development of policing in Taiwan from a comparative, environmental, historical, operational, philosophical, and political perspective; considers the role of the police in the democratic transition; and draws comparisons between police cultures in the East and in the West – both now and in the past. Taiwan operates as a modern country within an East Asian culture and this book shows that Taiwan's move towards democracy may have political ramifications for the rest of the nations in the area. Including references to literature on policing in China and the United States, this book about Taiwan police may serve as a springboard for academics and students to learn about similar cultures in this important area of the world.

Policing in Taiwan will be of interest to academics and students who are engaged in the study of criminology, criminal justice, policing studies, and Asian studies, as well as the general reader.

Liqun Cao (曹立群) is Professor of sociology and criminology at the University of Ontario Institute of Technology, Canada. He also holds an adjunct appointment at Hunan University and has published numerous refereed journal articles. He is the author of *Major Criminological Theories: Concepts and Measurement* (2004) and is a co-editor of the *Routledge Handbook of Chinese Criminology* (2014). His co-authored paper "Crime volume and law and order culture" (2007) won the 2008 ACJS Donal MacNamara Award for the best article of the year.

Lanying Huang (黃蘭媖) is an Assistant Professor in the Graduate School of Criminology at National Taipei University, Taiwan. Her research interests include policing, victimology, and restorative justice.

Ivan Y. Sun (孙懿贤) is Professor in the Department of Sociology and Criminal Justice at the University of Delaware. His research interests include police attitudes and behavior, public assessments of criminal justice, and crime and justice in Chinese societies. He has published more than 60 refereed journal articles since 2002 and is a co-editor of the *Routledge Handbook of Chinese Criminology* (2014). His most recent publications have appeared in *Justice Quarterly, Crime and Delinquency*, and the *Journal of Criminal Justice*.

Routledge Frontiers of Criminal Justice

1 **Sex Offenders: Punish, Help, Change or Control?**
   Theory, policy and practice explored
   Edited by Jo Brayford, Francis Cowe and John Deering

2 **Building Justice in Post-Transition Europe**
   Processes of criminalisation within Central and Eastern European societies
   Edited by Kay Goodall, Margaret Malloch and Bill Munro

3 **Technocrime, Policing and Surveillance**
   Edited by Stéphane Leman-Langlois

4 **Youth Justice in Context**
   Community, compliance and young people
   Mairead Seymour

5 **Women, Punishment and Social Justice**
   Human rights and penal practices
   Margaret Malloch and Gill McIvor

6 **Handbook of Policing, Ethics and Professional Standards**
   Edited by Allyson MacVean, Peter Spindler and Charlotte Solf

7 **Contrasts in Punishment**
   An explanation of Anglophone excess and Nordic exceptionalism
   John Pratt and Anna Eriksson

8 **Victims of Environmental Harm**
   Rights, recognition and redress under national and international law
   Matthew Hall

9   **Doing Probation Work**
    Identity in a criminal justice occupation
    Rob C. Mawby and Anne Worrall

10 **Justice Reinvestment**
    Can the criminal justice system deliver more for less?
    Chris Fox, Kevin Albertson and Kevin Wong

11 **Epidemiological Criminology**
    Theory to practice
    Edited by Eve Waltermaurer and Timothy A. Akers

12 **Policing cities**
    Urban securitization and regulation in a twenty-first century world
    Edited by Randy K. Lippert and Kevin Walby

13 **Restorative Justice in Transition**
    Kerry Clamp

14 **International perspectives on police education and training**
    Edited by Perry Stanislas

15 **Understanding Penal Practice**
    Edited by Ioan Durnescu and Fergus McNeill

16 **Perceptions of Criminal Justice**
    Vicky De Mesmaecker

17 **Transforming Criminal Justice?**
    Problem-solving and court specialization
    Jane Donoghue

18 **Policing in Taiwan**
    From authoritarianism to democracy
    Liqun Cao, Lanying Huang and Ivan Y. Sun

Policing in Taiwan
From authoritarianism to democracy

Liqun Cao, Lanying Huang and
Ivan Y. Sun

LONDON AND NEW YORK

First published 2014 by Routledge

2 Park Square, Milton Park, Abingdon, Oxon OX14 4RN
711 Third Avenue, New York, NY 10017, USA

Routledge is an imprint of the Taylor & Francis Group, an informa business

First issued in paperback 2016

Copyright © 2014 Liqun Cao, Lanying Huang and Ivan Y. Sun

The right of Liqun Cao, Lanying Huang and Ivan Y. Sun to be identified as the authors of this work has been asserted by them in accordance with sections 77 and 78 of the Copyright, Designs and Patents Act 1988.

This book is partially funded by a small grant from the Chiang Ching-Kuo Foundation for International Scholarly Exchange (本書由蔣經國國際學術交流基金會補助).

All rights reserved. No part of this book may be reprinted or reproduced or utilised in any form or by any electronic, mechanical, or other means, now known or hereafter invented, including photocopying and recording, or in any information storage or retrieval system, without permission in writing from the publishers.

Notice:
Product or corporate names may be trademarks or registered trademarks, and are used only for identification and explanation without intent to infringe.

British Library Cataloguing in Publication Data
A catalogue record for this book is available from the British Library

Library of Congress Cataloging-in-Publication Data
Cao, Liqun.
Policing in Taiwan : from authoritarianism to democracy / Liqun Cao, Lanying Huang and Ivan Y. Sun.
pages cm. – (Routledge frontiers of criminal justice ; 18)
Includes bibliographical references and index.

1. Police–Taiwan. 2. Democratization–Taiwan. I. Huang, Lanying. II. Sun, Ivan Y. III. Title.
HV8262.A2C36 2014
363.20951249--dc23
2013045404

ISBN 978-1-138-66603-0 (pbk)
ISBN 978-0-415-52977-8 (hbk)
ISBN 978-0-203-55074-8 (ebk)

Typeset in Times New Roman
by Sunrise Setting Ltd, Paignton, UK

Contents

List of figures	xii
List of tables	xiii
Preface	xiv
Acknowledgements	xviii
Abbreviations and laws	xix
Romanization of Chinese names	xx

1 Introduction: the great transition   1

    Taiwan: a brief history   4
    A few key terms   8
    The organization of the book   10

PART I
Historical developments   13

2 Policing under martial law   15

    The social and political environment of Taiwan
      before the repeal of martial law   15
    Police functions and powers under martial law   21
    Initial reform before the lifting of martial law   26

3 Policing during the democratic transition   30

    Legal mandates as sources of authority   31
    Dealing with a challenging work environment   35
    Community policing: innovation or new wine in old bottles?   38

4	**Policing in the new century**	43
	Minimizing political influence	44
	Attempting to enhance service quality	47
	Maintaining core missions	51

PART II
Critical issues 57

5	**Training, education, and promotion**	59
	The making of the rank-and-file	62
	The cultivation of police supervisors	64
	Promotion	68

6	**Police culture**	73
	Occupational outlooks	75
	Operational behavior	79
	Organizational cultures	82

7	**Police misconduct and corruption: déjà vu experience?**	87
	Policing underground societies	89
	Police misconduct in the Taiwanese context	92
	Electronic gambling machines, prostitution, and the gravel truck industry	95
	Controlling police misconduct and corruption	96

PART III
Emerging challenges 101

8	**Female officers on the move**	103
	From clerks in the office to co-workers on the street: the historical development of female officers	103
	Female officers in the literature	109
	Barriers facing female officers	113

9	**Policing socially disadvantaged groups: criminalization or victimization?**	118
	The socially disadvantaged groups	119
	Aboriginal governance	121

	Yesterday's criminals, today's victims? Policing immigrants	124
	Policing violence against women	127
10	**Confidence in the police**	132
	Police legitimacy and performance	133
	Citizen evaluations of the police	136
	Comparison with other societies in the world	139
11	**Coda: Taiwan's conundrum**	145
	Chiang Ching-Kuo's legacy	145
	Implication of Taiwan's democracy for China	148
	Democratic deficits of Taiwan's police	153

Appendix: Chinese names and nouns with their romanization   158
References   160
Index   183

Figures

1.1	The map of Taiwan	5
2.1	The confrontation during the Formosa Incident in 1979	18
3.1	Getting ready for the upcoming parade	33
4.1	Community policing: chatting with residents about their concerns	48
8.1	Number of male and female police officers (2001–12)	104
8.2	The selection rates for female and male applicants in CPU	108
8.3	The selection rates for female and male applicants in Taiwan Police College	108

Tables

2.1	Civil–police relations in Taiwan 1949–87	23
2.2	Backgrounds of presidents of Central Police University	24
3.1	Violent, property, and total crime rates, 1980–98	35
3.2	Number and percentage of assemblies and parades, 1988–2000	37
5.1	The ranks of Taiwan police	61

Preface

Policing in Taiwan is a significant and welcome contribution to the study of democratic policing. I would argue that it is a fine representative of what is now called comparative police studies. Although police studies have expanded to include a wide variety of countries and types of policing, what might be called democratic police charged with national security, with the exception of the London Metropolitan Police, have not been well-studied. Even given a long history of concern about policing in the context of democracy and studies of the French gendarmerie, the Royal Irish Constabulary, the Royal Ulster Constabulary, and the Garda of Ireland, few studies take up the role of the police in promoting democratic practices and how a democratic polity shapes policing. This remains true in spite of the early and important works of that sought police reform, in part because they examined well-established and long legitimated police systems, and in part because they focused on police administration rather than policing. Systematic police studies, those relying on a mix of observations, records, official statistics and historical records, perhaps can be benchmarked by the early work of Michael Banton (1964) and the foundational work of David Bayley on the police and political development in India (1969). These were powerful and illuminating studies with an implicit framework of governance, legitimacy, and public trust. Bayley examined the political context within which the police organization worked. Bayley and later scholars took Western European policing, and one of the faces of Peel's innovations in policing as a model. When it is called the "Peel model" in textbooks, it is a misleading solecism that conflates the dualistic nature of Peel's contribution: the security force, hidden, armed and dangerous, and the deterrence-based visible, unarmed, reactive police. Of course, everyday policing always portends violence. The tension between these two "faces" of the forces of order remains in all democracies.

Many important police studies published in English post-1970 were of single nations, especially historical analyses. In due course, the horizon of police studies widened and spread outside the European continent (Bayley's being an exception in the late 1960s). This shift in the horizon was facilitated by changes in communication (social media, the internet, cell phones, and cheap international interactions such as Skype), inexpensive travel, a new ease of crossing what once were international borders, European economic integration and international trade agreements. These served to decrease social distance across cultures and nations, and to confound time, space, and identity. These processes are indicated in part by "globalization," and encouraged scholars to broaden their horizons.

Scholarly interest in international, comparative and cross-cultural studies of policing escalated in part because of American expansionism and invasions of Iraq and Afghanistan and the efforts of the American government to export "community policing" now defined as a commodity (Brogden and Nijhar 2013). New research exploring democratic policing in various forms appeared, arising from disciplines such as anthropology and criminal justice. Economic developments in the pan-Pacific area and the South China seaboard (Macau, Taiwan, mainland China, and Hong Kong) raised the question anew the role of policing in development.

As these studies unfolded in the early years of this century, several things emerged. The idea of "democratic policing," a yet undefined concept, was featured in part because it had wide political appeal in developing nations. In due course, studies of democratic policing were based on a variety of materials-official data, attitude surveys, historical records, narratives, and media reports and pictures. The research somehow resembled pieces of a puzzle or answers to a question: what are the police good for? As a result, there is now a base of comparative, cross-cultural research on policing that shares some of these concurrent themes.

Now consider *Policing in Taiwan: from authoritarianism to democracy*. Cao, Huang, and Sun present us here with a well-argued and informative piece of the puzzle of comparative policing. They have carved out an imaginative analysis of the transformation of the police in Taiwan from 1945 to the present. This work builds on research, their own studies as well as relevant historical materials. The book includes an introduction, a historical overview of developments in the nation in this century, and further chapters on crime control, policing in the new century, police training, police culture, police misconduct, female officers, policing socially disadvantaged groups, confidence in the police, and a coda. The overall theme of these chapters is changes and adjustments in policing in the context of changes in governance since 1987. This means that the authors chart carefully changes in the political winds as they shape police training, practices, and leadership.

The thread of the development of policing is followed in this book from the arrival of the Guomindang (GMD) and Chiang Kai-Shek through the election of an alternative political party in 2000 and subsequent political changes. This is not a story without twists and turns of fate, including dealing with indigenous peoples, imposing and terminating martial law, managing a succession crisis revolving around the elevation of Chiang's son to leadership, and facing the consequences of massive rapid economic development. Politics, or questions of power and control, suffuse the story with life and new, unexpected contingencies. The book addresses themes of colonial conquest; cultural and nationalistic conflicts; international attention; and outbursts of violence that echo the democratization process in other nations, Ireland and South Africa, for example.

Perhaps the most telling aspect of the story Cao, Huang, and Sun construct is the close historic and socio-emotional connections between the people of the island and their rulers, both Japan and China, in the course of the previous century. The island has been considered a part of China and a Japanese province in the previous one hundred years. One might add, of course, the powerful effects of American economic and political support. There are a sizable number of indigenous peoples for whom policing remains problematic. As the authors write, "The principle of equality for all is not the dominant philosophical theme found in Confucianism." In addition, there is growing political interest in developing further the relationship between Taiwan and mainland China. As is the case elsewhere in the South China seaboard, the growing power of China is a somewhat unpredictable looming force.

The authors also describe changes in policing in the context of an emerging democracy, and tie this development to changes in party politics and elections, shifts in the global economy and the shaping of policing by traditional Confucian tenets or epigrams. As is shown in developed and other nations, in Taiwan, police organizations are facing the problem of ensuring equality of treatment of officers in regard to promotion, transfers, and perks of office; they have difficulty "managing" and controlling the lower participants; they are subject to media events and scandals of little scandals and big theatre or national media-amplified crises, and they struggle to get training right for policing in the rapidly changing world. The system remains strikingly two-tiered: officers are produced in the Central Police University, while lower participants, unlikely ever to achieve officer rank, are trained at the Taiwan Police College. The police top commanders support higher education and skills based examinations, and urge "professionalism" in the force, and these emphases will doubtless have continuing affects.

The most fascinating aspect of the lower participants' work is their enormous diligence, hard work, long hours, and low pay which are seen in the context of elegant modes of negotiation and mediation. This is also shown in studies in Taiwan by the anthropologist Jeffery T. Martin (Martin 2007). Cao, Huang, and Sun illustrate how the blend of Confucian ethics and civility unfolds in complex, potentially explosive situations. The vague notion driving many socio-legal studies, that police engage in "law enforcement," is shown to be irrelevant in this kind of nuanced problem-solving on the ground. The relationship between marginalized peoples and the police remain problematic and changing. Chapter 10 shows an uneasy distrust of the police according to attitude surveys, and the imbrication, intertwining, of procedural and outcomes-based policing in Taiwan.

The authors have pieced together the available data on trust and legitimacy to show a manageable acceptance of policing, even though attitudes of officers concerning their authority are likely to be more "traditional" than those of the public. Yet, the police remain close to the people they serve and are entangled in a web of obligation. In a culture governed still by Confucian "situational ethics" and a long and powerful tradition of gift-giving, especially during holidays, these exchanges are sanctioned, are culturally contexted, locally patterned, and exquisitely complex, given the role of the officer.

This book is the first systematic overview of recent developments in policing in Taiwan and it joins other studies in a rich environment of comparative and cross-cultural work on democratic policing. The authors have also brought to the surface the complex set of forces of the economy, party politics, and governance in general that shape police organizations and policing as a practice in Taiwan. It is significant that in the course of this narrative, the authors illustrate the growing concern with equality and justice in Taiwan as in other democratic societies. It might be argued, as did John Rawls in *The Laws of the Peoples* (1999), that democratic practices are inevitably culturally shaped.

Peter K. Manning
Elmer V.H. and Eileen M. Brooks
Professor of Criminology and Criminal Justice,
Northeastern University, Boston USA
November 14, 2013

Acknowledgements

We would like to offer our sincerest appreciation to Charles Chang, Charles Hou, Susyan Jou, Weide Mon, Jim Sheu, and their associates working in Taiwan. This book project is partially funded by a small grant from Chiang Ching-Kuo Foundation for International Scholarly Exchange. In terms of content and development of arguments, the book benefits considerably from the constructive criticisms provided by Professor Nicholas Lovrich of Washington State University. We also wish to thank the administrative assistance rendered by the staff headed by Hui-hua Lin at the Graduate School of Criminology, National Taipei University.

Thanks likewise go to the staff at Police Torch and the Central News Agency for their assistance in searching for suitable photos to represent different stages of policing in Taiwan. We especially wish to state our appreciation to Chen Hsiu Yuan for him allowing us to use his award-winning photo.

This project was facilitated by Liqun Cao's sabbatical leave of 2012–13 from the University of Ontario Institute of Technology. Liqun is appreciative of National Taipei University's provision of a grant for a short visit to the campus in May 2013. Hong Chen, Tzer-Chang Liu, Rui-Hung Yeh and Feilin Chen deserve credits for assisting Liqun in conducting various fact-finding and fact-confirmation tasks. Finally, Liqun Cao wants to dedicate his portion of the book to the fond memory of his grand-uncle Shaw Yuan-Bin (邵元彬, 1918–2013), who graduated from the Central Police Academy in Chongqing in 1939 and retired as a police superintendent in Taipei in 1983.

Tom Sutton, Nicola Hartley (2010–12) and Heidi Lee of Routledge were all very supportive of and helpful to this project. Tom and Heidi spent time in developing the most appropriate title for the book, and Heidi's skillful copyediting provided a professional and precise presentation of our ideas. We are grateful in having had you as our editors.

Abbreviations and laws

Accord on Anti-crime Collaboration and Mutual Legal Assistance across the Strait 海峽兩岸共同打擊犯罪與司法互助協議
Act Governing Relations between the People of the Taiwan Area and the Mainland Area 臺灣地區與大陸地區人民關係條例
Act of Gender Equality in Employment 性別工作平等法 (AGEE)
Assembly Law 集會遊行法
Anti-hoodlum Law 檢肅流氓條例
Child Welfare Law 兒童福利法
Chinese Community Party 中国共产党 (CCP)
Civil Organization Law 人民團體法
Civil Service Administrative Neutrality Law 公務人員行政中立法
Central Police University 中央警察大學 (CPU)
Democratic Progressive Party 民主進步黨 (DPP)
Domestic Violence Prevention Act 家庭暴力防治法
Guomingdang 国民党 (GMD, or Kuomingtang, KMT)
Jinmen Accord 金門協議
Juvenile Welfare Law 少年福利法
Law for the Punishment of Police Offenses 违警罚法
Local Autonomy Statute 地方自治法
Martial Law (戒嚴令)
National Police Agency 警政署 (NPA)
National Security Law 國家安全法 (NSL)
People's Republic of China 中华人民共和国 (PRC)
Police Law 警察法
Republic of China 中华民国 (ROC)
Social Order Maintenance Law 社會秩序維護法
Taiwan Garrison Command 臺灣警備總部
Taiwan Police College 台灣警察專科學校 (TPC)
The Provisional Amendment for the Period of Mobilization of the Suppression of Communist Rebellion (動員戡亂時期臨時條款)
Three Anti-Violence Act 防暴三法

Romanization of Chinese names

The problem of rendering Chinese ideographs into a romanized form raises several issues worth noting. The three most common ways to romanize Chinese names into English are: (1) the Wade–Giles system used on Taiwan; (2) the *pinyin* system used in mainland China; and (3) idiosyncratic spellings and English–Chinese name combinations adopted by individual authors themselves. This text uses the *pinyin* throughout (with some exceptions for personal names that are long familiar in the west, notably names such as Chiang Kai-Shek). It was chosen for use because it is the most widely used romanization system outside of Taiwan, and because there is no single authoritative system among the several in use in Taiwan.

To avoid undue confusion, all Chinese names and important terms appear with the *pinyin* for the first time. The Romanization Table in the Appendix provides the name of each Chinese as used in the text; the same name appears in the Wade–Giles system; and the name is given in *pinyin* system.

1 Introduction
The great transition

One of the most significant social and political changes taking place in the course of the last quarter of the twentieth century was the *third wave of democratization* (Huntington 1991; Zhao and Cao 2010). The high point of this historical development occurred when the Soviet Empire collapsed in the early 1990s. Before the demise of the former Soviet Union, Eastern European nations as well as many East Asian nations such as Taiwan, South Korea, and the Philippines either transformed into or began the process of taking form as functional democracies without a great deal of blood of their citizens being shed (Cao and Dai 2006). By the mid-1990s, the number of democratic nations had surpassed the number of non-democratic societies in the world for the first time in human history (LaFree 2007).

While the removal of the Soviet threat was a primary facilitating condition for the democratic changes being made in Eastern Europe, the democratic transformation in Taiwan shortly before that period of tumult was a considerably more complex case of democratization involving the interaction of domestic and global milieus and a series of intensive confrontations between the long-time ruling party and newly formed opposition parties. The rapid economic growth experienced in the late 1950s and throughout the 1960s in combination with the unfavorable international political environment in the 1970s gave rise to a mounting demand for democratic change in Taiwan. Riding the third wave of democratization, "the great transition" as it is known in Taiwan (Tien 1989) has been slow but steady toward democratic political development. This change could not have taken place in a relatively peaceful manner without the neutral roles played by the military and the security apparatus – the police being a major part of that apparatus – since both uniformed forces had been frequently mobilized by the ruling Guomingdang (GMD, 国民党) or nationalist party to suppress political dissent and contain the influence of opposition groups. While almost all aspects of Taiwan's democratic transition have been studied extensively and a large volume of often excellent research is available to researchers, thus far the police have received very little attention in this connection. With a focus on the police in Taiwan, this monograph contributes to a better understanding of Taiwan's transition to democracy by addressing the following four major questions: (1) Why did the police behave the way they did during the democratization period? (2) What aspects of police work have changed during the transition? (3) What remains the same as the past for the police as a social control institution? and (4) What are the new challenges for the police since the institutionalization of democracy in Taiwan?

Taiwan was selected as the research project first and foremost because of the political ramifications for the rest of the nations in the area, in particular China, North Korea, and Vietnam. Taiwan operates as a modern nation within an East Asian culture which features a long tradition of despotism and contains the religious heritages of Buddhism, Confucianism, and Taoism. The political regime's legitimacy before the democratic transformation was based primarily on violence and intimidation, and relied only secondarily on persuasion of the population and consultation with societal elites. The mantra associated with the ruling party was that "the gun and cannon" engendered the government. For thousands of years of Chinese history, people who emerged from the periodic power struggles to become the rulers were in general the more violent and the more vicious among the competitors, and within limitations they could maintain their mysterious mandate from a vaguely understood "heaven" overseeing the competition. The prevailing Western explanation of the East Asian proclivity toward authoritarianism points to the underlying culture. The political scientist Lucian Pye (1985), for example, posits that the "Chinese mentality" is responsible for the sustained and seemingly unbreakable authoritarian rule witnessed in Chinese societies. It is argued that Chinese culture is fundamentally different from Western culture in a number of important respects, and it is not conducive to the values of individual rights and social freedoms that undergird Western civil society and thereby permit the development of democracy. This thesis of *cultural exceptionalism* is not new. It bears an impressive social-science pedigree, harkening back to the political sociology of Max Weber. Taiwan's case, however, shows that democracy can indeed grow and prosper on Chinese cultural soil. Its democratic transition may set up an example for China – whose relationship with Taiwan is perhaps best described as "inseparable separation" (Huang 2010). We extend the analysis, wherever it is relevant, to include the literature on policing in China and the US, offering a general comparison of the challenges of policing in the East and the West at present and into the foreseeable future.

Second, Taiwan was selected because of its relatively moderate dislocations experienced during the country's democratic transition. Unlike the precipitous fall of Marcos in the Philippines, or the large-scale unrest taking place in South Korea in the mid-1980s, Taiwan's transition to democracy was relatively peaceful and orderly. As was the case in these other Asian nations, Taiwan was under the authoritarian rule of Guomingdang (GMD) until 1987. With the passing of the GMD's long-time leader Chiang Kai-Shek (蔣介石) in 1975, the regime embarked on its slow but steady journey toward democracy. The speed of the democratic transition greatly accelerated after the death of Chiang Kai-Shek's successor and son, Chiang Ching-Kuo (蔣经国) in 1988. Taiwan became a full-fledged democracy by any standard when the oppositional party – the Democratic Progressive Party or DPP (民进党) – won the general presidential election in 2000. All these large scale changes were accomplished with minimum blood being shed and without any societal catharsis taking place.

This monograph aims to accomplish a deeper understanding of this unique society situated within the East Asian culture zone through a focus on the police. It is essential for students in the throes of globalization to understand the variations of police behavior to be found in societies that are quite different from their own. Taiwan is a good choice for such study because it is situated in a dynamic area of the world experiencing dramatic economic growth and may represent a typical case of democratic transition for fast-developing East Asian societies as a whole. Sen (1999a), for example, argues elegantly that economic development by its very nature entails an increase of freedom and the expansion of individual choices in life, and by extension, moves a society toward democracy. To put it somewhat differently, democracy is possibly a political concomitant to modernity. Taiwan's record of parallel economic and democratic development would seem to lend support to this line of argument (Chao and Myers 1998; Lipset 1959; Tien 1989; Weller 1999). Therefore, Taiwan may serve as a springboard for students to learn about similar cultures in this important area of the world. To address our research questions listed above, we use mainly historical and comparative analytical methods.

The police represent the principal subject matter of this research project for several reasons. First, police behavior generally reflects the values and norms of the society that creates formal law enforcement institutions. One of the criticisms of the existing literature on the democratic transition in Taiwan is that these elsewise important works (e.g., Chao and Myers 1998; Copper 2005; Dickson 1998; Moody 1992; Rigger 1999; Weller 1999) focus on the change in content of *high culture* – that is, the ideological and philosophical changes at the top of societal intellectual thought. What is too often missing in this literature are the critical institutional changes that link the prevailing political culture with ground-level activities affecting the lives of citizens. In this connection, the police are arguably the most important institution of formal social control in society. In general, the police as an organization tend to be conservative and supportive of the status quo (Zhao 1996). Why/how did the police in Taiwan maintain a neutral role in the democratic transition is one of the most important questions addressed in this book. Additionally, the police matter greatly in societies experiencing the democratic transition because predictable setbacks and disappointments associated with the process have a marked tendency toward inspiring violence and extreme actions, and because the police itself needs to adapt to a new model of *democratic policing* (Cao and Dai 2006). During the transition when demonstrations and civil disorder were virtually daily events, it was extremely difficult for the police to carry out their duties when all newly freed media eyes were upon them and the going was roughest on the street-level cop and their superior officers. The democratic transition was accompanied by a combination of increased crime, heightened social tensions, and elevated public sensitivity to both. It was a time when police work was peculiarly complicated and required a delicate balance of values. Their work "can sustain or erode the quality of democratic life" (Manning 2010: vii). Consequently, we examine the critical role of the police during the

4 *Introduction: the great transition*

democratic transition, and portray the police as a key point of linkage between the state and civil society.

Finally, and a fortiori, the democratic principle of the rule of law is best reflected in the practice of the police. This study of the police in Taiwan features the authoritarian or undemocratic policing practices employed before 1987, democratic policing practices institutionalized after 2000, and the transitional policing practices carried out in-between. This assessment of policing provides a vantage point for examining the democratization of Taiwanese society as a whole. The democratic reform of the police must take into account cultural factors. It has to address the problem of resistance to the change – with that change requiring moving away from the traditional and Confucian cultural heritage at the ground level in regards to employing female officers, the management of corruption, and the lack of commitment to the observance of universal human rights. We now begin our narrative on the police of Taiwan with an historical overview.

Taiwan: a brief history

Taiwan is an island surrounded by the East China Sea, the Philippine Sea, the South China Sea, and the Taiwan Strait, located off the southeastern coast of China, see Figure 1.1. The Taiwan Strait is approximately 200 kilometers wide, separating the island from mainland China and keeping Taiwan at arm's length from China's direct political influence. Taiwan has maintained a status of de facto independent political entity after the GMD government was defeated in the Chinese Civil War (1946–9) and retreated to the island in 1949. The geographical area of Taiwan is 35,980 square kilometers, slightly smaller than the combined areas of Maryland and Delaware in the US (Lai *et al.* 2010). Currently, there are nearly twenty-three million people living in Taiwan.

The earliest Chinese settlements on Taiwan began in the seventh century CE, coming chiefly from the mainland provinces of Fujian and Guangdong. The island was reached in 1590 by the Portuguese, who named it Formosa (i.e., beautiful island). The Dutch assumed control of the entire island in 1641. They were forced to abandon Taiwan in 1662 when Zheng Chenggong (Koxinga 郑成功, 1624–62), a general of the Ming Dynasty of China who was forced to flee from the Manchu invasion, invaded the island, defeated the Dutch, seized the entire island, and established an independent kingdom. That island kingdom was short-lived, however, falling to the Manchu regime of China (the Qing Dynasty) and becoming part of China again in 1683 as a prefecture of Fujian Province.

In 1885, the Qing elevated the status of Taiwan from a prefecture of Fujian to Taiwan Province, the twentieth in the empire, with its capital in Taipei. This elevation of Taiwan's status was accompanied by a modernization effort that included building Taiwan's first railroad and starting the modern postal service. These actions on the part of China were interpreted as an anxious reaction to Japan's earlier successful annexation of Ryūkyū Kingdom, which had been a tributary nation of China. Japan renamed the kingdom Okinawa, and made it a prefecture of Japan in 1879.

Introduction: the great transition 5

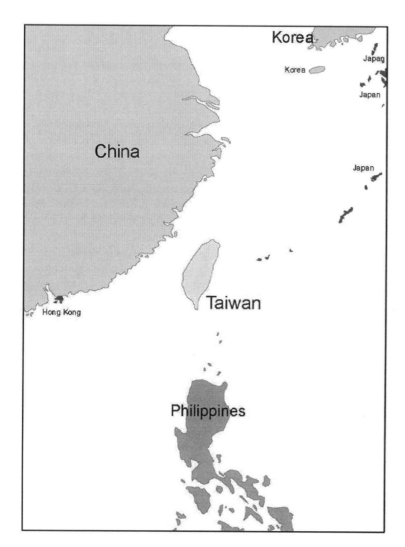

Figure 1.1 The map of Taiwan.

A mere ten years later, however, Japan acquired Taiwan by the *Treaty of Shimonoseki* (1895) as an outcome of the Jia-wu Sino-Japanese War. The Japanese occupation represented a watershed event in Taiwan's history. Before this period, Taiwan was largely unruly and ungovernable, engaged in frequent battles with the aborigines, with foreign invaders, with the central government, and among groups on the island. In accordance with *The Cairo Declaration of 1943* and *The Potsdam Conference of 1945*, China regained sovereignty over Taiwan and made it a province after World War II. In 1949, the Chinese Communist Party (CCP) gained complete control of the mainland and founded the People's Republic of China (PRC). Chiang Kai-Shek and the GMD were forced to take refuge on the island, continuing to use its official name – the Republic of China (ROC).

It is interesting to note that both the GMD and CCP were considered Leninist parties which shared a similar ideological beginning (Cheng 1989; Dickson 1998; Moody 1992; Tien 1989). Chiang Kai-Shek formally resumed his duties as the President of ROC on March 1, 1950. Since that time, there have been two separate, independent regimes sharing Chinese culture and historical connection facing each other across the Taiwan Strait.

Along with two million mainlanders, the GMD government also brought martial law to the island, which was initially declared in the mainland in 1932. On May 19, 1949, General Chen Cheng (陈诚), who had been sworn in as the governor of Taiwan, ordered that martial law become effective the next day at zero hours on the grounds that communist troops were moving into Fujian province, thus threatening Taiwan which had been designated a combat area in China's civil war. As the Chinese Civil War continued without truce, the GMD built up military fortifications throughout the island while it implemented three major economic policies: (1) price stabilization; (2) import substitution behind a protectionist tariff; and (3) land-to-the-tiller reform in agriculture, which greatly improved the lives of the peasants by allowing tenant farmers to purchase their own land. With US aid, Taiwan enjoyed spectacular economic growth after 1950. The economic boom greatly increased the middle class of the country and fundamentally changed the social structure of the society. One of the positive consequences of the Leninist-style party was that the GMD government popularized education through competitive examinations, which has always been an important vehicle for social mobility in Confucian society. With successful economic development, increased access to education (Lipset 1959), and a limited experience with grass-roots elections (Chao and Myers 1998), Taiwan was ready for further political change toward democracy in the 1980s.

The process of broad-scale liberalization and democratization began in Taiwan soon after the death of Chiang Kai-Shek in 1975 and the succession to power by his son Chiang Ching-Kuo (1978–88). Under the pressure of mass social movements and some actual defiance of police authority, the younger Chiang initiated a series of reforms, including lifting the imposition of martial law in 1987. Li Denghui (李登辉), a Taiwan native, succeeded Chiang Ching-Kuo as president in 1988 and began to accelerate the process of democratization. In the 1991 election for a new national assembly, the ruling GMD held on to a majority but the Democratic Progressive Party (DPP) won nearly a third of the seats, forming a credible opposition party. In 1996, the first direct election of the president was held and Li Denghui was duly elected as the president. In the 2000 presidential election, a GMD split resulted in the election of the opposition DPP candidate Chen Shuibian (陈水扁), signaling the completion of Taiwan's democratic transition.

The police system in Taiwan represented an extension of the police in mainland China. It was also influenced by the Japanese system of the *koban*, mini-station, established during the Japanese occupation of Taiwan between 1895 and 1945 (Alarid and Wang 2000; Martin 2007; Sun and Chu 2006). As the GMD was a Leninist-style party in nature (Dickson 1998; Moody 1992), it borrowed many practices, typical of high policing, from the former Soviet Union. The primary allegiance of the police force was to the GMD and to supreme leader Chiang Kai-shek, not to the civil society, nor even to the duly established civilian government. The Soviet advisors also introduced to the military and the police the *commissar system* as a method of control by the political party. The police in Taiwan were trained to see themselves as "a revolutionary force," guarding the republican ideal of its founding father Dr Sun Yat-sen. The effective suppression of political dissent, moreover, was viewed by President and Generalissimo Chiang Kai-shek as an integral part of policing.

As Taiwan's authoritarian regime underwent a slow process of "softening" (Winckler 1984) since Chiang Ching-Kuo's tenure (1977–88), the practice of celebrating the revolutionary force role had become largely irrelevant and police professionalism began to emerge in the country. The corresponding change in time to democratic policing practice represents a common path of adaptation to the external environment at the most general level (Zhao 1996). Consistent with the prevailing democracy, current law enforcement forces in Taiwan can be seen as a paramilitary force operating fully within a civilian government and are committed to being accountable to the rule of law, and ultimately to the democratically elected Legislative Yuan. Surviving the democratic transition largely intact, the police have been seen increasingly as "the thin blue line." This concept of the thin blue line (Brogden 2005) captures the idea that when major state structures suffer from varying degrees of stress and from legitimacy crisis, the police acting as a neutral and professional institution can play a key role in preserving the social order and promoting the regaining of legitimacy on the part of governmental institutions.

Under the authoritarian regime, the social order was maintained through often draconian measures – the "white terror" – and the legal system was built principally on fear as opposed to the careful building of consensus and shared values. With the demise of the authoritarian regime, the people of Taiwan have become the masters of their own fate, and they have for the first time in their history enjoyed freedom of choice in their government. Ideally, a liberal democracy is defined by "the extent to which a political system allows political liberties and democratic rule" (Bollen 1993: 1208). The enforcement of contracts, regulations, protection of freedoms, and sole claim on the legitimate use of violence allow the state to protect its citizens and guard their freedoms. Via these functions, the state is able to create the space for each citizen to live a "good" life. In time, the recrudescence of ethnic intolerance and inflated political conflicts, such as those of natives versus "out-provincials" (*waishengren*, 外省人), resurfaced in Taiwan during the transition to democracy. The opposition party portrayed Taiwan as being occupied largely by "foreign" invaders who came from mainland China in 1949; meanwhile they defined people who came to or lived in Taiwan before 1949 as "natives." Their strategy was successful, and the political partisan divide has become the major "official" line of alignment ever since. During the democratic

8 *Introduction: the great transition*

transition, a new social order based on the principles of civil society had not yet been built up to replace the old mechanisms of social control. As the last thin blue line, the police in Taiwan lived up to the task of carrying out neutral, equitable, and effective maintenance of order assignments during the bumpy democratic transition period.

In summary, Taiwan has prospered and become one of East Asia's economic "Tigers." From 1951 to 2007, the gross national product (GNP) per capita has ascended more than one hundred-fold, from US$145 to US$17,542 (National Statistics, ROC Taiwan, 2009). The government and people of Taiwan not only have succeeded in creating an economic miracle, but they have also completed a challenging journey to democracy as well (Cao and Dai 2006; Clark 2001; Copper 1997).

A few key terms

Confucius regards the *rectification of names* as the first task of government. "If names are not correct, language will not be in accordance with the truth of things" (Xia *et al.* 1996: 209) and this failure at name rectification in time would lead to the end of justice, to anarchy, and ultimately to war. Before we discuss further the police in Taiwan, a brief introduction of the contemporary societal role of police will help place the issue in an appropriate historical context and lead to an appreciation of the rectification of names phenomenon in Taiwan.

The contemporary police all over the world share a common goal of crime prevention as their dominant theme (Cao and Hou 2001). The police represent the technological and organizational answer to the Hobbesian question of social order, the *deus ex machina*. Beneath this rather superficial similarity, however, the nature and practice of policing vary a great deal across nations (Lai *et al.* 2010). The most fundamental dividing line is the practice of *high policing* versus *low policing* historically (Bordue 1968; Chapman 1970) and democratic policing versus undemocratic policing contemporarily (Cao and Dai 2006; Liang 1992; Manning 2005, 2010).

The concept of police originates in France. The police as an organization should be seen as one facet of a culture broadly construed within a particular sociocultural, historical, and institutional environment (Loader and Mulcahy 2003). This does not mean that there were no precursors of the police in Chinese history. Indeed, there were similar organizations and mechanisms of social control (see Dutton 1992). As a professional institution, however, the principles underlying modern Chinese police organization were imported from Western culture.

Historically, there are two distinctive models of police in the West known as high policing and low policing (Bordue 1968; Brodeur 1983; Chapman 1970; Manning 1997). High policing (or political policing) traces its roots back to Roman law and regards the police created in France in 1667 under Louis XIV as the first police organization comparable to modern forces (Brodeur 1983; Chapman 1970). The police are one major by-product of the consolidation of power in a national or imperial government. Members of the police organization were selected, trained, and compensated by the central government. Police agents owed loyalty not to kinship groups or local leaders, but rather to the central government. The police thus served the political government of the day. The national police devoted considerable attention to control and investigation activities targeted at political opponents and enemies of the state; their duties included intelligence gathering, the regulation and arrest of "subversives," and censorship and the distribution of regime-supportive propaganda.

High policing is an all-inclusive style of social control that seeks out potential threats in a systematic attempt to preserve the existing distribution of power in a given society. It refers to "police interventions in the struggles taking place inside society over the possession and exercise of state power" (Brodeur 1983: 507). In the pursuit of order, high policing is ready to subdue the haughty and unruly by force. The contemporary version of high policing can be found in all communist states, such as the former Soviet Union, and all autocratic regimes in the world, including Taiwan before 1987. It is dubbed "undemocratic policing" in contrast to "democratic policing" in the Western comparative policing literature (Manning 2005; Skolnick 1994).

The concept of low policing can be regarded as a reaction to high policing and to the often repressive consequences of high policing. The development of low policing can be traced back to Sir Robert Peel's preventive police initiated in Great Britain in 1829. Low policing activities were limited by having to operate within the bounds of the reinforcement of criminal law and the gathering of information about public sentiments (Brodeur 1983). The quest for order by peaceful means is the preferred style of low policing, and low policing is regarded as one of the cultural traits of a common law civilization. Manning (2005) argues that Anglo-American policing is democratic policing. All existing contemporary police organizations operate in the space between these two models of policing, with democracy practicing mainly low policing and autocracy relying heavily on high policing.

Democracy is "a system of governance in which those who exercise government power are subject to the electoral control of citizens by majority vote" (Zimring, Hawkins, and Kamin 2001: 183). It is a pre-condition for a *more accurate* public opinion (LaFree 2003) as well as more accurate crime data (Cao 1999; He and Marshall 1997). In addition to periodic, multi-party elections, liberal democracy is based on the twin principles of liberty and equality for all (Fukuyama 1992). Political liberalism can be defined as the rule of law that recognizes certain individual rights or freedom from government control. Any systematic discrimination of any identifiable groups within a society is against the principle of liberal democracy.

Although the idea of democratic policing remains somewhat in dispute (see Manning 2010), in general terms it is agreed that the proper criterion for democratic policing is whether the police in a society are answerable to the rule of law (Skolnick 1994), and whether public opinion matters in the formation of public policy in that society (Cao and Dai 2006; Garcia and Cao 2005; Manning 1997). Consequently, two pillars of democratic policing are accountability and transparency (Liang 1992). Building on John Rawls, Manning (2010: 3) posits that democratic policing is "a kind of redistributive mechanism resting on notions of trust, equality, and legitimacy."

Traditionally, Confucian societies include China, Hong Kong, Japan, Korea, Macau, Taiwan, and Vietnam (Moody 1988), while the concept of East Asian values cover more area to include such nations in southeast Asia as Cambodia, Laos, Malaysia, the Philippines, Singapore, and Thailand. With the arrival of modernization in these societies, the influence of Confucianism, which is viewed as a consummatory value system, began to decline. To different degrees, all Confucian societies have been influenced by Western ideas and institutions; all are penetrated by the world economy and technologies, and all have taken different political labels – e.g., Japan, that of a democracy and North Korea, that of a socialist state. Despite the changes undergone and the infusion of Western influences, residues of Confucianism continue to have social and political importance today. Compared with the West, these societies remain heavily family-oriented and allow the state to avoid some of the welfare costs necessary to be borne in the West. The checks on state power are more moral than instrumental. Politics is embedded in *guanxi* (關係) or relational practices rather than in civil society. These commonalities have caused these societies to be labelled as "post-Confucian societies" (Moody 1988), of which Taiwan is one.

The organization of the book

Taiwan emerged triumphantly as a new democracy as a result of the third wave of democratization. The transitional period spanning the period from 1987 to 2000 was turbulent, but short of any large-scale blood or violence, which was typical of any major change in Chinese history. The police as a professional force were able to maintain their neutrality for the most part, at least on the surface, during even the most tumultuous periods, a fact which greatly facilitated the peaceful transition of power from a long-dominant party to a fledging opposition. This monograph combines democratic theories of policing with a practical concern for responsible and professional police work on the street, in their offices, and training academies. By subjecting the police in Taiwan to the broader environment of the East and the West, and to the larger political philosophies of democratic policing versus authoritarian policing, this research project represents an historical analysis of the police in an Eastern society. The book consists of eleven chapters, with Chapter 1 constituting an introductory chapter and Chapter 11 representing the concluding summative and forward-looking chapter with respect to future research and likely avenues of political development in post-Confucian societies. The rest of the nine chapters are grouped along three broad themes: historical developments, critical issues, and emerging challenges.

We first trace and compare the historical developments of policing before, during, and after the democratic transition in Taiwan, placing an emphasis on changes in philosophy, law, authorization, functions, organization, environment, and tactics (Chapters 2 to 4). We provide a general discussion of police practice and legal philosophy used for the purpose of social control, then describe the latest developments and permutations, and examine the techniques, methods, and the principal environmental and political constraints faced by the police in Taiwan In an attempt to answer why the police were able to maintain their outward neutrality during the democratic transition, we highlight several specific police organizational changes taking place before and during that process.

As we mentioned earlier, the contemporary history of Taiwan can be generally divided into three distinct phases. The first phase features the sustained authoritarian rule which ran from 1945 to 1987 when martial law was finally lifted. Chapter 2 discusses this period, during which time the police in Taiwan were unquestionably an integral part of the repressive police state engaged in high policing.

The second phase of democratic transition began with the repeal of martial law along with the advent of free news media and the legal formation of opposition political parties in 1987. Chapter 3 covers this period. The focus of political life in Taiwan shifted from establishing governmental roots in Taiwan to the process of democratization. All overt attempts on the part of the police to interfere with elections were forbidden through a series of executive orders. The first direct presidential election was held in 1996. Four years later, Taiwan's democratization process was crystallized with the popular election of Chen Shuibian, representing the opposition DPP, as the president of Taiwan. The election in 2000 symbolized the first peaceful transition of power in the 45 years of Taiwanese history, and also in the 5,000-year history of Chinese government.

The third phase of democratic consolidation is the period after 2000. The 2000 presidential election may have completed the transition to procedural democracy, but the democratic consolidation phase has only just started. Huntington (1991) defines consolidation as acceptance and routinization of power transfers from one party to another. In 2008, another milestone of democracy was achieved in Taiwan. Ma Yingjiu (馬英九) the GMD candidate, won the majority of votes in the presidential election and became the president. Chapter 4 describes major developments within police organizations, including the de-politicalization of the force, the implementation of quality management programs, and the development and maintenance of the new core missions associated with democratic policing.

Next, the book examines three critical dimensions of policing in Taiwan: police training and promotion, police culture, and the handling of police misconduct. In Chapter 5, the unique police educational system is described. We endeavor to develop a balanced evaluation of both its strengths and weaknesses. Chapter 6 describes police culture in Taiwan, and discusses its similarities and differences with the police cultures found in Japan and in the US. The culture of the *paichusuo* (PCS) is among the most unique characteristics of policing in Taiwan. Chapter 7 focuses on police misconduct and identifies the complex cultural milieu within which complicated relationships with both law-abiding residents and underground societies take place throughout Taiwan.

In all these substantive areas of policing, we see repeatedly signs of strong cultural resistance to the principle of democracy and the rule of law on the part of police administration. Indeed, at the very top political echelon, the clash between

12 *Introduction: the great transition*

East and West results in the total triumph of democracy as a form of government; all political parties in Taiwan have agreed that democracy is the only way to govern. At the bottom on the level of "life politics" (Giddens 1991), however, tensions between Eastern ways and Western ways remain to be reconciled. It is apparent that the existence of informal social sectors in Taiwan does not reproduce the "civil society" phenomenon found in the West, but nevertheless provides strong impetus toward a form of democratization consistent with the persistence of informal social sectors (Weller 1999). These ubiquitous informal social ties resulting from Confucian culture are the "alternate civilities" that constitute the principal sources of social and cultural capacity for social self-mobilization in the Taiwanese setting.

Finally, we cover three emerging challenges facing contemporary policing: (1) the full integration of female officers into the police force; (2) policing socially-disadvantaged groups; and (3) citizen evaluations of the police. Unlike the issues discussed in the previous chapters, these challenges of policing are more universal because they exist in all Western democracies to one degree or another. Chapter 8 introduces the historical development of women in Taiwanese police and, more importantly, examines barriers and difficulties that female officers have faced and continue to face in their police careers. The patriarchal culture, Confucian or otherwise, is singled out as one of the main obstacles in the full integration of women into the police force. Chapter 9 is devoted to the principle of equal policing which comes with democracy. Democratic government is the form of governance least apt to abuse and ignore the rights of the most helpless and disadvantaged in society. Accordingly, the police force in a democracy must adopt appropriate measures for dealing with aborigines, foreign workers, and the victims of domestic violence. Citizens' evaluations of the police and their comparisons to those in mainland China and other nations are the topics discussed in Chapter 10. It is concluded that the gap between the perception of ineffective policing and actual police effectiveness is rather huge in Taiwan, and that this gap can be narrowed substantially if police leaders are able to do a better job of reducing widespread cynicism within the police force. They must also overcome the cultural inertia favoring secrecy by opening themselves up for more extensive public scrutiny on an on-going basis.

The book's final chapter confirms the significance of Taiwan's democratization experiences. Taiwan remains a safe society governed under democracy, and its economic prosperity is further safeguarded by its effective management of the democratic transition. Democracy is most certainly not a panacea and life in Taiwan did not become "a paradise" after democracy became a social reality, but it is undeniable that there was no great uncontrollable turmoil often accompanying the democratic transition – as can be witnessed in the Middle East after the onset of the "Arab Spring" changes in Libya, Egypt, Tunisia, and Syria. The regime's internal legitimacy is strong, and the continuity is largely beyond a doubt. While the idea of democracy is Western one, the democracy created by Taiwan is genuinely homegrown: it can perhaps best be viewed as a universal system with a local variant. Let us begin our enquiry into an orderly transition to democracy with a study into the creation of reliable and competent police administration.

Part I
Historical developments

2 Policing under martial law

Our narrative begins with Taiwan returning to China as a province after World War II in accordance with the *Cairo Declaration of 1943* and the *Potsdam Conference of 1945*. In 1949, as the Chinese Communists won military control of the entire mainland of China, the Nationalist government of Chiang Kai-Shek and the remnants of his army took refuge on the island of Taiwan.

The social and political environment of Taiwan before the repeal of martial law

The Republic of China on Taiwan was sworn to follow the dictates of the Constitution promulgated in 1947 in Nanjing. The actual operation of the government on Taiwan, however, was circumscribed by a series of emergency laws, administrative decrees, and constitutional interpretations by the *Council of Grand Justices* (one of two branches of the Judicial Yuan, which is equivalent of the Supreme Court of Taiwan). *The Provisional Amendment for the Period of Mobilization of the Suppression of Communist Rebellion* (動員戡亂時期臨時條款), commonly known as the *Temporary Provisions*, was promulgated by the ROC while still on the mainland on May 10, 1948. These "provisions" permitted the president's tenure in office to exceed indefinitely the two-term restrictions prescribed in the constitution. For 38 years, the *Temporary Provisions* and marital law colored every aspect of Taiwan's politics and social life. These laws and executive decrees created two powerful institutions – the *National Security Council* and the *Taiwan Garrison Command* – entities which existed entirely outside the 1947 Constitution, and which conferred virtually unlimited authority on the Office of the President.

As a Leninist-style party, the Guomingdang (GMD) completely monopolized power within the government, the armed forces, and the police force. Interlocking relations among leaders of the party, the government, and the legislative institutions also extended to the economic field. There was little separation between the party and the state. The party and the state were simply combined to constitute "*dangguo*" (党国) or the "party-state" in English. Note also that in this association, the party prioritizes itself over the state, meaning that the GMD could override the state and the constitution in the *dangguo* setting. The connections woven between the party and all centers of power in Taiwan subsequently resulted in a vast range of assets being owned by the party in the name of the state. Separating the state-owned assets from the party-owned assets occasioned a substantial amount of corruption, and in due course led to many criminal charges being brought against high-ranking government and party officials, including ex-Presidents Li Denghui and Chen Shuibian.

Once in Taiwan, Chiang Kai-Shek initiated a fundamental reorganization of the nationalist party. The primary aim of Chiang was to recuperate from his military loss and create an economic and military bastion against his community adversaries in the yet unfinished Chinese civil war. For that purpose, all party members had to be registered anew. Those persons considered disloyal, suspected of enemy connection, or found guilty of corruption were purged at all levels of the party and the government. Once the comprehensive "house cleaning" was accomplished, the GMD began a process of penetrating the institutions of civil society, both spying upon and seeking to take control of all existing voluntary associations. Before Chiang Kai-Shek's death in 1975, the "white terror" (i.e., the oppression of communist sympathizers and political dissents) had prevailed as the governing reality on the island. There was no serious and organized political opposition; only a precious few isolated voices articulated criticism of the regime, such as those of Lei Zhen (雷震), and Bo Yang (柏杨), prominent individuals who had some influence among intellectuals on the island. Given the ubiquitous system of control commanded by the GMD, such bold voices had no real chance to reach out for grassroots support.

Two small legal parties were allowed to exist, but they were essentially satellite operations which relied on the GMT's financial subsidy for their survival. In the political arena, all the top positions were occupied by people from the mainland. In climbing bureaucratic ladders within the government, speaking *guoyu* (国语) became a necessity. This was hard for many Taiwanese who grew up in an environment of either speaking their native tongue or Japanese. The Taiwanese native tongue is a dialect of Minnan, a language which most Chinese outside the area could not understand.

Inspired by their Leninist and Marxist understanding of class conflicts, the GMD government launched the land-to-the-tiller reform in the 1950s in order to promote industrialization and expand capitalist markets (Huang 2006). The reform allowed peasant tenants to purchase their own land under lenient terms from the government. The government also traded stocks in state-owned enterprises for lands owned by long-established big landlords. The land reform program's success paved the way for subsequent industrialization, but at the same time it buried the seeds of discontent among the native gentry-elite class of Taiwan, the societal sector which later formed the basis of the Taiwan independence or *dangwai* (党外) or "outside-the-GMD" movement.

Taiwan modernized quickly during the martial law period, with the concept of modernization understood as a continuing process involving the broad transformation of traditional and local values together with changes in institutions and behavior patterns. Such change has indeed taken place across the economic, political, social, and cultural sectors. While the modernization of Europe and the USA took some two centuries, in Taiwan "that time span has been compressed into a few decades, dating back to the late decades of Japanese colonial rule" (Tien 1989: 42). This process of modernization also added strain to the local gentry-class whose lifestyle had not changed much for hundreds of years.

As a protectorate of the US before 1979, Taiwan was never a fully Leninist society. It did have many trappings of the totalitarianism found in mainland China – namely a centrally planned economy, a ubiquitous ideology, and a government and party organization that kept the population constantly mobilized while attempting to remodel its people into "ideal citizens." A major difference, however, was that the political system in Taiwan was authoritarian with some limited measures of democracy, such as the holding of local popular elections beginning in the 1950s. Its political system was more authoritarian than democratic on the totalitarian–authoritarian–democratic continuum (Gastil 1987), but significantly more tolerant and much less bloody than the totalitarian system in place on mainland China. In Beijing, Mao Zedong established the social device of the "carceral," which was "a network of a single figure discourses and architecture, coercive regulations and scientific proposition, real social effects and invincible utopia, programmes for correcting delinquents and mechanisms that reinforce delinquency" (M. Foucault, cited by Dutton 1992: 245). Chao and Myers (1998) labeled the system in Taiwan as the "inhibited political center" based on single party rule, marital law, the jury-rigged amendments to the 1947 constitution, and limited democracy, which permitted competitive local elections and competition of ideas – so long as those ideas did not include Marxism, socialism, Taiwan independence, or delegitimizing criticism of the regime. The limited form of democracy kept the seeds of democracy alive and served to prepare people in Taiwan for their final direct presidential election in 1996; in contrast, the carceral, like the Gulag in the former Soviet Union, exerted total control over its population.

Taiwan was clearly an authoritarian system which emphasized the centralization of power, the flow of decisions from the top down rather than of demands from the bottom up, deference to authority, strictly limited pluralism and the ready use of violent oppression when other methods of co-optation and control fail (Chao and Myers 1998; Moody 1992; Tien 1989). As of the early 1970s, however, the international environment became increasingly unfavorable to the authoritarian rule of the GMD. Taiwan was forced to withdraw from the United Nations in 1972. The US rescinded its formal tie with Taiwan, and established direct diplomatic relations with China in 1979. The de-recognition of the GMD government as the sole representative of China undercut Chiang Kai-Shek's dream of the reunification of China under a Nationalist government. In due course increasingly open opposition to the GMD emerged, first among overseas Taiwan natives (Tien 1975) and subsequently began to infiltrate Taiwan after Chiang Kai-Shek's death in 1975. The watershed incident was that of the Formosa Incident (also known as the Kaohsiung Incident) in 1979 when *Formosa Magazine*, the flagship magazine of the opposition (Chen 1998) headed by veteran opposition Legislative Yuan Legislator Huang Shin-chieh (黃信介), held a demonstration commemorating

18 *Historical developments*

Human Rights Day (see Figure 2.1). The military police marched forward and closed in on the demonstrators. The GMD authorities used the incident as an excuse to arrest virtually all well-known opposition leaders. Subsequently, the arrested groups were tried and sentenced in three separate groups. Many involved became the bellwethers of the opposition party later.

The other landmark in Taiwan's long march toward democracy was Jiang Nan's assassination (江南命案) in 1984. Jiang Nan was a writer, a journalist, and a vocal critic of the GMD. He was most famous for writing an unauthorized biography of Chiang Ching-Kuo. As a naturalized citizen of the US, he resided in Daly City, California, where he was assassinated by mob members who had been reportedly trained by ROC's military intelligence. The GMD's mishandling of the event and subsequent investigation further weakened the legitimacy of the authoritarian government of the GMD.

Democratization is a dynamic process of change (Giddens 1991; Rawnsley and Rawnsley 1998; Tien 1989). Initial democratization often involves some measures of media liberalization, an action which tends to erode the legitimacy of authoritarian governance. At this stage, the non-democratic state is increasingly challenged by a growing opposition from within the state and from elements of civil society. The moment of democratic breakthrough occurs later, when political competition is first institutionalized and the authoritarian regime agrees to play by the new democratic rules of the game.

Figure 2.1 The confrontation during the Formosa Incident on December 10, 1979.

Source: Photo provided by the Central News Agency.

Three years after Chiang Kai-Shek's death in 1975 his son, Chiang Ching-Kuo, became the president and he started a gradual process of democratic change. One important step he took involved transferring authority over the approval of new publications from the Taiwan Garrison Command to the Government Information Office. The loosening of the GMD's grip over the press signaled the advent of significant new rules of the game for public discourse. The Formosa Incident in 1979 represented the first organized challenge of authoritarian rule in general, and of censorship in particular. All involved were charged and sentenced by the military courts. The trials were widely reported in domestic and international media. After that incident, the government further changed its techniques for handling the press. Instead of charging the journalists in court and ordering the imprisonment of publishers, it used financial pressures to shut them down and issued a huge fine. Even so, short-lived opposition magazines sprang up and enjoyed a boom between 1980 and 1985 (Chen 1998). For example, Kang Ningxiang (康寧祥), a publisher and legislator, launched five influential magazines between 1975 and 1986 (Fulda 2002). Together with similar magazines of the period, these regime critics created an environment of "emancipatory politics," a term developed by Anthony Giddens to describe the kind of normative politics that often characterizes regime transition toward democracy (Giddens 1991). The interaction of the regime-challenging media with the "emancipatory politics" of the day combined to weaken authoritarian rule (Rawnsley and Rawnsley 1998).

The scattered activities of the groups making up the *dangwai* movement, which did not have a specific social base, finally found their commonality in pro-independence by demanding democratic reform, and eventually their collective efforts culminated in the audacious formation of the Democratic Progressive Party (DPP, 民主進步黨) on September 28, 1986. The bold announcement of the founding of the DPP caught the GMD off their guard.

At this particular point in history, Taiwan was at the crossroads of future political life. All eyes focused on the reaction to the formation of the DPP by the GMD, or by President Chiang Ching-Kuo (1978–88) more specifically. To the surprise of many, including the DPP founders, the ruling party publicly took a conciliatory public stance regarding the formation of the opposition party. Behind closed doors, however, ailing Chiang Ching-Kuo rejected the GMD conservative wing's suggestion of suppression, and he insisted that the GMD must accommodate to the changed environment and accelerate its reforms aimed at loosening the grip of control and permitting the development of democratic institution.

Thus, a potentially bloody crisis was averted, and Taiwan's progress toward democracy looked promising. The emergence of democracy was dependent, in part, upon interactions between domestic and global cultures. Domestic cultural factors associated with modernization were noteworthy, but they were not sufficient for explaining democratization in Taiwan. The GMD's need to democratize to enhance its legitimacy vis-à-vis the Chinese Communist Party was probably not a determinative factor either. The DPP's demand for political participation was likewise an inadequate explanation. One of the key factors was Chiang Ching-Kuo's attitude toward democracy and toward the inevitability of democratic change in Taiwan.

Chiang Ching-Kuo was the last strong man who could have followed Franco in Spain or Kim in North Korea to choose the non-democratic road. He in fact could be said to have possessed all three forms of authority described by Max Weber – traditional, rational-legal, and charismatic. He was at once widely respected and greatly feared (Chao and Myers 1998). He enforced the "white terror" in the 1950s, rebuilt the National Security Bureau (the central intelligence coordinating body), and was ruthless toward his enemies as he pursued his path to the top of the political pyramid.

The law was on the side of Chiang Ching-Kuo. With martial law in effect, the military and the police were under his tight control. As the paramount leader, Chiang Ching-Kuo enjoyed complete support from the GMD. In fact, there would have been no serious objections from his top aides had he decided to use violence to crush the opposition. He most certainly did not have to ride the democratic tide to maintain his hold on power. Indeed, when facing a somewhat similar situation three years later in 1989, his one-time schoolmate Deng Xiaoping (邓小平) of China decided to use the army to smash the popular anti-corruption social movement at Tienanmen Square.

The decision was by no means an easy one. External factors contributed to an atmosphere of siege at that time. This may lead the embattled leader either to harden its current grip to power, or to ride the popular demand by slowly loosening up his grip on power. Fortunately, Chiang Ching-Kuo chose the latter course and Taiwan took the road of democracy without experiencing major bloodshed.

After Chiang Ching-Kuo's death in 1988, his hand-picked successor Li Denghui's historical choices were less critical because he never faced comparable historical crossroads. He was a leader in the sense that he could influence the speed or the way of democratization in Taiwan, but he was never in the position to exert much influence over the direction of democratization. That task fell solely on the shoulders of Chiang Ching-Kuo, and once it was done Taiwan would never have to face that type of decision again. Chiang Ching-Kuo thus goes down in history as an enlightened and era-breaking leader, one who continues to be respected in Taiwan and abroad (Du 2011). The formation of the DPP in 1986 initiated a profound, irreversible structural transformation in Taiwanese governance, a genuine peaceful regime change soon followed.

In a bid to improve its international image and soften political oppositions at home, the GMD Central Standing Committee announced on October 15, 1986 its intention to lift the emergency decrees. Emboldened, the DPP defied the existing laws and held its first party congress on November 10, 1986. On July 15, 1987, a new state security law formally replaced the martial law decree. Censorship of the press was formally ended, mass demonstrations were permitted, strikes and collective bargaining were legitimized, and visits to China by ordinary Taiwanese were allowed.

Thus, the answer to our first question as to why the police behaved the way they did during the democratic transition was that the democratization in Taiwan was not a one-way track. While the push from the *dangwai* movement was indeed important, it is also the case that democratization was also partially a top-down reform promoted by Chiang Ching-Kuo.

Since the early 1970s Chiang Ching-Kuo had been thinking about Taiwan's identity, wondering how to implement political changes so that Taiwan could be consistent with its slogan as "free China" (Copper 2005). Taiwan's polity was, at that time, authoritarian with a thin democratic façade, a regime which could hardly differentiate itself from that of mainland China.

In contrast, in many other nations that have experienced democratic transitions from an authoritarian past, entrenched autocrats often resisted the pressure to the point of resorting to violence or to the point of its own collapse. Chiang Ching-Kuo never seriously considered the suggestions to use the military and the police to crack down on the *dangwai* movement after the scandal of the Jiang Nan Incident in 1984 (see Chao and Myers 1998). The GMD government responded to the popular demand, or even coopted portion of the political agenda set up by the DPP (Chao and Myers 1998), and survived the democratic transition – even winning the national elections, first in 1991 and then again in 1996.

The raison d'être for why Taiwan, but no other part of China, has experienced democratization can also be found in the logic of the core philosophy that underlies both regimes. For Taiwan, the GMD and the ruling elite established an "inhibited political center" of authoritarianism and limited democracy "committed to promoting full democracy but without a timetable" (Chao and Myers 1998: 8). Democracy is one of Three Principles of the People (三民主义) advocated by the founding father Dr Sun Yat-sen. In contrast, the mainland China regime under Mao has established "uninhibited political center" or the "carceral" (Dutton 1992) with no commitment whatsoever to accomplishing a full democracy.

Police functions and powers under martial law

The police we are discussing in this book are the general police, not the secret police or the special police that were in existence before 1988 when there were "close to a dozen secret police organizations" (Pye 1986). These secret police forces are beyond the scope of this book. Currently, there are basically two principal police agencies in Taiwan: the National Police Agency (NPA) within the Ministry of Interior and the Investigation Bureau within the Ministry of Justice (Sun and Chu 2006). Both law enforcement organizations are centralized forces within the central government's executive branch, with the latter being comparable to a combination of the American FBI, DEA, ATF, and Secret Service. Our discussion concerns mainly the mission and the principal activities of the NPA.

During the era of martial law, military generals controlled police organization with no provision made for civilian supervision. While the GMD exerted a degree of civilian control over the police through the party system, the police remained an active ingredient of the centralized party–military-police complex, both in politics and society. Both Chiangs, father and son, had extensive military experience. The primary allegiance of the police during the martial law period was to the GMD, not to the civilian government. The police were trained to see themselves as "a revolutionary force," guarding the ideal of its founding father Dr Sun Yat-sen's (孫中山) Three Principles of the People (三民主義). The suppression of political dissents, moreover, was seen by Chiang Kai-Shek as an integral part of policing. In the name of anti-communist "social mobilization," the GMD governed Taiwanese society as a unified entity possessed of organic political dynamics, which the state should properly capture and cultivate towards political-economic goals. The criminal justice system was viewed as an adjunct subservient element to the GMD's aggressive, military-run, party-engineered national-security mission.

Chiang Kai-Shek emerged to the top power in the context of a Hobbesian world of civil and military turbulence in China in the 1920s. He understood that his political survival depended on military strength being placed at the service of the state. It is not a coincidence that Chiang Ching-Kuo was appointed Minister of Defense before he was appointed to the office of Premier.

The state of civil-police relations in Taiwan under martial law is summarized in Table 2.1. In that graphic, we contrast democratic policing practices with the actual policing practices in Taiwan before 1987. These differences are further grouped into three key areas: political neutrality, democratic control, and social impartiality. The second column of Table 2.1 lists the indicators of democratic policing, while the third column represents the actual status of the police in Taiwan until 1987.

First, in a democracy, the police are supposed to swear allegiance to and be loyal to the constitution. In Taiwan before the lifting of martial law, the police were specifically instructed to pledge their loyalty to the GMD, and to Chiang Kai-Shek himself before 1975. There was no way for a non-GMD member to rise to the top position in the organization (Sun and Chu 2006).

In a democracy, each profession in civil society has separate tracks for promotion, and they generally do not overlap a great deal (if at all). In Taiwan, once at the top, all party cadres were highly interlocked. As the police were considered to be an extension of the military forces, the top positions of the police, including the Director-General of the NPA, were all filled by military generals until 1990 (C. Chang 2012). Their GMD loyalty, more than their law enforcement professionalism, determined their promotion. In a democracy, there is a clear distinction between the military and police, with police leaders not necessarily having military experience. The police are not involved in the selection of government officials, elected or appointed, while under martial law the consultation system involved the police being used for vote-mobilization efforts and being part of the official appointment process.

In a democracy, the police have the clear and defined mission of enforcing criminal law and maintaining order, and of remaining neutral in politics. In Taiwan, the police were explicitly instructed to share the task of the internal security mission of supressing communist rebellion and minimizing opposition to the regime. In a democracy, an independent police culture is a part of police forces and greatly influences police behavior, while in Taiwan this sense of an independent police professionalism only began to emerge in the late 1970s and early 1980s.

Table 2.1 Civil–police relations in Taiwan 1949–87

	Indicator	Status
Political neutrality	Loyalty to the constitution	Loyalty to the GMD and Chiang, not the government
	No appointment of active duty officers and limited involvement of retired officers in civilian government	A highly interlocking system where senior domestic posts are filled by active and retired officers
	No involvement in selection of government officials, either elected or appointed	Participation in vote-mobilization efforts and the official appointment process
	Clear and defined mission of enforcing criminal law and maintaining public order	Explicit internal security mission of suppression of communist rebellion and opposition to the regime
	Professional police culture	Growth of professionalism in late 1970s and 1980s.
	Police force is broadly representative of society at rank levels	Officer corps dominated by mainlanders, not Taiwan natives
Democratic control	Constitutional supremacy of chief executive as commander-in-chief	Constitutional separation, but overruled by the Temporary Provisions
	Legislative oversight and monitoring	Effectively none, due to the lack of opposition being represented in the Legislative Yuan
	Civilian expertise in security affairs	No civilian research centers or experts
	Internal autonomy of the police	Extensive GMD political involvement within all of the police
Social impartiality	Reconciliation and healing for past abuses	Silence on 2-28 Incident and partial participation in the "White Terror"
	Demilitarization of culture	Mandatory military education program in all schools
	Transparency of police activities	Police ownership of media assets and most information is highly classified

In a democracy, one ideal which is pursued is that *the public are the police and the police are the public*. Local representation of the police is strongly emphasized, while in Taiwan the police organization was centralized and it ran as a closed system from its inception and remains so to this day. Chiang Kai-Shek

24 *Historical developments*

considered the police as an extension of the military. In the combination of military-police, the military overrides the police. All of the police chiefs of the NPA, such as Zhou Zhongfeng (周中锋), Zhou Jucun (周菊村), Kong Lingcheng (孔令晟), He Enting (何恩廷), and Luo Zhang (罗张), had been military generals before their appointment to head up the national police organization. All except Wang Minning (王民宁) were non-native Taiwanese. Beginning with Wang in 1947, all were military or military-security generals (Xi 2012).

Chiang Kai-Shek also founded the Central Police College in 1936 in Nanjing. He was the first president of the college and stayed in that position until 1947. All the presidents of that police college thereafter until Yan Shixi (颜世锡) in 1987 were military generals, and all the presidents were mainlanders until Cai Dehui (蔡德辉) was appointed in 2001 (see Table 2.2).

Ideally, whether a person is native or not should not be a criterion for selecting a president of a university, be it a general university or a police university. In the period during martial law, mainland origin was an unspoken criterion, and thus it could be one of the criteria for a short period immediately after the lifting of martial law. Currently, after more than a decade of democratic consolidation, this aspect of a person's background should become entirely irrelevant. Similarly,

Table 2.2 Backgrounds of presidents of Central Police University

Names	Tenure	Background
Chiang Kai-shek (蔣介石)	Sept. 1936–Oct. 1947	Military
Li Shizhen (李士珍)	Oct. 1947–Feb. 1949	Military
Chen Yushui (陳玉輝)	Feb. 1949–June 1949	Military
Li Qian (李謇)	July 1949–Apr. 1950	Military
	Apr. 1950–Oct. 1954	Suspension
Le Gan (樂幹)	Oct. 1954–Apr. 1956	Military, mainlander
Zhao Longwen (趙龍文)	Apr. 1956–Nov. 1966	Military, mainlander
Mei Kewang (梅可望)	Dec. 1966–Dec. 1973	Military, mainlander with PhD
Li Xingtang (李興唐)	Dec. 1973–Apr. 1983	Military, mainlander
Zhou Shibin (周世斌)	Apr. 1983–May 1987	Military, mainlander
Yan Shixi (顏世錫)	May 1987–May 1995	Police Academy, mainlander
Yao Gaoqiao (姚高橋)	May 1995–June 1996	BA in Police, mainlander
Cheng Bi (陳璧)	June 1996–July 1997	Police, mainlander
Xie Ruizhi (謝瑞智)	July 1997–Aug. 2000	Police, mainlander with PhD
Zhu Zhenmin (朱拯民)	Aug. 2000–Aug. 2001	Police, mainlander
Cai Dehui (蔡德輝)	Aug. 2001–Mar. 2006	Police, Taiwan native with PhD
Xie Yindang (謝銀黨)	Mar. 2006–Aug. 2008	Police, Taiwan native
Hou Youyi (侯友宜)	June 2008–Dec. 2010	Police, Taiwan native with PhD
Xie Xiuneng (謝秀能)	Mar. 2011–present	Police, Taiwan native with PhD

whether a person has a police background or not should not prevent him/her from being a competent candidate for the president of the police university. In principle, the standards for their positions were set up by the Examination Yuan. This was an issue because there was a heavy penetration of the military into the police until 1987, which is most evident in the appointment of the top police leaders. According to the civilian supremacy principle in a democracy, a civilian without much of a link to the police should also have an opportunity to be selected as the president if the police university is going to be more academic than professional. This type of civilianization has not taken place in Taiwan.

In the second area of contrast, constitutional supremacy, this is a well-established principle in a democracy. In Taiwan there was such constitutional separation, but the 1947 constitution was overruled by the proclamation of the *Temporary Provisions*. In a democracy, the police are described as subjecting themselves to "impossible mandates" (Manning 1997) because the officers are held accountable to the legislative body and the public as well as to their own police administration. Officers are required to act according to well-defined rules and stay within precise limits and act within prescribed powers. They operate within the laws of the state and the regulations of the administration, and they are personally liable for breaches of the law. In Taiwan, effective oversight from the legislative did not exist due to the lack of real opposition representation in the Legislative Yuan. Effective supervision from the public was also missing. Police officers were only held accountable for their actions by their supervisors. The primary code of the police was the *Law for the Punishment of Police Offense* (違警罰法) which authorized officers to detain violators for up to two weeks in local holding cells, to shut down businesses, and to apply a variety of other forceful sanctions without any requirement for judicial oversight and review. In other words, the police were able to prosecute, judge, and jail an accused person under a number of circumstances. Entrusted with such arbitrary power, some officers used their prerogatives for personal aggrandizement (Huntington and Moore 1970). In the case of Taiwan, various informal "regulatory fees," "grease water," or "A-money" were mechanisms used by some corrupt officers (Martin 2007).

In a democracy, civilian expertise is widely sought and readily available for police education. In Taiwan, the police operated in a closed system with its own training academies. Both the Taiwan Police College and the Central Police College (renamed in 1995 the Central Police University) belong to the Ministry of Interior, not the Ministry of Education. All of the police cadets were given a monthly stipend, were obligated to serve a certain number of years as officers and were not liable pay tuition. The Central Police College was allowed to offer up to the master's degree. The ideological indoctrination of the police was quite thorough. Officers who graduated from the TPC and the CPU had to pass rigorous exams in Sunnist doctrine of Three Principles of the People (or collectively *San-min Doctrine*). The Sunnist doctrine is a comprehensive political philosophy developed by Dr Sun Yat-sen as part of a philosophy for allowing China to develop into a free, prosperous, and powerful nation. This philosophy has been claimed as the cornerstone of the Republic of China's policy as carried by the GMD. The three

26 *Historical developments*

principles also are featured in the first line of the National Anthem of the Republic of China. The three principles are often translated and summarized as nationalism, democracy, and the livelihood of the people.

No civilian research centers dealing with the police or independent experts on policing existed outside this closed system. No civilian has ever become the president of the Central Police University (see Table 2.2) or was appointed as a police chief. This situation has not changed, even after the democratic transition and during the period of democratic consolidation.

In a democracy, the police are internally autonomous and operations are based largely on professionalism. In Taiwan, the involvement in political activity by all ranks of the police was extensive. Without showing their absolute loyalty to the ruling party, an officer's chance to move up the promotion ladder was near zero. Almost all police officers were members of the GMD (Sun and Chu 2006).

Finally, in the area of social impartiality, the tasks of the police in a democracy include social reconciliation and healing for any past abuses. In Taiwan, the police were silent about the 2/28 Incident even though they were the triggering factor at first and played a critical auxiliary role to the military later (Chen 2010; Xi 2012). They were deeply involved in the subsequent "White Terror" during the martial law era of policing. In a democracy, the police are a paramilitary force, but over the years there is a tendency toward the demilitarization of the police culture. In Taiwan before 1987, mandatory military education programs were rigorously enforced in all high schools and universities. In a democracy, there is an emphasis on transparency of police activities. In Taiwan, the police was largely a small subsystem of society existing in a world of its own. Most information disseminated was highly classified. The police owned and operated the police radio station (C. Chang 2012) and the magazine for the police (《警光杂志》) (Chen 2011).

In all of the above areas, the police in Taiwan under martial law were qualified as an armed force organized to practice high policing (Cao and Dai 2006; Manning 1997). Most of the functions under the authoritarian regime needed to be reformed during the democratic transition, and indeed, in the following years tremendous changes have taken place in this regard.

It must be made clear that our description of democratic policing represents the ideal type in the Weberian sense (Weber 1947). Policing, like all social institutions, is both "made and imagined" (Unger 1998). In practice, democratic policing varies in degrees among the long-term stable democratic nations (Manning 1997; Bayley 1985) and among different police departments within a single nation (Wilson 1968). Bayley (1985: 24) observed that "police work has a distinctively different character in different places."

Initial reform before the lifting of martial law

The structure of the Taiwanese police can be traced to the Japanese *hoko* system developed during the Japanese occupation of Taiwan between 1895 and 1945 (Alarid and Wang 2000; Cao and Dai 2006; Lai *et al.* 2010). Gentarou Kodama (兒玉源太郎) became the Governor-General of Taiwan in 1898, and with the help of his talented civilian assistant Shimpei Goto (後藤新平) the central administration of the police was completely reorganized to ensure that civil officers, including the police, functioned in true independence from military command. The *hoko* system, which was based on the local village organization known as *baojia* (保甲), was established during this time period and persists into the current field stations called *paichusuo* (派出所, PCS) throughout Taiwan. *Baojia*, as a type of Frankpledge system, became an appendage of policing methods.

When the GMD government took over Taiwan in September of 1945, Hu Fuxiang (胡福相) was appointed as the first head of the Taiwan provincial police. He brought with him some 1,000 police officers from the mainland to assume leadership positions over the roughly 13,200 Taiwanese police personnel. He also brought in many police practices from mainland China. On October 27, 1945, Hu established the Taiwan Provincial Police Training Center (台湾省警察训练所), which in the due course became the current Taiwan Police College.

During the period of martial law from 1949 to 1987, the Nationalist government practiced centralized "high policing" and treated the police as a key extension of the military forces (Cao and Dai 2006; Sun and Chu 2006). After a few years of uncertainty when the central government was relocated into Taiwan, Chiang Kai-Shek's government eventually gained some stability because of the Korean War and because of the American commitment to Taiwan's defense. The passage of the 1953 *Police Law* (警察法) provided the police with the first formal legal document. The law specifies that a centralized administrative office within the Ministry of Interior is in charge of all provincial and direct-municipality police affairs. The tasks of the police include riot control (peace protection, or *bao-an*, 保安), external affairs, national boundaries and maritime policing, criminal affairs, and all other specialized police units. The duties of the police are to maintain public order based on law, to protect social safety, prevent all harm, and to promote the people's welfare. The powers of the police include the promulgation of public safety ordinances, the punishment of violations of the law, and assistance in the investigation of crimes.

With minor adjustment and reforms over the following years, the 1953 law was the governing document from its enactment up to 1987. The process of liberalization and democratization began when Chiang Ching-Kuo became the premier in 1972, accelerated after the death of Chiang Kai-Shek in 1975 and under his tenure as president (1978–88). In 1972, the highest police authority shifted from the provincial police to the National Police Agency, with Zhou Zhongfeng as its first chief (Chen 2010). The conceptual shift from serving as a "revolutionary" police force standing for an explicitly articulated ideological position to a "professional" police force dedicated to the relatively content-free ideal of "maintaining law and order" (治安, *zhi-an*) was one fraught with complications.

President Chiang Ching-Kuo appointed Kong Lingcheng (a marine commanding general who had previously managed the restructuring of the presidential bodyguard units) as the Director-General of the NPA in 1976 and charged him with the mission of orchestrating police reform. Kong thereupon introduced his plans for a "Police Modernization Movement" employing the "C3I Management Theory" that he had learned over the course of two years of study in American military colleges. This reform package focused on using a cutting-edge telecommunications network, computerized information management, and motorized patrol to enable a centralization of police operations, taking officers out of their neighborhood substations and consolidating them with the city-level precinct offices where they would be accessible to citizens through a newly implemented telephone emergency-response system. These furtive reform measures were broadly considered a failure because they met with strong resistance from neighborhood PCSs or field stations (Lai *et al.* 2010; Laio 1991; Martin 2006). A centralized patrol system never was established, and police patrols remain in the hands of the PCSs to this day. With Kong's departure as the chief in 1980, this reform program was quickly ended and soon forgotten. The reforms, however, did infuse the police with much new equipment and advanced technology, such as helicopters, radios, and cars for law enforcement; more importantly, there was a new emphasis on political neutrality for the police in dealing with political protests or domestic riots (Guo 1999). This value of political neutrality proved to be important as Taiwan transformed itself into a new democracy.

Beyond the effort to promote police reform, Chiang Ching-Kuo adopted two measures to boost popular support for the ruling elites: the Taiwanization of political decision-making bodies, and the acceptance of incipient pluralism and liberalization. The former led to the increase of Taiwanese representation in the top state apparatus, the police included, and the latter curtailed restrictions on political activities, increased tolerance of opposition forces, and abolished some features of authoritarian rule (Kuo 1997).

As Taiwan's authoritarian regime underwent a process of "softening" under Chiang Ching-Kuo (Winckler 1984), many revolutionary measures (special means developed to suppress all communist party or anti-government activities) had become irrelevant and out-of-date. Police professionalism began to emerge in the wake of their demise. With the Garrison Command withdrawing from the penetration and control of civil society, the police were empowered with a new law, the *Anti-hoodlum Law* (檢肅流氓條例) in 1985. This statute allowed the police to designate violent suspects as hoodlums and permitted sentencing them to reformatory education through forced labor and/or one to two years of imprisonment (Cohen 1988). The courts seldom challenged these types of cases presented by the police (Sun and Chu 2006). Thus, the police had much more discretion and authority than their counterparts in Western nations during the democratic transition.

In 1985, the former chief of the Garrison Command, Luo Zhang, was appointed Director-General of the NPA. He introduced the last police reform coming under martial law, the "Five Year Plan for the Police Administration." The plan addressed five aspects of policing administration, including organizational structure, education and training, remuneration, equipment, and legal ordinances (Zhu 2001). The timely reform measures proved to be effective in Taiwanese police adaptation to the subsequent, and oftentimes agitated, political liberalization process.

President Chiang's decision to lift martial law as well as his determination to end the ban on opposition political parties marked the start of Taiwan's transition toward democracy. Getting the secret intelligence agencies under control was not an easy task. Chiang used his personal authority and consistently directed the associated changes up until the time of his death. During this period of political change, the military as well as the police remained a potent force in domestic politics. Taiwan's transition to democracy occurred without overt resistance from the armed forces through a coup d'état or other silimar action. The reason, as we argued previously, was that the reform was partially top down as well as bottom up. As a well-trained paramilitary force, the police dutifully took orders from above.

In summary, at the outset of democratization, Taiwan was a post-Confucian society where the state was subject to little legal constraint. The executive branch had de facto law-making power; it enjoyed wide discretion in its choice of procedure and regulatory content. The state power was invested in a person rather than in legal institutions. The role of the police under the authoritarian regime before 1987 was radically different from their role in a healthy democracy (Wiatrowski and Goldstone 2010). Under martial law, the main function of the police was to protect the GMD regime rather than to serve the people. They were highly politicized, with appointments being part of the patronage system that rewarded regime loyalists. In the name of defending Taiwan from the communist threat, police officers spent a great deal of time spying on the populace in an effort to unmask political opposition; crime against citizens was less of a concern. The police were deployed to hundreds of PCSs and officers were assigned to their beats with instructions to collect information on anti-government activities. The GMD controlled the flow of the news and the news media. Abuse of police authority and corruption were quite common because supervision and monitoring were lacking, and because officers were not held accountable for their actions. With the democratic transition, the police finally began to change their foci and strategies. We will discuss these changes in detail in the next chapter.

3 Policing during the democratic transition

The development of policing in Taiwan entered a major new era in the late 1980s when a higher degree of liberalization in the political life of the country was finally achieved. The opposition or *dangwai* movement culminated in success on September 28, 1986 when political dissents announced the formation of the Democratic Progressive Party (DPP). The then President Chiang Ching-Kuo decided not to crush the fledging DPP, and instructed GMT senior officials that "times are changing; the environment is changing and the tide is changing" (Taylor 2000, cited in Hu 2005: 42). Less than a month later, Chiang revealed his intention to end martial law and legalize new political parties during his interview with Katherine Graham of the *Washington Post*. Martial law was officially lifted in 1987 after having been in place for more than 37 years. The Taiwanese press was no longer controlled and censored, mass demonstrations were permitted, strikes and collective bargaining were legitimized, and the GMD was no longer the sole legal political party permitted to organize and operate.

In the early afternoon of January 13, 1988 Chiang Ching-Kuo passed away and Li Denghui, a Taiwan native, took the oath of office the next day as the fourth president of the Republic of China. A new era in Taiwan's history began with this momentous event. Li succeeded to the leadership of the government, officially ending the authoritarian rule of Taiwan by the two Chiangs (i.e., Chiang Ching-Kuo and his father Chiang Kai-Shek) since 1949. Political invective swept over the island amid the death of Chiang Ching-Kuo. Taiwan moved steadily toward democratic governance in the 1990s. Two party politics with several minor parties emerged after the 1992 legislative election when the DPP received about 30 percent of the votes cast. Taiwan held its first direct election for president in 1996, and the opposition DPP won the presidential election in 2000. The country has clearly evolved from a society with a single prevailing ideology into one where people hold diverse views reflecting a variety of values and interests.

Taiwan's transformation from an authoritarian regime to a democratic modern state has posed great challenges to the police. As part of the political system, the police had to reform to enhance their legitimacy, and most importantly to maintain neutrality in the increasingly confrontational politics associated with the transition to democracy. The political control exercised by the GMD began to shrink. The police had to discontinue some of their practices, such as the administrative sanctions developed under the *Law for Punishment of Police Offences*. These practices were ruled unconstitutional by the Council of Grand Justices (i.e., the Judicial Yuan). Meanwhile, the police had to shoulder some new responsibilities, such as airport and seaport security checks and immigration monitoring (which used to be under the control of the military), empowered by the laws promulgated during the post-martial law era of political governance.

The most noticeable change is the evolution of the police role from primarily being a control agency that emphasizes the maintenance of the status quo to a professional institution that stresses the protection of individuals' rights and shows proper respect for the maintenance of political neutrality. Police professionalism in Taiwan entailed the enhancement of legal education and training for police recruits, a refocusing of police responsibility on core missions, the promotion of community policing, the use of modern technologies and methods in solving crimes, the establishment of a set of more specialized units to meet the needs of the citizens, and the improvement of the integrity of the force (Sun and Chu 2006). While the formation of a politically-neutral police force was far from fully accomplished, it marked the first time in the history of Taiwan policing that protecting the interest of the general public, rather than the GMD, became an influential force in shaping police organizational strategies and operational behavior.

This chapter discusses major developments in Taiwanese policing for the period 1987 to 2000. The evolution of policing in the areas of philosophy of operation, legal authorization, societal function, organizational form, environmental influences, and tactics is the focal concern (Kelling and Moore 1988). The discussion of these critical dimensions is organized along four sections. The first section focuses on changes in legal mandates, and the impact of such changes on police functional scope and organizational developments. The second section touches upon the complex and difficult working environment that police face in performing their duty. The third section involves the application of community policing in Taiwan, and assesses the effect of this concept on police practice. The last section summarizes the key information discussed in this chapter.

Legal mandates as sources of authority

The democratic-transition era of policing was highlighted by a period of relatively rapid change brought on by the promulgation of new laws and regulations, and the additions of amendments to existing laws and rules. The passage of relevant laws and regulations in policing, which could be viewed as part of a broader political reform during the post-martial-law era in Taiwan, represented the key source of authority that provided the mandates and resources for the police to operate as a professionalized law enforcement community. The rule of law, or restriction to only those actions permitted by legal mandates, in general and the protection of human rights in particular have emerged as the overall guiding principles for Taiwanese policing.

To fill the void left by the repeal of martial law, the Legislative Yuan enacted the *National Security Law* (*NSL* 國家安全法) in 1987. Several articles in the new law are directly related to the police, including: (1) the Bureau of Entry and Exit

Administration was transferred from the Taiwan Garrison Command (TGC) to the National Police Agency (NPA); (2) the right of public assembly and association is to be observed, but actions in this area must not violate the constitution and they must not involve advocating communism or the division of the national territory or the independence of Taiwan from China; and (3) civilians will not be tried in military courts. The *NSL* signalled the end of the dominant role played by military agencies (e.g., the TGC) in domestic security and governance, and established a civilian-controlled and police-centered model of democratic law enforcement.

Two other laws pertinent to the *NSL* are the *Assembly Law* (集會遊行法) and the *Civil Organization Law* (人民團體法). Promulgated in 1988, the *Assembly Law* represented the first time in Taiwan's history that citizens were given legal protection for their assembly rights and the police were provided with administrative regulations to guide their use of discretion in maintaining order during public demonstrations (Wong 2005). Protestors are required to obtain a permit first from the police district station wherein the assembly is to take place. The *Civil Organization Law* was revised in 1991 to govern political, social, and professional organizations. Police are given permission to work with neighborhood residents to form organizations for the purpose of crime prevention and dispute settlement.

In 1991, the *Social Order Maintenance Law* (社會秩序維護法) was enacted to replace the *Law for the Punishment of Police Offenses*, which was enacted in the mainland during the Sino-Japanese War (1937–45) and brought to Taiwan after taking over Taiwan from Japan. It was widely criticized for the violation of human rights because it authorized the police to arrest, prosecute, and punish offenders who committed minor crimes without any judicial approval or review. It was ruled unconstitutional in 1980 by the Council of Grand Justices but continued to be used sporadically until its use was ended by the president in 1991.

The *Social Order Maintenance Law* greatly reduced the scope of police power and signalled the government's legislative move toward democratic policing (Martin 2007). Another important development is the revision of *Article 100* of the ROC *Criminal Law*. Two broad offenses prescribed in the *Article*, "conspiracy to incite insurrection" and "public promotion of insurrection" which had been used the most commonly to sanction political dissents were repealed.

Changes in legislation had a direct influence on police functional and organizational developments, resulting in a refocusing of police responsibilities, a move toward professional leadership, the establishment of more specialized units, and the enhancement of local control of police. The refocus of police responsibilities referred to the separation of some traditional functions shouldered by the police in Chinese societies, such as household registration, fire fighting, maritime security, and private security, from the Taiwanese police to other governmental or private entities. It also entailed the expansion of police involvement in the prevention and sanction of violence against women and the abuse of children. Specifically, the 1989 *Juvenile Welfare Law* (少年福利法), the 1993 revised *Child Welfare Law* (兒童福利法), and the 1998 *Domestic Violence Prevention and Control Act* (家庭暴力防治法) all required the police to play a much more active, and often controlling and punitive, role in governmental response to domestic violence and to work collectively with social service agencies, prosecutors and courts, public health, education, and household registration to provide better protection to children and women. The three pieces of legislation are extremely important, representing a victory of human rights over the Confucian patriarchal culture – which for thousands of years guarded the privacy of family against societal regulations – and bringing the Taiwanese legal system on a par with the most advanced democracies. They also signal that the police are moving away from a continental legal system that emphasizes the administration of a wide array of social functions to the Anglo-American system that focuses on a narrower range of responsibilities relating to criminal sanctions (NPA 2002: 50).

A shift toward professional leadership is most evident in the appointment of career police officers as the Director-General of the NPA. Between 1949 and 1990, all Director-Generals but one (who served the post for only eight months) were former military generals with little police training and extremely limited knowledge of street-level policing. The penetration of the police leadership from the military officially ended in 1990 when a career police officer with a background of criminal investigator, Zhuang Heng-dai (莊亨岱), assumed the position of Director-General. Not only have Director-Generals been promoted from career officers in active duty since then, but also they have also become much more accountable for mistakes and misconduct by police officers. Three Director-Generals stepped down between 1996 and 2000 because of high profile cases involving corruption and poor police performance. Although the independence of police leadership from military influence promoted great aspirations for career officers who were upwardly mobile-minded, it also made the position much more vulnerable to a heightened demand for political accountability.

Figure 3.1 Getting ready for the upcoming parade (June 28, 1993).
Source: Photo provided by the Central News Agency.

Several specialized units were established to handle emerging police concerns. In 1990, the Fourth and Fifth Peace Preservation Police Corps (PPPC, also known as Special Police Fourth and Fifth Headquarters 保安警察第四、第五總隊) were formed in *Gaoxiong* and *Zhanghua*. Along with the First PPPC, which is deployed in northern Taiwan, the Fourth and Fifth PPPC serve mainly as mobile task forces in middle and southern Taiwan, respectively. Under the direct supervision of the NPA, these corps' main responsibilities include riot control, special weapons and tactics, and counterterrorism. The formation of these specialized units reflected the need to control large-scale demonstrations and maintain social order during the first few years after martial law was revoked, and when the police and citizens were figuring out how to behave toward each other under the newly implemented *Assembly Law*. In 1992, a special safety protection force, the so called *wei-an* (維安) squad, was formed within the First PPPC, with its main missions being counterterrorism, high-profile hostage rescues, and the protection of presidential candidates and domestic and foreign dignitaries.

At the local level, the passage of the *Domestic Violence Prevention and Control Act* in 1998 required each police district to assign a detective (at the rank of sergeant or above) to serve as the domestic violence officer, whose primary responsibilities include applying for protection orders for victims and informing officers at local stations about the nature (e.g., time and place) of the protection orders, assisting victims in seeking legal actions against offenders, compiling and analyzing case-related data, conducting contacts with victims and making referrals to counselling and shelter services, and administering training in handling domestic violence (Sun and Chu 2010). The assignment of full-time officers to handle domestic violence reflected NPA's commitment to offering better police services to victims of family violence.

The last noticeable change during the democratic transition is the enhanced local control of police. Taiwan had a highly centralized police force with the NPA having administrative jurisdiction over all police units. The central control of police received progressively greater challenge from elected city mayors and country magistrates, officials who wanted to have some decision-making authority over the appointment of local police chiefs and some influence over the allocation of police budgets. In 1989, seven DPP and independent city and county executives formed an alliance to fight for more control over local police administration. Between 1989 and 2000, local executives in Taipei City, Yilan County, Xinzhu County, and Jiayi County refused to accept the police chiefs appointed by the NPA and the Ministry of the Interior (MOI). Their collective efforts against the central government's control of police and the resulting ruling by the Council of Grand Justices finally made the NPA and MOI concede some of their personnel appointment powers to the local governments. The *Local Autonomy Statute* (地方自治法) was eventually passed by the Legislative Yuan in 1999, giving the localities a veto power in the appointment of local police chiefs. Police chiefs are now chosen by city and county administrators from a list of candidates recommended by the NPA. City mayors and county magistrates are responsible for evaluating the performance of the police chiefs in their jurisdictions, and if they are not satisfied with the job being done by their local police chiefs they can request a transfer of the police administrators in question. This action has rarely occurred, though it is likely to serve as an ever present reminder to the local police executives.

Dealing with a challenging work environment

On its way moving toward a more politically and economically open society, Taiwan inevitably experienced some challenges that threatened the stability of the country. Indeed, crime control and order maintenance during the democratic transition were not always as smooth as policy makers and police administrators would prefer; this was likely the case because of several discernible reasons. First, rapid social changes have given rise to a continued increase in crime rates. As reported in Table 3.1, Taiwan's total crime rate rose more than 40 percent between 1980 and 1987. The rate doubled during the democratic transition, skyrocketing from 41.89 per 10,000 residents in 1988 to 88.58 in 1998. Both violent and

Table 3.1 Violent, property, and total crime rates, 1980–98

Year	Total crime[a]	Violent crime[a,b]	Property crime[a,c]
1980	29.67	3.84	15.91
1981	28.54	3.15	16.77
1982	24.39	2.89	14.32
1983	27.66	3.16	16.03
1984	27.64	3.01	15.25
1985	31.37	3.12	16.21
1986	48.14	5.73	26.04
1987	42.42	5.43	18.34
1988	41.89	5.35	20.00
1989	42.17	5.33	20.49
1990	42.48	4.72	20.56
1991	56.48	4.61	21.17
1992	62.75	3.02	18.83
1993	62.86	4.01	16.66
1994	53.92	4.58	15.97
1995	76.27	9.49	34.55
1996	88.51	3.78	45.32
1997	88.42	8.35	44.57
1998	88.58	7.13	47.92

Source: *Crime Statistics* （刑案統計） published annually by Criminal Investigation Bureau, National Police Agency, Republic of China.

Notes
a Percentage per 10,000 residents.
b Violent crime includes homicide, rape, robbery, and aggravated assault.
c Property crime includes larceny, auto theft, and fraud.

property crimes showed a downward trend between the late 1980s and mid-1990s, and then an upward trend after the mid-1990s (NPA 1988, 1998). The total crime rate is less comparable after 1998 when the inclusion of drug-related offenses occurred, significantly inflating the official crime rate. In addition to an increase in the amount of crime occurring in Taiwan, new types of crimes (e.g., computer, environmental, and international), including those more common in developed countries (e.g., drug crimes and financial fraud), also emerged on the scene for the attention of law enforcement (O'Leary and Sheu 1992). Crime control became more challenging because of democratization.

Second, although the localization of policing has enhanced police accountability to local politics, it has also made the police force much more vulnerable to local political influences. Specifically, police operations against illegal businesses, such as gambling and prostitution, are frequently hampered by members of the local city/county councils who have close ties with owners of questionable businesses. In 1996, the Ministry of Justice estimated that out of the 858 city and county councilors in office, 286 were known underworld figures (Chin 2003). Police are often asked by councilors to "give a break" to illegal activities. Councilors could place constraints on the police budget if the police failed to pay attention to their requests. The protection of questionable businesses by legitimate elected political figures has become a major barrier for the police in dealing with vice-related crimes in many towns and cities.

Third, the large number of assembly, parade, and demonstration cases caused a great burden for the police who, under the provisions of the *Assembly Law*, not only have to review and approve (or disapprove in a small number of cases) the applications, but also they must act as the first-line responders to ensure that these gatherings were lawfully and peacefully conducted. As shown in Table 3.2, the numbers of assemblies and parades varied greatly between 1988 and 2000, understandably spiking in election years (i.e., 1989, 1990, 1994, 1995, and 1998) and receding in non-election years. On average, the Taiwan police had to handle over 5,000 assemblies and parades annually. Compared to the 1980s, the police were better prepared (e.g., the establishment of the Fourth and Fifth PPPC) and more thoroughly trained to handle large-scale demonstrations and violent confrontations between police and the participants of assemblies. Even so, bloody incidents were not unheard of; in 1995, after violent confrontations between taxi drivers from two competing companies erupted in Taipei, the Director-General of the NPA announced that the era of soft enforcement of the *Assembly Law* was over and "protecting legal (approved) assemblies and parades and sanctioning illegal ones" became the guiding principle of handling of parades and assemblies (C. Chang 2010: 30). During the process of democratization in the 1990s, the police were continually seeking the most appropriate ways of dealing with participants in demonstrations when maintaining social order and protecting the rights of assembly became equally important for the police.

Fourth, how to handle crime and disorder problems associated with legal and illegal foreign migrant workers effectively emerged as a critical issue for the police (a topic that we will further discuss in depth in Chapter 9). The shortage of labor

Table 3.2 Number and percentage of assemblies and parades, 1988–2000

Year	Assembly		Parade		Total
	No.	%	No.	%	
1988	1,144	79.8	289	20.2	1,433
1989	4,971	91.5	460	8.5	5,431
1990	7,595	97.7	180	2.3	7,775
1991	3,403	88.5	443	11.5	3,846
1992	3,760	89.4	445	10.6	4,205
1993	5,428	90.9	543	9.1	5,971
1994	10,207	90.4	1,087	9.6	11,294
1995	6,108	91.5	570	8.5	6,678
1996	2,940	82.2	637	17.8	3,577
1997	3,500	85.0	619	15.0	4,119
1998	6,660	85.8	1,099	14.2	7,759
1999	1,110	87.7	155	12.3	1,265
2000	1,812	78.6	492	21.4	2,304

Sources: *Assembly and Parade Handled by Police Organizations* (警察機關處理集會遊行發生數) published monthly by National Police Agency, Republic of China.

problem for Taiwanese businesses led the government to permit the entry of foreign workers from the Southeast Asian countries of Indonesia, the Philippines, Thailand, and Vietnam. Foreign workers were first allowed to work in Taiwan in 1989, and the number of legal foreign workers increased dramatically during the democratic transition, rising precipitously more than 100 times from 2,999 in 1991 to 326,515 in 2000 (Council of Labor Affairs 2010). While foreign workers were much less likely than Taiwanese to be involved in crime, and the majority of offenses that they committed were simple thefts (Chen 2005), policing a marginalized population represented a demanding and challenging task for Taiwanese police because of the cultural and language barriers to be confronted, the absence of relevant prior work experience, and the shortage of foreign affairs officers. Even worse was the fact that, along with the increase of legal foreign workers, the number of runaway foreign workers overstaying their visas, partly resulting from the hefty referral fee collected by the brokers, increased quickly to an estimated number of 50,000 by the end of 1996 (Lu 2000). Their high mobility of moving from job to job and vulnerability to predators made the detection and investigation of their possible involvement in criminal behavior and their victimization extremely difficult.

Finally, increased international migration also took place between the two Chinese societies across the Taiwan Strait. Taiwan's decision to allow its citizens to visit relatives in China led to much greater cross-strait activity since 1987. Some Taiwanese criminals found safe haven in China because of the absence of agreements on criminal activity between the two societies, making the investigation of cross-border crimes and the apprehension of suspects and fugitives almost impossible. In 1990, in reaction to these problems both sides reached agreement (the so-called *Jinmen Accord* 金門協議) on repatriating criminals, smugglers, and fugitives under the spirit of humanity, safety, and convenience.

Substantial population migration from China to Taiwan also occurred in this period. The large wage gap between Taiwan and China created an economic incentive for mainlanders to seek employment opportunity on the island that shares the same culture and written language. Unlike foreign workers from Southeast Asia, the majority of mainlanders entered Taiwan illegally, mainly through smuggling channels. The influx of illegal Chinese workers reached a peak between 1989 and 1993, with an average of about 5,000 mainlanders arrested annually by the police and immigration authorities (Huang 2008). The number of illegal Chinese immigrants started declining after 1993, averaging about 1,500 arrests and deportation in the late 1990s, chiefly because the passage of the *Act Governing Relations between the People of the Taiwan Area and the Mainland Area* (臺灣地區與大陸地區人民關係條例) legalized the entry of Chinese citizens under certain circumstances. In addition, the rapid economic development taking place in China in recent years has created many more higher-paid domestic job opportunities for mainlanders, hence reducing the lure of Taiwanese employment opportunities.

In addition to the large number of illegal workers from China, a spate of airline hijackings took place in the 1990s which also caught the Taiwan government and the police off guard. Between 1993 and 1994 alone, fourteen mainlanders were involved in seven hijackings of commercial airlines from China to Taiwan. Until the late 1980s, mainland hijackers, especially military pilots, were hailed as freedom fighters and they were heftily rewarded by Taiwan. However, more recently, the government has adopted a tough policy of sending hijackers back to China after they have served prison terms in Taiwan. Although smuggling incidents and hijacking incidents have either receded or discontinued entirely after 2000, while they were occurring they created lot of extra work for the police who had little experience in managing such incidents before the lifting of martial law.

Amidst all these challenges, police salaries were raised substantially during the tenure of Premier Hao Bocun (郝柏村). Low salaries and long working hours were often given as the major reasons for police disciplinary problems. In order to attract higher quality applicants into a rapidly expanding police force, officers' salaries were adjusted upward to compensate for the long and irregular working hours. The increase in overtime pay greatly improved police morale at a time when so many demands were being made on the police. The policy initiative also helped strengthen the hand of police leadership who were determined to ride out the wave of democratic change to a successful conclusion of creating a truly professionalized police force.

Community policing: innovation or new wine in old bottles?

Community policing has become pretty much a worldwide movement for police since the 1980s. Though the concept was first introduced to the world by Western scholars, police practitioners in several Asian societies, in particular China,

Taiwan, and Japan, have embraced some of the key principles of community policing (e.g., cultivating close ties between citizens and the police and focusing on neighborhood-level disorder) for decades now (Bayley 1999; Lovrich 1978). The concept was first brought to Taiwan in the mid-1990s by several Western-educated (mainly in the US) police scholars at a time when the idea of democratic policing was in need of a boost. The NPA has promoted some community policing initiatives, such as foot patrols and bike patrols, use of community service cards, enhanced patrol around houses whose owners are away, volunteer neighborhood-watch programs, and community-police problem-solving meetings throughout the country. A number of jurisdictions have implemented intensified localized activities along these lines (C. Chang 2002). The impact of the community policing philosophy is evident. However, notwithstanding these activities, community policing in Taiwan has rarely evolved into any tangible transformations in police strategies or organizations. Unlike many US police agencies, the NPA has never officially declared community policing as a guiding strategy of the Taiwan police. Most community policing initiatives in Taiwan have been operational programs rather than attempts to promote philosophical changes and bring about major administrative reforms.

The lack of an agency-wide transformation toward community policing is mainly due to the fact that community-based organizational structures and field practices have been in place for many decades, making the official adoption of such reform less needed. It is posited that the sub-district station (the so-called *fenzusuo*, FZS 分駐所) and field station (*paichusuo*, PCS 派出所) officers, who are assigned to police operational beats (*Jingqinqu*, JQQ 警勤区), made up a Taiwanese version of community policing that can be traced back to the *koban* system established during the Japanese occupation of Taiwan between 1895 and 1945. Similarly, the patrol and watch system launched in Nanjing, China, in 1929 (Yeh 1999) had clear connection to community policing concepts. The PCS is the lowest formal organizational unit in the police hierarchy, and JQQ is the basic operational unit for the Taiwan police.

An FZS is a sub-district station located in villages, towns, and small cities where there is no district police station, while a PCS is a field station within mid-sized to large cities where the hierarchy runs from the city or county police headquarters, to a few district stations, and to many PCS units. In general the size of a FZS is larger than a PCS. Other than this, the functions of the two types of stations are virtually the same.

In the mid-1990s, there were approximately 221 FZS and 1,333 PCS units with 15,482 JQQ throughout the country, averaging one FZS or PCS per 23 square kilometers (Lee 1994; Yeh 1999). The FCS and PCS system deeply penetrated the civil society during the period of authoritarian rule, but under the democratic regimes it allows the police to be deployed close to the citizens they serve. The change in tenor is based on philosophy underlying policing: whether the police were in the community to monitor political dissidents or regime enemies or they are in the community to prevent crime and serve citizens.

According to the NPA policy, each JQQ is manned by one FZS or PCS officer, who is normally in charge of approximately 500 households or 2,000 residents. JQQ officers' main duties include: (1) patrol; (2) making periodic household visits; (3) in-station duty (e.g., manning reception desk, taking inquiries, and filing reports from citizens, and maintaining the security of the station); (4) back-up duty (e.g., taking temporary assignments, replacing absent officers, and transporting and guarding suspects); and (5) community service. Rapid urbanization since the 1980s has brought a large number of migrants into cities, making some urban JQQs much larger than 500 households and some rural JQQs much smaller. PCS officers, especially urban ones, carry very heavy duty loads. It is common for them to work twelve hours a day and six days a week out of the PCS. Although PCS officers were required to spend at least two hours on patrol and two hours on household visits, they were burdened with an array of duties and various special assignments and paperwork, making it almost impossible for them to be attentive to their JQQ.

Research on community policing in Taiwan has focused primarily on introducing basic concepts and elements of community and problem-oriented policing, with a limited number of studies touching upon evaluation and documenting the effects of this police innovation. As with findings from research conducted in the US, evaluative studies on the impact of community and problem-oriented policing in Taiwan showed some encouraging results. For example, one study examined the effects of the redesign of the JQQ assignment in a PCS in Taipei County (Yeh 1999). The experiment divided all officers in the PCS into two groups, with one being JQQ specialists and the other regular PCS officers. JQQ officers were required to spend at least six to eight hours on patrol, household visits, and community service, while regular officers performed traditional PCS work exclusively. Community survey data collected before and after the experiment indicated that citizens expressed higher levels of satisfaction with the police, greater sense of safety in the neighborhood, greater familiarity with JQQ officers, and an overall more positive impression of JQQ officers (Yeh 1999). It should be noted that similar experiments (e.g., a redesign of the JQQ system) were conducted in five other counties and cities. None of the experiments, including the one in Taipei County, have lasted for more than a year due to the absence of support from other units and personnel, the co-existence of both JQQ officers and regular officers within the same PCS, the lack of sufficient manpower, and the NPA switch from a focus on police–community relations to officer performance (Yeh and Li 2003). The abandonment of the specialized JQQ design echoes the failure of team policing among US police agencies in the 1970s, which revealed that police reform would not be successful without winning the hearts and minds of rank-and-file and middle managers, integrating the innovation into the main operation of the department, and rendering appropriate and timely training to all parties involved.

Two other studies assessed community policing programs implemented in Taipei City (C. Chang 2000a; Lin *et al.* 2000). One study found that residents in two neighborhoods that were subjected to higher levels of police problem-solving interventions (e.g., enhanced patrol, entrance surveillance, and household visits) tended to experience lower levels of actual and perceived crime rates and fear of crime, and to report higher levels of satisfaction with police compared to residents in two comparable neighborhoods without any police intervention (Lin *et al.* 2000). The other study showed that residents in a neighborhood expressed slightly better evaluations of the effectiveness of community policing and satisfaction with police compared to citizen sentiments collected a year prior. Officers were largely receptive to community policing, but they were also concerned about the extra workload created by community policing-related assignments (C. Chang 2000a).

Summary

Political development entered a new phase in the history of Taiwan when martial law was lifted in 1987. In this context, Munro (1995) observed three major transitions of Taiwan police – namely, from martial law to civil control, from regime police to professional police, and from police leaders as administrators to police leaders as managers/change agents. What is meant by the term regime police is that the government, the police, and the ruling party used to be indistinguishable (see Chapter 2). By practicing high policing, the police officers enjoyed great power. Since the lifting of martial law, the police have been dealing with a new democratic reality entailing working with less power and with more accountability for their actions. The top police leadership was no longer made up of former military generals, but rather career police officers who largely supported the democratic change. The transition, however, was not complete as the GMD's influence within the police (the so-called Liu Zhong-shin Branch of the GMD, 劉中興黨部) was largely intact. The DPP repeatedly accused the police of violating its neutral standing in politics, and indeed the top leaders within the GMD repeatedly defended the police as being a neutral force. In reality, most GMD's influence was hidden instead of open as in the past.

The Taiwan government had to promulgate a series of laws in the post-martial law era of political and social order in the island. The most significant of these statutes are the 1989 *Juvenile Welfare Law*, *Child Welfare Law*, and the 1998 *Domestic Violence Prevention and Control Act*. The new laws began to regulate family relationships which were long considered sacred and virtually the last stronghold of Confucian ethics. In time, with the transition to democratic governance the police inevitably and gradually shifted their main roles from assuring the maintenance of the status quo to the active protection of individuals' rights and legal mandates; in time their new role became their source of legitimacy in a democratic Taiwan.

New legislation since the lifting of martial law has led to noteworthy developments, both in police functions and in police organizations; a refocus of police responsibilities, a move toward professional leadership, the establishment of more specialized units, and the enhancement of local control of police are among the most prominent. As a paramilitary organization, the police played their role as a stabilizer well. The transformation into a democratic police force is not an easy task, especially during a period of rapid social and political changes. Many times police agencies resisted the changes, or did not give up established ways until a new legislative enactment was adopted. In addition to the series of internal reforms resulting from the changing political environment, the Taiwan police faced great challenges in performing their duties because of a continued increase in crime rates, their vulnerability to political influences, a large number of assembly and parade cases, and the influx of legal and illegal foreign and mainland workers. Police responded to these challenges by increasing the use of modern technologies and methods in solving crimes, improving legal education and training for the police officers and recruits, establishing mobile response forces, and enhancing cooperation with the mainland Chinese police authorities.

Community policing is embraced as a useful set of programs and has been widely adopted, but it did not impact too greatly on what the Taiwan police had been doing during the post-martial law era of policing. Various community policing initiatives have been launched throughout the country to improve police–community relations. The majority of them were operational programs which lasted only for a short period of time, and none of them have entailed major organizational or strategic innovations. Crime control was still largely reactive, driven by individual incidents reported to the police. Motorized patrol coupled with household visits remained the main tactics utilized by PCS officers in carrying out order maintenance and crime fighting functions within their operation beats. Despite some difficulties and fits and starts, the NPA accepted often reluctantly the changed legal environments and adapted itself to the changed working environment. In a relatively short period of time, the police in Taiwan successfully transformed themselves into a largely professional and civil service agency, responsive to local governments and the local control as well as being accountable to the NPA and the rule of law.

4 Policing in the new century

The development of policing in Taiwan entered yet another era when the opposition Democratic Progressive Party (DPP) candidate Chen Shuibian won the presidential election at the turn of the century. The election results officially ended more than fifty years of the domination of the Guomindang (GMD) and formally established a fledgling two-party system. Unfortunately, the DPP was poorly prepared to be the ruling party of the country. The 2004 presidential election was a tight race from start to finish. Chen survived a mysterious shooting a day before balloting. While campaigning in his home county, Tainan, Chen was shot once, causing minor injury to his abdomen. Nobody heard the gun shots fired at the scene because of the loud noise generated by firecrackers. Some Taiwanese suspected that Chen staged the shooting to illicit public sympathy and boost support for the DPP. The police identified a single suspect who committed suicide before the police got a chance to interrogate him. The case was officially closed in 2005, leaving many questions unanswered. Chen was eventually re-elected by merely a 0.2 percent margin over the GMD candidate, Lian Zhan (連戰). Chen's popularity faded quickly over his second term, mainly because of widespread corruption and the DPP's inability to pass important legislation at the Legislative Yuan which remained under the control of the GMD majority.

Chen was in office for a period of eight years, from 2000 to 2008, a period which represented the first time in Taiwan's history that the police were under the direct supervision of a non-GMD central government. Traditionally, DPP's relations with law enforcement agencies were weak at best given its long-term opposition status. The DPP frequently accused the police of failing to maintain a neutral position during prior political elections. How to improve its relations with the police and, perhaps even more importantly, expand its influence on the force emerged as a vital issue for the party once it won its first national election. An improved relationship, however, cannot be achieved overnight. Under the DPP's rule, the National Police Agency (NPA) was led by four different Director-Generals, signalling unstable governance and even distrust in the NPA top brass.

The inexperienced ruling party was eager to establish an image of open, honest, and effective governance by, for example, promoting a quality management movement in all government agencies to enhance services to the public. Police departments took the challenge seriously by initiating various quality

44 *Historical developments*

enhancement programs around the country. Despite the launching of a number of such initiatives, the NPA focused on law and order as the principal concern of the Taiwan police. Another challenging area for the DPP government is its relations with mainland China. DPP's pro-Taiwan independence orientation led to a strained Taiwan–Mainland relationship, a development which inevitably hindered the progress of cross-strait police cooperation. In 2008, GMD's Ma Yingjiu won the presidential election and a more progress toward the development of cross-border cooperation in policing has been noted as a direct consequence.

This chapter discusses some major developments in Taiwan policing since 2000 – a period which is also known as the *democratic consolidation* when power transfers from one party to another become *routine*. Since the turn of the century, Taiwan has shown characteristics of a consolidated democracy, with reversion back to authoritarianism being highly unlikely and democracy becoming increasingly routinized and more deeply internalized in all aspects of social and institutional life (Linz and Stepan 1996). Indeed, Taiwan has evolved from a "high power distance society" wherein the public expects that legal authorities will exercise decisions with little input from citizens to a "low power distance society" wherein the public expects to have input into governmental decision making and exercise influence in how they are governed (Hofstede 2001).

The following discussion is divided into four sections. The first section touches on political influence in Taiwanese policing, with a focus on how such interference has been minimized in certain areas but has remained largely unchanged in others. The second section describes NPA's efforts to improve the quality of police services, and highlights program characteristics similar to those of comparable reforms carried out in Western police forces. The third section presents various programs introduced by NPA's five Directors-General since 2000, and explains the police's responses to fraud and theft and how collaboration with the Chinese law enforcement authorities has developed over time. The final section provides a brief summary of key points delineated in previous sections.

Minimizing political influence

One of the most important goals associated with the transition to democratic policing is to reduce political influence over the police. During the martial-law era of policing, the GMD penetrated deeply into all segments of society, with political units and representatives being directly embedded in the military, police agencies, public schools, and state enterprises. Two of the most famous and influential units of the GMD were the Huang Fuxing Branch (黃復興黨部) and Liu Zhongxing Branch (劉中興黨部), with the former representing the veterans and their families and the latter existing in police departments. The NPA's Director-General, local chiefs, and members of supervision divisions commonly had served in posts in such political units and they were routinely involved in decision making regarding performance evaluation, promotion, and the disciplining of police officers. These political units were extremely active during elections, mobilizing the entire police force and available administrative resources to ensure successful campaigns of GMD candidates. Despite constant scrutiny by reformist academics and the opposition party (Chen 1992), many police officers still engaged in assisting GMD candidates during the early years of the post-martial-law era of Taiwan politics.

In theory, the police should be allowed to work independently, largely free of the governing party's interference. In practice, however, a close tie between local politicians and the police is often the case when such a connection benefits both parties (Kelling and Moore 1988). In Taiwan, political influence is most apparent in two areas: the promotion of high ranking officers and the involvement of the police force in elections for public office. Many police officers believe that promotion, particularly advancement to higher commanding positions, is determined primarily by connections to politicians rather than professional qualifications, leading those ambitious officers to ally themselves with particular political parties (Yang 2000). In turn, officers who were promoted because of their political connections are expected to support certain candidates and be involved in campaign activities during elections.

A good example to illustrate a reciprocal relationship between the police and politicians could be found during the 2000 presidential election. The commander of Taipei's Beitou Police Bureau, Wu Zhenji (吳振吉), was reprimanded for meeting with the DDP candidate Chen Shuibian in his police station (Liu 2010). Wu was previously promoted to the commanding position when Chen was mayor of Taipei City. Not unexpectedly, Wu's open welcoming of the opposition candidate at a police station stirred harsh criticism, even though similar visits by GMD candidates were not unheard of in the past. Wu's befriending Chen paid off handsomely for him after Chen won the presidential election. He was promoted swiftly to several higher positions, including that of the director of presidential residence security and the chief of the Jilong Police Bureau. Wu formally joined the DPP in 2003, and was appointed as the first Director-General of National Immigration Agency in 2007. He took early retirement in 2008 after GMD's Ma Yingjiu became the President.

Apparently, a complete separation of the political parties and the police was not an easy task, particularly given that the GMD has exercised nearly total control over the police for decades. Although the NPA and the ruling party have repeatedly declared that "maintaining a politically neutral force in enforcing the law" was a firm policy and top priority (Mon 2003), many people continue to entertain serious doubt about such exhortations. No legislation was proposed during the democratic transition between 1987 and 2000, nor during the Chen's government during the period 2000 to 2008. The lack of institutionalized control of power partially reflects the nature of a post-Confucian society.

A noticeable advancement of political neutrality occurred in 2001 when the Liu Zhongxing Branch officially departed from police agencies. While the GMD was not ready to loosen its association with an unassailable pillar of government control, such a development was inevitable because of the election of DPP candidate Chen as Taiwan's President in 2000. After the 2001 national and local elections, the NPA's Director-General Wang Jinwang (王進旺) proudly announced that "this is the election that the police officers have followed the principles of administrative neutrality most strictly over the past decades" (Chen 2001). It is probably correct to say that political interference in the police affairs has been greatly curtailed after the withdrawal of the GMD from police agencies, and that the impartial enforcement of violations of election rules (particularly voter bribing) regardless of the candidate's party affiliation has prevailed. Nonetheless, there is yet a long way to go in terms of establishing a police force that is totally free of political influence in a post-Confucian society such as that of Taiwan.

Indeed, the path toward political neutrality was not as smooth as the police or the public would have preferred. The first experience of control of the central government between 2000 and 2008 provided the DPP with tremendous opportunities to extend its party influence into all aspects of policing. In 2003, eight high-ranking police officers pledged their loyalty to the DPP during an open ceremony where more than 50 "social elites" were inducted into the party. Observers of this spectacle criticized that the DPP, which as an opposition party in the past had been a strong advocate for the separation of the party and the police, fell into the danger of politicalizing the police in a way similar to what their GMD counterparts had done before.

The final institutionalized separation of partisan politics from the police came when the *Civil Service Administrative Neutrality Law* (公務人員行政中立法) was passed in 2009 under the GMD-dominated Legislative Yuan. The law furnishes all government officials with a clear set of guidelines to perform their duties lawfully, justly, and *neutrally*. It explicitly stipulates, inter alia, that civil servants are permitted to join any political parties and groups, but they cannot hold posts concurrently in such groups or the campaign offices of public office candidates and should not participate in any kind of political activity during business hours. Political activities that civil servants are prohibited from engaging include: (1) using administrative resources to print, disseminate, display writings, drawings, or other items for promotional purposes and related activities; (2) hanging up, putting up, wearing, or showing a flag, emblem, or clothing of a particular political party, group, or candidate for public office in the office space; (3) hosting an assembly, initiating a demonstration, or leading a signing petition; (4) advertising through mass media by title or name; (5) giving orders to persons related to the civil servants' posts or other subjects related to such posts; (6) showing support in campaign or demonstrations, or soliciting vote for public office candidates in public; and (7) other actions prohibited by the orders of the Examination Yuan after consulting the Executive Yuan. The enactment of the neutrality law in civil service was another signal milepost on the road to democracy. The advancement in question is what Cooney (2004) called the thin rule of law versus the thick rule of law; that is, it is possible to process alleged cases of favoritism in a legal process nowadays, while in the past such complaints were poorly regulated by administrative orders and condemned largely in terms of change in moral tone and similar non-adjudicated actions.

While Taiwan has made significant strides in tackling the problem of political influence, the issue continues to surface from time to time in the arena of policing. Public office and political representative elections remain the most troublesome events where the police are scrutinized for whether they fairly and justly enforce election laws related particularly to the investigation of voter bribing. Rank-and-file officers often complain that it is not they who wish to avoid the responsibility for impartial enforcement of election laws. Rather, the heart of the problem rests with some police commanders who have deep connections with some politicians, are sometimes explicitly or implicitly in favor of certain candidates, and are concerned that aggressive enforcement of such laws may jeopardize their future career (Liu 2004).

Given that the police are an integral part of the political system, and as long as reciprocal relationships beneficial to both politicians and the police are possible, political influence will be, more or less, a necessary evil in policing (C. Chang 2000b). On a positive note, such improper influence is negligible in Taiwan street-level officers' decision-making processes during their daily encounters with the public. As in other democracies, elective officials such as the president, city majors, and county executives all have the authority to participate in the selection of officers who they believe to be the most suitable persons for various commanding positions. This is a common practice in democracies worldwide. As such, it is important that elected officials are aware of the detrimental effect of favoritism in choosing police commanders, and they should strive to ensure the integrity, openness, and fairness of the police promotion system. Police administrators should keep in mind that political connections cannot always guarantee a smooth path to career advancement given that a two-party political system has been established whereby the control of a city, county, or national government could change hands at some point in their careers. It follows that the best option for any individual officer with leadership aspirations will be a strong commitment to neutrality and professionalism (C. Chang 2004).

Attempting to enhance service quality

Another development that has swept rapidly through police agencies at the turn of the century involved initiatives aiming at enhancing the quality of police services. These organizational improvements were part of a nationwide movement promoted by the Executive Yuan to implement such business management strategies as *Total Quality Management* (TQM), *Quality Circles* (QCs), *Business Process Re-engineering* (BPR), and standards published by the International Organization for Standardization (known as ISO) in all government agencies (C. Chang *et al.* 2008). Similar to the US professionalism movement which transformed policing in the US in the early twentieth century, these various organizational reform strategies were widely used in the private sector before being introduced to the arena of policing in a number of Western countries.

Based on the general idea that quality of service is the top priority of an organization (Deming 1986), Western police departments incorporated some key elements of quality management strategies, including trained and qualified employees, quality leadership, participatory management, and customer-oriented service programs into their internal and external operations (Chen 2004). The rise of community policing in the US facilitated the adoption of elements of a

48 Historical developments

TQM system, which stress a customer-focused agency that involves all officers in continual improvement. Indeed, the command-and-control or top-down style of leadership became broadly viewed as obsolete when community policing advocates for greater participation of rank-and-file officers in departmental decision-making processes. Police supervisors were encouraged to blend police managerial practices with TQM skills, a combination which tends to optimize community policing techniques (Stevens 2001). Quality leadership may be exemplified by displaying such preferred traits as vision, trustworthiness, inspiration, empathy, loyalty, cleverness, and most importantly, a servant-centered propensity that requires police administrators to internalize leadership as a calling to serve subordinates before self (Gardner and Reece 2012).

One of the most well-known programs that incorporated the principles of quality management into community policing was launched by the Madison, Wisconsin, Police Department during the late 1980s. The implementation of quality leadership and participatory management significantly improved officers' satisfaction with work, supervision, and the department (Wycoff and Skogan 1994). Quality Circles or QCs, which refer to small groups of non-supervisory officers who meet regularly to identify, analyze, and recommend solutions to problems relating to their work, were also adopted by some US police agencies. In the US setting, QCs were found to strengthen small-scale services and improve work-unit morale and management-by-objectives (MBO) showed substantial potential for motivating police managers to improve service outcomes and citizen satisfaction with service

Figure 4.1 Community policing: chatting with residents about their concerns (April 10, 2011).

Source: Photo taken and provided by Hsiu Yuan Chen.

delivery (Harty and Greiner 1984). In the UK, QC programs were set up in a number of police agencies to promote greater officer participation and involvement, stimulate the personal development of officers, and generate practical benefits to the British Police Service and officers through more effective problem solving (Shaw 1989).

The basic principles of quality management strategies meshed well with the transition from the authoritarian to the democratic style of policing in Taiwan. Although law and order remains as the central theme during the democratic era of policing, an emphasis on the quality of police service has inevitably emerged. In addition to strong support from the Executive Yuan and Ministry of the Interior, an undivided commitment to quality management by top and middle managers of the NPA became the essential impetus for organizational improvement. Indeed, while quality management stresses the importance of a client-centred and bottom-to-top approach in organizational decision making, the willingness of top commanders to buy into the ideas and serve as initial change agents is essential. A solid foundation of successful planned changes was laid for quality improvement to the credit of a professionalizing police force.

In 1999, the Foreign Affairs Division of the Taipei City Police Department became the first police unit in Taiwan to receive the ISO quality management certificate. Managerial support reached the peak of attention in 2001 when "The Promotion of the ISO Quality Management System among Police Agencies" was listed as the NPA's mid-range administrative plan for four years between 2002 and 2005. Before launching the initiative as an agency-wide change effort, the NPA designated one police field station (PCS) in Taipei City, Taipei County, and Taoyuan County Police Departments, respectively, as the experimental sites of the ISO system. Taking into consideration local characteristics and crime and disorder problems, these sites designed their own quality management plans and the NPA provided supplemental funds to support the proposed changes. By 2005, the initial system was established in all of the NPA's 152 police district bureaus and their PCSs (C. Chang *et al.* 2008).

Although the ISO systems established in all police districts and field stations were not entirely identical, they shared a similar operational framework, which included three phases: *input, process,* and *output*. The input stage refers chiefly to citizen demands, task requirements, and legal mandates. The process can be either direct or indirect; the direct process involves actions directly serving the public, and the indirect process represents resources and procedures supporting the operation of the direct process. Output is the result or outcome generated by the direct process of serving the public (C. Chang *et al.* 2008). The Quality Control Circle (QCC) was an essential element of the direct and indirect process implemented in many departments. For example, in Taizhong County Police Department, two groups of QCC were set up with one group focusing on research and development and the other stressing operational learning. The concept of QCC was also integrated into quality management programs launched in Taidong County Police Department and Jiayi City Police Department (Chen 2011). These three police departments received the first-place, nationwide award from the Executive Yuan for initiatives and reforms in enhancing the quality of their services.

Evaluations of the impact of various quality management programs were largely encouraging (Chen 2005; Lin 2004; Wu 2002). A study of the ISO quality management system implemented in nine police departments revealed some interesting findings about police officers' and citizens' attitudes regarding the effects of these changes (C. Chang *et al*. 2008). More than half of the officers reported that the ISO process promoted the beautification of their work places, the reallocation of work space, and the management of work files. Over 40 percent of the officers believed that the system improved the quality of police service, the image of police, and the process of file management. The system, however, was less effective in enhancing rank-and-file officers' job satisfaction. On the citizen side, over 60 percent of citizens surveyed expressed favorable attitudes toward how officers responded to their reports of crime, the process through which their cases were handled, and the mechanisms that could be used to file complaints against poorly performing officers. Citizens on average displayed more favorable evaluations of many aspects of policing than their police counterparts, but it is unclear whether their favorable assessments could be linked directly to the ISO system (C. Chang *et al*. 2008).

The quality management movement shared some similar characteristics with police reforms in Western countries. First, they tended to be short-lived, lasting from several years to normally less than a decade, and then being replaced by newer programs or initiatives. A good example would be the team policing movement that rose quickly in the US in the late 1960s, but was largely abandoned in the 1970s. Taiwan's development of its quality management system seemed to follow the same general pattern, reaching the peak from 2002 to 2005 and then losing its popularity gradually after that. There haven't been any reports about the system or related new programs since 2010, marking the waning of the ISO system. A second and related point is that the movement can be characterized as predominately transactional change, one which entails interventions directed toward structure, systems, management practices, work climate, and motivation of an organization; transformational change, in contrast, targets organizational culture, strategy and mission, and leadership (French and Bell 1995). A recent example is the post-9/11 reforms of US policing when virtually all organizational changes undertaken by state and local police agencies in reaction to 9/11 were transactional in nature (Marks and Sun 2007).

Police agencies, including the Taiwan police, undoubtedly have transformational change in mind when implementing organizational reform. Nonetheless, such change is difficult to achieve and could be costly and time-consuming because it requires changes in some of the underlying cultures and professional goals of the police organizations. Indeed, after roughly a decade of the quality management movement, there is no concrete evidence showing that police cultures and fundamental missions and goals have actually been modified in Taiwan. To be fair, positive improvements in strengthening the processes and procedures of internal operation and furnishing quality service to external clients should be acknowledged. Whether such organization change could persist in the future policing in Taiwan remains an open question, however.

Maintaining core missions

Looking back at the first decade of the new century, *law and order* remained the top mission for the Taiwan police (C. Chang *et al.* 2011; Mon and Liang 2011). Such an orientation, however, was not always evident across times and places in the country because of a quick turnover of NPA top leadership and the emergence of greater local autonomy in policing.

When the DPP was in power between 2000 and 2008, four different career police officers were appointed as leaders of the NPA. Not surprisingly, when each of them came into office they would characteristically continue some existing tactics and programs and advocate a few new ones for all police departments to follow. In 2003, for example, the then Director-General Wang Jin-wang promoted a new "maintaining law and order capability" system, one which used different colors of light to indicate whether violent crime and theft rates had increased or decreased greater than a 5 percent margin over the past year. This system took a figurative back seat when the next Director-General Zhang Siliang (張四良) launched a SAFE (Satisfied service, Anti-terrorism, Forensic expertise, and Electronic information) project in 2004. The goal of this effort was to increase crime clearance rates by 60 percent, to reduce criminal cases by 5 percent, and to decrease traffic accident deaths by 3,000 per annum. Zhang's short tenure caused his ambitious SAFE project to disappear upon his replacement. In 2005, a nationwide campaign of law and order was launched under the supervision of Director-General Xie Yindang (謝銀黨). His successor Hou Youyi (侯友宜) continued the anti-crime efforts of his successor by strengthening the investigation of Internet-related crimes and initiating a countrywide crime victimization survey (C. Chang *et al.* 2011).

The current NPA Director-General Wang Zhuojun (王卓鈞) took office in 2008 after the GMD regained its control of the central government. Wang proposed four major goals for the police to fulfill, including human rights protection, effectiveness enhancement, discipline strengthening, and image improvement. Five specific directions set out to accomplish these goals were: (1) establishing a model of administration by law; (2) dedicating to law and order and traffic enforcement; (3) building an upright and professional police image; (4) striving for intra-agency support to form collaborative, cross-strait anti-crime mechanisms; and (5) rendering service to the public with true sincerity (C. Chang *et al.* 2011). While law and order was still highlighted, there were additional competing themes in policing. Other important initiatives during Wang's tenure included incorporating public affairs outreach into policing by enhancing media relations, expanding legislative contacts, domestic and international visits, and police-initiated charitable and voluntary activities, and increasing enforcement efforts to prevent and prosecute traffic violations by utilizing new technology and improving service quality in handling traffic accidents (C. Chang *et al.* 2011).

As mentioned in Chapter 3, local control of the police has been substantially enhanced after the passage of the *Local Autonomy Statute* in 1999. Under the direct supervision of mayors or county executives, police chiefs are much more likely to design and then implement localized policing strategies and tactics based on the characteristics of each locality. For example, in Taidong County, which covers mainly agricultural and largely rural areas, order maintenance and services rather than crime fighting constitute the core missions of the police since crime is of a much less concern for local residents. While police departments by and large adhere to the general guidelines set by the NPA in terms of their missions, the rise of strong local control of the police has made police forces much more diversified in terms of setting the priorities of local law enforcement and selecting the principal goals to be sought in policing.

Two other developments related to maintaining core missions are also worth mentioning. First, as in the past, the evolution of Taiwan policing in the twenty-first century was driven chiefly by *exogenous forces*, developments in the broader society which subsequently triggered *endogenous* forces of change. As part of an open system that operates within a highly complex environment, the police are influenced by some changes in their social, political, and economic environments. The evolution of policing practices thus often entails organizational adaption to changes in a larger environment or a survival tool utilized by the police to maintain their organizational legitimacy (Crank and Langworthy 1992; Zhao 1996). How the Taiwan police have handled two types of crimes perhaps illustrates this point well. Telephone fraud and consumer scam crime became a widespread phenomenon as of the early 2000s, driving the total fraud cases up steadily from 37,191 in 2003 to 43,023 in 2005 (NPA 2013). Public outcry and political pressure pushed the police to move swiftly to tackle the problem. In 2005, the "165 anti-fraud consultation hotline" was established and a joint service platform was created to integrate police counter-fraud practices with these of financial institutions and telephone companies. The NPA also worked closely with foreign governments (in particular China and Philippines) to conduct joint crackdowns on phone fraud syndicates. The total fraud cases dropped dramatically to 20,421 in 2012 (NPA 2013).

The other offense would be theft, which has been the most common crime in Taiwan for decades. Along with the rapid economic development, thefts have shown little sign of receding before 2000. To combat the problem, the NPA implemented several programs specifically aimed at dealing with residential invasion and vehicle thefts. Vehicle owners were encouraged to have their car and motorcycle parts engraved with codes, making the selling of stolen property harder and the detection of such crime easier. After initially favorable results were noted, a similar program was extended to agricultural and fishing tools and machines. Official statistics have shown a downward trend for total theft in recent years, decreasing from 330,655 in 2003 to 100,264 in 2012, more than a two-thirds reduction. Both automobiles and motorcycle vehicle thefts have dropped as much as 80 percent during the same time period (NPA 2013). These reductions were attributed mainly to the NPA's vehicle parts engraving program and aggressive enforcement against the selling and buying of illegal property. Additionally, patrol officers were equipped with palm-size personal computers which allowed them to quickly check a lost-vehicle database onsite and detain the vehicle and driver if a positive match was found (Jiang 2011). Although the accuracy of these official crime reports remains somewhat in doubt (Hebenton and Jou 2014), the police have clearly demonstrated their capacity to suppress crimes with more reliable data – namely, data on homicide rates. Indeed, homicide rates have shown a downward trend since 1998, even during the democratic transition from a high of 781 cases in 1998 to 385 cases in 2011 (Hebenton and Jou 2014).

Second, the last decade has also witnessed greater international and regional cooperation in crime fighting between Taiwan and foreign authorities. The best example and fastest development is the cross-border cooperation between Taiwan and China. As mentioned in Chapter 3, in 1990 Taiwan and mainland China signed the *Jinmen Accord* to regulate the mutual repatriation of criminals, smugglers, and fugitives by sea. The agreement was a breakthrough as it represented the first time that Taiwan and mainland China authorities jointly resolved a security concern by setting aside political differences and pursuing a mutually beneficial common ground. Repatriation operations, however, were often slow because the accord was signed by non-governmental organizations (i.e., the Red Cross for both sides), resulting in a weak binding power (Cheng and Sun 2013). The accord also lacked specific guidance as to how to handle other aspects of crime fighting and legal assistance. Without having a standardized operational procedure to which to adhere, requests for non-repatriation assistance have been handled entirely on a case-by-case basis.

The relationship between Taiwan and China then plummeted in the mid-1990s when China launched missiles close to Taiwan and Taiwan's President Li Denghui visited the US in what was seen as a near state visit. Political disagreements and a bitter relationship between Taiwan and mainland China extended into the new century when the DPP came into power amid a great need to strengthen collaboration in cross-strait law enforcement for the Taiwan government. Since Taiwan is a post-Confucian society where the civil society is weak and political parties do not have a specific social base (Moody 1992), attitudes toward unification became a rallying point for the DPP, a fact which stimulated the nerves of the Chinese government on the other side of the Taiwan Strait. As a response to the continuous movement toward the functional, de facto independence of Taiwan, China kept the interaction with the DPP to the minimal level possible during the eight years of Chen's government.

After several years of negotiation and many working meetings, finally in 2009 both sides reached agreement on the *Accord on Anti-crime Collaboration and Mutual Legal Assistance across the Strait* (海峽兩岸共同打擊犯罪與司法互助協議). Based on the general principle of "comprehensive cooperation and focused strike" both sides agreed to target telephone/Internet fraud, economic crimes, drug trafficking, and human smuggling. The accord significantly expanded cooperation in policing between the two Chinese societies by formalizing the exchange of crime intelligence, the provision of legal documents, investigation and evidence collection,

54 *Historical developments*

the delivery of evidence and property, and the granting of permission for human rights visits (Mon and Liang 2011). In 2010, the NPA delegation led by Director-General Wang Zhuojun met with China's Minister of Public Security, marking the first time in history that top police leaders of both Taiwan and China have met in public. Conferences on policing attended by practitioners and researchers from four Chinese societies – China, Hong Kong, Macao, and Taiwan – have been held annually since 2006. In addition, police delegations from many major Chinese municipal and provincial police departments have visited Taiwan in recent years.

An improved cross-strait relationship is clearly beneficial to regional stability and Sino-American relations. But from time to time cross-strait relations become strained because of US support for Taiwan. Relations are jeopardized because China is still selective in investigating cases or arresting suspects/fugitives as requested by Taiwan. An example is the case of Chen Youhao (陳由豪). Chen was a successful businessman in Taiwan who maintained good relations with top officials in both the GMD and the DPP, making generous cash contributions to candidates of both parties. During the 1990s, Chen's enterprises borrowed about US$4 billion collectively from a number of banks in Taiwan. Due to over-expansion, his businesses experienced severe financial crises and went into bankruptcy in 2001, resulting in a total of US$2 billion in defaulted loans. In 2001, Chen fled Taiwan using his US passport and later settled in China. In 2003, Chen was officially charged with fraud and embezzlement and put on Taiwan's ten most wanted fugitives list. Chen successfully rebuilt a new business enterprise in Xiamen, China. He maintained great relations with Chinese officials and became a major local tax payer. Despite repeated requests from Taiwan's legal authorities, China didn't make any move to detain him. Chen later obtained China's ID card and China has declined Taiwan's repatriation requests on the grounds that Chen has become a Chinese citizen. Despite a few cases such as those of Chen, it would be safe to predict that cross-strait cooperation will continue to grow as long as both sides are willing to put aside political considerations and focus on crime and justice concerns.

Summary

"Taiwan remains a high social control society with a low crime rate" (Huang and Sun 2014: 280). The ability of police to control crime has been consistent and was not affected adversely by the most important political development in Taiwan in the beginning of the twenty-first century when the DPP won the presidential election due to a split within the GMD. The DPP's coming into power has forced the GMD to officially withdraw its political machine out of police departments, a change which constituted a major advancement in terms of law enforcement political neutrality. At the same time, the DPP was eager to expand its representation in the police by actively recruiting top-ranking officers into the party through open ceremonies, a practice that had rarely been explored in the past. The promulgation of the *Civil Service Administrative Neutrality Law* in 2009 finally changed the atmosphere of politics as usual in the post-Confucian society, and it provided clear instructions for government officials to follow and moved the battle field for the processing of complaints from the moral arena to the legal arena. Despite clear signs of progress toward democratic policing, elections for public office continue to be a problematic area where the police are scrutinized for whether election laws are being fairly and justly enforced.

As part of a nationwide reform, quality management programs were implemented by various police departments throughout the country. An emphasis on service quality meshed well with the transition from an authoritarian to democratic style of policing in Taiwan. Similar to the reforms implemented in Western police forces, the quality management movement in the Taiwan police tended to be short-lived, lasting from several years to normally less than a decade, and most changes accomplished were transactional rather than transformational in nature. Evaluations of the impact of various quality management programs on police and public attitudes were largely encouraging, but their long term influences on policing remain rather unclear.

Crime rates, best illustrated by the homicide rates (Hebenton and Jou 2014), continue to decline as democracy takes root in Taiwan. Law and order remained the top mission for the Taiwan police in the twenty-first century. Such a consistent focus was not always evident, however, because of a high rate of turnover in top leadership and the emergence of greater autonomy in local policing practices. Four career officers assumed the positions of NPA Director-General within the space of eight years. They each kept some existing tactics and programs intact, but each successive NPA leader also advocated some new ones to be adopted by the entire force. Policing was driven chiefly by exogenous forces which, in turn, triggered endogenous forces of change. The NPA responded to phone fraud and residential and vehicle theft proactively and aggressively, leading to reductions for both types of crime over the past several years. The DPP's strained relations with the Chinese government jeopardized police cooperation across the strait for a number of years. Nonetheless, a major breakthrough was achieved recently with the signing of an agreement on mutual collaboration in crime fighting and legal assistance. Cross-strait cooperation is expected to grow as long as political considerations can be deliberately de-emphasized.

Part II
Critical issues

5 Training, education, and promotion

The recruitment of police officers through education is a practice unique to Taiwan, with strong initial influences in this regard coming from Germany and Japan. Because Chiang Kai-Shek saw the police as an extension of the military, the early years of the police after the 2/28 Incident bear a reflection of the belief in the inseparability of the military and police. The main goal of the police was to guard the GMD's regime and to be ready to recover mainland China at the earliest possible time. Since the late 1970s, the promotion of police professionalism has emerged as a priority, and in the new century, the idea of democratic policing has been firmly established in Taiwan.

Currently, the National Police Agency (NPA) functions within the Ministry of the Interior. It has approximately 1,600 *paichusuo* (and *fenzhusuo*) or police field stations located in Taiwan's 26 cities/counties. Although the nature of the police has been recast from high policing to low policing, the centralized structure of the police has been modified only slightly at the end of democratic transition in 1999 with regard to the active participation of local elected officials in the process of the appointment of city/county police chiefs. All other aspects of the centralized national police force remain intact. The police in Taiwan take a national character, wearing the same uniform regardless of their jurisdictions and are subject to a similar set of rules and regulations in their operation and their management. Compared with the period during martial law, the military's control over the police has been withdrawn and the agency is much more professional and more independently run as a consequence. It has likewise become a much more apolitical force in domestic politics. As of 2012, the police force employs more than 80,000 officers, and it is pursuing greater diversity in its ranks. Approximately 7 percent of officers in the force are female, compared to only 3.4 percent in 2004; similarly, greater diversity in ethnicity and language is being pursued as well.

In the US, there is no unified policing system. With the growing but still limited influence of the US Justice Department, policing in the US remains a very loosely coupled system without central direction, authority, or financing (Manning 1997). Consequently, the problem of generalization from American police practices is most difficult. This difficulty applies equally for the processes relating to the recruitment, selection, training, and retention of US police officers. There are many ways that American police departments recruit their junior officers.

60 *Critical issues*

Depending on the location (size of department, rural versus urban setting, county versus city jurisdiction), most police departments require an educational background of a high school diploma/GED as a minimum, and police cadets have to spend three to six months at a police academy. Even the most prestigious police training institution – the FBI Academy – does not offer any educational degree, such as a BA or MA. There is a clear separation between professional training, which the academies do best, and higher education offered exclusively by independent colleges and universities. Beyond the police academy, it is up to police officers themselves as to whether they are interested in pursuing an academic degree. Since the 1990s a few states, such as Ohio, have required a minimum of associate college degrees for all new officers. A few cities require a minimum of a bachelor's degree. Mostly, however, having a BA degree is a plus and honor; it is not required, and it does not necessarily relate to a promotion to a higher rank or administrative position. In some cases, it is not even associated with an increase in base salary. Similarly, even for the police chief, a master's degree is not compulsory, but simply a bonus. Many small town police chiefs, especially in the nation's rural areas, are simply a veteran patrol officer. Simply stated, in the US in general, experience is viewed as more important than academic degrees in most local jurisdictions; the exception would be the largest cities and state and federal law enforcement positions where academic degrees are increasingly required for initial appointment. In the US it is extremely rare to find a police chief with a PhD degree, but it is fair to say that MA degrees are rapidly becoming a requirement for the more prestigious police executive positions across the US – namely, in the nation's major cities and in state police executive ranks.

The concept of police is an imported idea in Taiwan; its design has been gradually grounded with a strong local taste. Taiwan is largely a post-Confucian society (Moody 1988), which not only has a centralized system of law enforcement, but also emphasizes educational achievement through competitive examinations for all its civil servants, the police included. These public sector competitive examinations are viewed as so important that there is an Examination Yuan (考试院), an official entity that represents one of the five pillar *yuan*s or branches of the government promulgated in the constitution of ROC. The other four *yuan*s are the executive branch, the legislative branch, the judiciary branch, and the control branch. These five *yuan*s reflect Sun's Yat-sen's attempts to merge Chinese and Western institutional forms. The Examination Yuan and Control Yuan (which monitors and sanctions the behavior of public officials) are based on institutions found in the traditions of Imperial China.

One of the most important contributions of Chinese civilization was the invention of the competitive examination system which would ensure that all people may have a chance to rise to the top of the social hierarchy based on merit alone. Police officers, as civil servants, are no exception to this general rule. As Manning (1997) states, policing in many respects represents an action out of the collective conscience. In Taiwan, the collective conscience in practice requires that all police officers have to go through many examinations in the process of their occupational training and they are required to have an equivalent of at least an associate degree before hitting the street as rookie cops.

It is interesting to note that Bayley (1985: 50) has observed that the East Asian forms of modern policing were in fact the world leaders in developing and implementing a systematic educational program for police officers and enlisted personnel. The most prominent characteristic of the current police educational system is that there is a strong connection between the educational degree and the level of responsibility to be assumed, which may be one of the most deep-seated national traditions in policing in Taiwan (Hebenton and Jou 2008). Basically, a two-track educational system is utilized, resulting in two different groups of police officers – namely, *street-level* officers and *management* officers. Both tracks emphasize the importance of formal education, and they qualify people based on their ability to pass the relevant examinations. Taiwan Police College (TPC 台灣警察專科學校) has the mission to train the rank-and-file officers, while the Central Police University (CPU 中央警察大學) is responsible for cultivating police leaders who will climb the administrative ladder over the course of their careers in policing. After graduation with a bachelor's (CPU) or associate bachelor's (TPC) degree, police cadets begin their two separate tracks for their police careers. Without getting into the CPU to obtain a bachelor's degree or complete supervisory in-service training, TPC graduates are mostly likely to be stuck at the level of frontline officer for life.

Taiwan has developed a police bureaucratic hierarchy of three levels featuring 13 ranks (see Table 5.1). The three levels are *officer* (警佐), *inspector* (警正), and *superintendent* (警監), with four ranks in each level and a special level for the last group (see Table 5.1). The current entry-level rank for TPC graduates is Police Officer Rank Two (警佐二級), whereas CPU graduates start their career at the level of Police Inspector Rank Four (警正四級). Using the rank structure of the New York City Police Department (NYPD) as a comparison, Police Officer Rank One is roughly equivalent to NYPD's sergeants and Police Inspector Rank Four is close to NYPD's lieutenants. A district commander normally carries a rank of Inspector Three or Four, similar to a captain or deputy inspector in charge of a

Table 5.1 The ranks of Taiwan Police

Police Superintendent General (警監特級)
Police Superintendent Rank One (警監一級)
Police Superintendent Rank Two (警監二級)
Police Superintendent Rank Three (警監三級)
Police Superintendent Rank Four (警監四級)
Police Inspector Rank One (警正一級)
Police Inspector Rank Two (警正二級)
Police Inspector Rank Three (警正三級)
Police Inspector Rank Four (警正四級)
Police Officer Rank One (警佐一級)
Police Officer Rank Two (警佐二級)
Police Officer Rank Three (警佐三級)
Police Officer Rank Four (警佐四級)

NYPD precinct. Promotion opportunities in such a pyramidal structure are highly limited, particularly for TPC graduates. Without an academic degree from Central Police University, it is very difficult to move to the level of inspector, and it is impossible to move to the level of superintendent. We will examine the details of career mobility and advancement in the following sections.

In this chapter we discuss the police educational system and police promotion practices. The discussion is divided into three parts: the making of the rank-and-file, the cultivation of police supervisors, and the character of promotion processes.

The making of the rank-and-file

As the Taiwan police remain a highly bureaucratic and largely centralized institution, police reform measures tend to be implemented from the top down to the bottom. Accordingly, police training has been formalized from the top down from day one. On October 27, 1945, Hu Fuxiang (胡福相) established the Taiwan Provincial Police Training Center (台湾省警察训练所), which in due course became the current Taiwan Police College. Over the following years, the institution's name changed several times. On April 1, 1948, it was reorganized and renamed "Taiwan Provincial Police Academy." After the Police Education Statute was amended and implemented on June 9, 1982, the Academy began to grant associate degrees to its graduates. On July 1, 1986, the Taiwan Provincial Police Academy changed its name to the Taiwan Police Academy. On April 16, 1988, "The Organizational Statute of Taiwan Police College" was passed during the eighty-first session of the Legislative Yuan. Then, on June 15, 1988, the "Taiwan Police Academy" was formally upgraded to that of "Taiwan Police College."

Recently, President Chen Lianzhen (陈连桢) of Taiwan Police College traced the college's roots back to "Police and Correction Officer Training Center of the Taiwan Governor" (1898–1945) (台湾总督府警察及司狱官练习所) (Chen 2012: 38). He further encourages professors and students at TPC to learn from many wise police practices stemming from the period of the Japanese rule. Some of the relevant good practices in question, such as Japanese Guidelines for Speech Patterns in Taiwanese, have been translated into Chinese (Wang 2012a, 2012b).

In 1986, shortly before the repeal of martial law, the supervision and control of the Taiwan Police College (TPC) was transferred from the province level to the National Police Agency (NPA), Ministry of the Interior. Since then, it has been financed and run by the NPA. Currently, the TPC is in charge of training all of the entry-level police officers in the country. All of its cadets, once admitted through entrance examinations, enjoy both scholarships (tuition wavier) and stipends (monthly payment). After graduating, they have to pass the national civil service examinations to qualify as serving police officers. If they fail to pass these mandatory civil service examinations, they become "wandering cops" (流浪警察). The stakes are even higher for those cadets who invested four years of their lives in the Central Police University than for those who studied two years in the TPC.

A second or "special" way to become enrolled in the TPC is to participate in the national civil service examinations for the police as a first step. If applicants pass the highly competitive examination, they are admitted into the TPC as special examination students (特考生), who will not only enjoy similar benefits (free tuition and a stipend), but also have their years at the TPC count toward their total civil service years upon their retirement. Gender quotas were lifted for this group of students by the Examination Yuan in 2011 (NPA 2012). As many as 40 percent of those admitted to the college were female applicants in that year (Chinese Women's Research Network 2013).

All applicants for the college must graduate from a high school and must be younger than 28 years old. There is also a lower limit on height; for males, it is 1.65 meters (5 feet, 4 inches) and for females it is 1.6 meters (5 feet, 2.5 inches). In the US, height and weight requirements have been a highly controversial issue in the past (Walker 1999) because such standards do indeed discriminate against women and against many Asian and Hispanic applicants. While the weight and height requirements have been replaced in most jurisdictions by the rule of a *reasonable proportion between height and weight* in the US, such requirements surprisingly have not been challenged in Taiwan up to now.

Gender equity remains an issue for the police force in Taiwan. The TPC's traditional route or regular class annual cohort (i.e., students who take the entrance exam first, then the civil service examination at the end of their academy training) features only 10 percent female cadets, a quota set by the NPA. This quota persists even though female applicants tend to do significantly better on their competitive examinations than their male counterparts. Differential treatment of female applicants continues for the time being, but will likely become a more contentious issue in the future as gender equity becomes a more widely shared value in post-democracy Taiwan.

Once passing the entrance examination, students are accepted into one of the TPC's five majors: Department of Police Administration, Department of Criminal Investigation, Department of Disaster Management, Department of Traffic Management, and Department of Maritime Police. The education and training received over the course of two years include both classroom training during regular academic semesters, and FTO (field training officers) supervised, on-the-job type training at *paichusuo* (PCS) or police field stations during summer months.

The content of the police education curricula has changed significantly since the lifting of martial law. All ideological indoctrination political courses have been abolished during the course of the democratic transition. The new curriculum is geared toward knowledge acquisition and skill building in preparation for being a police officer. The educational goal, according to the TPC website, is

> ...based on the principles of "integration of theory and practice" and "equal emphasis on knowledge and skills," to cultivate grassroots law enforcers who are equipped with professional knowledge and capability, strong physique, humanistic cultivation, integrity and morality, organizational discipline.

The perspective lies in cultivating excellent police officers and building the distinguished brand.

(TPC 2014)

In addition to training entry-level police officers, the TPC also runs two short-term educational programs: police in-service training programs, designed to promote professional skills and increase working efficiency and effectiveness; and an advanced class, designed for the senior officers with the purpose of improving their knowledge and ability to fit their new jobs after receiving a promotion. The latter has rarely been conducted in recent years since this assignment has largely been given to the CPU.

Once graduating from the police college and passing the national civil service examinations for law enforcement officers, these cadets are assigned to work throughout Taiwan as police officers of Rank Two. There are four ranks within the police officer level (see Table 5.1). Rank Three and Rank Four became out-of-date once the TPC moved to the NPA in 1986, and offered only associate degrees. In the past, the TPC also recruited from among junior high school graduates, and after two years of training these graduates began their careers at Officer Rank Four.

From Officer Rank Two it usually takes line officers an average of eight years to move to Rank One, and this is only if opportunities for promotion become available. To be promoted to the next level of inspector, officers have to take a special examination and subsequently receive eight months of additional training at the CPU. Alternatively, they can go through an internal promotion examination process managed by the Ministry of the Interior. Finally, they can work to obtain an academic degree from the CPU. If they do not wish to engage in any of these courses of action, they are unlikely to be promoted beyond Officer Rank One. They cannot, moreover, go beyond Police Inspector Rank Two without first obtaining a bachelor's degree. Such qualifications could be waived only for special promotions (the so-called break-rank promotions 破格晉升), which occur occasionally as a way to reward officers for uncommon bravery or noticeably heroic actions.

The graduates from the TPC educational process constitute eighty percent of Taiwan's low ranking police personnel, forming the core foundation of the force. They work at PCSs located throughout the country, and they have, among all police officers, the most frequent contacts with the public. Any police force is only as good as the aggregate of its rank-and-file members; and equally true is the observation that a police force is only as strong as its weakest or least professional officers.

The cultivation of police supervisors

In addition to attending the TPC, high school graduates can take more competitive entrance examinations to go directly to Central Police University (CPU). Taking this route, by the time they graduate they will receive a BA degree. While receive a full range of training and education, they still have to pass the national civil service examinations to qualify for placement in a law enforcement leadership position. This final requirement has created some problems for a small number of cadets, who after four years of education and training fail to pass the national civil service examinations and thus cannot be sworn in as a police officer. Heavy reliance on the written examinations, and downplaying the importance of other qualifications such as oral ability, physical and psychological fitness, and law enforcement-related background result in this misfortunate situation.

For the overwhelming majority of those who pass the national civil service examinations, they will start their career as an Inspector Rank Four. There are four ranks within the inspector level, and through hard work and due diligence in carrying out their duties these "rookies" can expect to move up in ranks in due course. More often than not, a short cut for accelerated promotion is the earning of a master's degree. The acquisition of advanced degrees becomes imperative later in their careers if CPU graduates aspire to be one of the 26 police chiefs in Taiwan.

Unlike Taiwan Police College, the CPU is not under the direct supervision of the NPA, but rather stands as a parallel unit within the Ministry of the Interior. The CPU president enjoys an elevated rank comparable to that of the Superintendent General of the NPA. The mission of the CPU is to train qualified cadets and police officers to be leaders in all of the nation's police organizations. At its beginnings, the CPU's education reflected the values and styles of continental European police system rather than those characteristics of common law societies. Since the CPU moved to Taiwan, it began to take on more of the characteristics of Confucian society; in particular, it came to emphasize the use of examinations more and accorded less weight to other qualifications and personal attributes.

On September 1, 1936, by merging several existing police training schools, the GMD government established the Central Police Academy in the town of Ma-qun near Nanjing for the purpose of unifying the police educational system and cultivating police administrative personnel. At that time, two- and three-year police education programs were available in China. At the breakout of the war with Japan in 1937, the fledging school was moved west to *Danzishi* in Chongqing – the war-time capital of China.

After the triumph experienced in the Sino-Japanese War in 1945, the school was moved back to Nanjing outside Guanghua City-Gate. In accordance with national policy, the training for army officers who would become police administration and other specialized public safety professions, was expanded. Besides Nanjing, six additional schools were established in Xi'an, Guangzhou, Dihua, Chongqing, Beijing and Shenyang, and two officer training centers were founded in Shanghai and Taiwan. The multi-campus school flourished for a time, with a student body of more than 12,000 at its apex. Toward the end of the Civil War (1946–9), the school was forced to move to Guangzhou, then to Chongqing, and finally to Taiwan where it was consolidated with the Training Course for Police Officers in Taipei. In June 1950, the school founded in 1936 was closed.

In October of 1954, the Academy reopened and classes resumed. In 1957, it was expanded into a four-year college. The college began with two departments, those of Police Administration and Criminal Investigation; thereafter, the establishment of other departments of Public Security, Crime Prevention and Corrections, Household Administration, Fire Service, Traffic Science, Foreign Affairs Police, Military-Service Administration, Administrative Management, Information Management, Border Police, Maritime Police, Forensic Science and Law all followed in due course.

In 1970 the CPU began to offer the MA degree in police administration through its graduate school. This represented an important step to illustrate one of the core characteristics of a Confucian society. In common-law societies, no police academy can grant an educational degree, while in Germany and France police academies do not grant educational degrees beyond the bachelor's degree because they consider police education to be a professional training process, not a formal education. In other Confucian societies, such as South Korea and Japan, it is now possible to get a master's degree from a police college.

In 1987, Yan Shi-xi (顏世錫) became the president of the Central Police College and he changed the name slightly in Chinese (Yan 2012) to reflect the democratic nature of the institution: it changed from the Central Police Officers' Academy (中央警官学校) to the Central Police Academy (中央警察学校). The slight change in wording is intended to connote the idea that police officers are now equal in status to the citizens they serve, not above them as bureaucrats enjoying a superior status. It was also during his administration that the school began to develop a PhD program in criminology – the first of its kind in the world to be offered by a police institution.

The graduate school of the Central Police Academy began to offer the PhD degree to students in 1994. This was a truly major innovation. No other police colleges in the world had attempted to make their mark on the world in this way up to this point. About ten years later, the Chinese People's Public Security University followed suit. At this point, these two universities are the only police educational institutions that offer a PhD degree – initiating another symbolic tradition in the global process of professionalization in policing (Hebenton and Jou 2008).

In addition to establishing research institutes and holding regular courses, the Academy holds seminars for the promotion of in-service police officers and organizes specialized professional seminars on a wide range of topics. It also admits foreign students, cooperates with foreign universities, exchanges teachers and students, holds frequent academic seminars, and takes active part in international academic organizations and global scope police professional activities. Approved by the Legislative Yuan on December 12, 1995, the school, with roots going back to Nanjing in 1936, was formally renamed Central Police University.

Three distinct kinds of students attend the CPU. The first kind is high school students who pass competitive written, oral, and physical examinations and are recruited for the four-year bachelor degree program. The second kind is commissioned police officers with an associate college degree who have already served some time in uniform. The program provides an opportunity for these officers to receive a higher academic degree, and more importantly, to achieve promotion in ranks in their career. Upon successful completion, the commissioned cadets return to the police organization from which they came and are promoted to the position of inspector (警正). Finally, in the new century, the third kind of students can enter the university by taking the national civil service examinations for the law enforcement. In general, CPU professors do not prefer this type of students, favoring instead their own students for the most part. These professors sit in the Examination Yuan and participate in designing the examination items. Some critics believe that they use all the influence at their disposal to privilege the training of their own students and help them score well on standardized tests.

After the successful completion of their education and upon passing the national civil service examinations, the cadets are assigned as an Inspector Rank Four to PCSs throughout the country. Successful graduates then begin to climb the police hierarchy.

After so many decades of women's social movement globally, it is a bit unexpected that gender equity has never been high on the agenda of the police administration. The NPA has arbitrarily set each year's new recruits to reflect a proportion of 9 to 1, meaning only ten percent of new cadets are female. The resistance to accepting women as equal partners in policing in Taiwan partially reflects the influence of the patriarchal culture worldwide, and the enduring influence of Confucianism which favors longstanding practices that tend to perpetuate institutional injustices. With the advent of democracy, the time may have come to integrate policewomen fully into the force (see Chapter 8 for more detailed discussion).

Democratic policing may also raise the issue at some time in the future of the eventual civilianization of the police university so that it could be run more academically. Sam Houston State University in the United States, a formal partner university which engages in frequent exchanges with the CPU, is a potential role model in this regard. It is a comprehensive state university with a strong focus on criminal justice education and offers various programs for training of police and correctional officers in the state of Texas. Although the university grants academic degrees, these degrees are not necessarily associated with professional development for law enforcement officers. Most of its PhD students, for example, will take faculty positions in other universities rather than move up the ladder into executive law enforcement positions.

In Taiwan both National Taipei University and National Chong Cheng University offer degree programs in criminology/criminal justice. These educational institutions produce graduates who are capable of serving the need of police officers who wish to earn a graduate degree. Emerging from the military-led police past, some critics of the current police education system argue that there is no need to have two police-only educational institutions in a democratic society, and they maintain furthermore that the Taiwan police should not continue to operate the closed system resembling the military system. The strict hierarchical culture based on seniority within the police is seen as detrimental for the development of open mindedness, which is broadly believed to be a necessary condition for a scholar and likely a good quality in police executives. Education is different from training; the essence of education is to expand knowledge through innovation.

But innovation cannot be prescribed from above. By definition, innovation does not arise from following existing routines. It requires individual autonomy, and can flourish only when students feel free to express their ideas regardless of what the prevailing authorities believe. Institutions, such as the TPC and the CPU, have a long tradition of strict hierarchical order and the maintenance of an authoritarian atmosphere; both of these conditions tend to stifle creativity. Little in the way of scientific research initiatives, and more in the way of white-washing products from the officially sanctioned CPU are the natural consequences of too much control on what scholars are allowed to do and how they are permitted to do it. To be fair, even if some professors want to do or are able to do an impartial research project, their positions in the political embedded universities have foreshadowed their results.

Alternatively, the CPU can focus exclusively on police training, and not take upon itself the degree granting role. The Taiwan Investigation Bureau within the Ministry of Justice has set up a role model in that regard. For special agents working in the Bureau, they do not have their own specialized college or university. Instead, the Investigation Bureau runs its own academy and offers non-degree programs ranging from a week long in-service training to nearly a year long new agent training.

As the police transition from an all-inclusive revolutionary force to guard the regime stability to a democratic professional force to provide police services, the military drills in training and in daily activities seem to be somewhat out of place. Civilization of the police most likely needs to begin with the police training provided at the outset of their career. There are, of course, naysayers in any reform effort, especially when one's own individual interest is at stake. Without dismantling the police university, however, the image of the police state from the past authoritarian regime will continue to persist for many citizens of Taiwan.

Promotion

As is the case elsewhere in the world, Taiwan law enforcement agencies are organized along quasi-military lines. That is, they resemble the military in some but not all respects of their operation. Like in the military, police officers wear uniform, have ranks, and carry firearms. The police command structure is hierarchical, with commands flowing from the top to the bottom of the authority structure. The police are divided into subunits such as platoons, squads, and details. In their chain of command, officers do not report directly to the highest ranking officers but rather to their immediate supervisors; in the case of police officers, in most cases sergeants and lieutenants are the supervisors in question. The organizational style is authoritarian, with stiff penalties for failing to obey lawful orders. Officers have legal authority to intrude into citizens' lives, to restrict their liberty through detention or arrest, and to use physical (even deadly) force if necessary. Unlike the military, however, the police serve a citizen population rather than fight a foreign enemy. They often provide services designed to help people, and these services are frequently requested by individual citizens. They are constrained by laws protecting the rights of citizens. Finally, they routinely exercise individual discretion in carrying out their professional duties.

Taiwan police operate on a dual-track system featuring one form of education for front-line officers and the other form of education for police managers. There is a high correlation between the degree received and the pace of promotion experienced in a career. In general, getting an additional degree beyond that of a BA will accelerate promotion. This is most particularly true if the aim is to hold one of the 26 local police chief positions at the superintendent level. However, 80 percent of line officers who do not hold a bachelor's degree do not have much chance for further promotion. Ironically, only about 20 percent of CPU graduates focus their attention on promotion in ranks.

There is considerable controversy over whether the commonly used tests in policing select the best-qualified people (Walker 1999). Written examinations, for example, test factual knowledge but may not indicate the applicant's potential for working as a supervisor. Oral interviews may compensate for some of the inadequacy of written examinations, but they could also be subjective and reflect the biases of the interviewers. Likewise, in an unprofessional and unethical police department, officers with high standards of integrity could receive low performance scores from their supervisors. Physical and psychological fitness tests can contribute to a more comprehensive evaluation of a police leader, although these forms of fitness at one point in time are not conclusive indicators of fitness to come as the stresses of police work are experienced in actual practice.

A survey conducted by the CPU in 1998 concluded that most of its students are "males from a lower- or middle-level socioeconomic family status" (Tarng et al. 2001). It also documented that the reasons given for selecting a career in the police force are in the following order: good salary and fringe benefits, influence of parents, job security, followed by desire to help people and desire to fight crime. These reasons are quite universal in law enforcement.

The police in Taiwan during the period of martial law were organized as an all-inclusive revolutionary force, whose main task was to safeguard regime stability. The role for women was quite limited. The first female police officer was appointed as early as 1931 in mainland China (Chu and Sun 2006). The primary duties of female officers were to protect women and conduct crime preventive activities and to perform some intelligence work. After the military retreat to Taiwan and re-establishment of the central government in 1949, the GMD government recruited a few women police officers in 1949. The Taipei City Police Department was the first to institute the "women's police squad" in 1952. The main responsibilities of this unit included working at the service desk at police headquarters and conducting investigations on specific businesses. In 1974, the Central Police Academy began to recruit female cadets (Mon and Liang 2011).

Although, Taiwan's society and its police organization can be described as democratic in many respects, the police culture in Taiwan lags behind the societal changes brought about through modernization and democratization. The fact that the status of women within the police profession has not changed much exemplifies this gap (Huang and Cao 2008). Female officers in the past worked primarily in gender-segregated units, such as the Juvenile Affairs Division or women's and children's protection division, and they dealt with the issues that were more suitable for women who were viewed as the weaker gender. Women and men were viewed essentially as dichotomous in character and abilities. Since the democratic transition, job opportunities have increased substantially for women, but women are still not truly equal partners in Taiwan society (see a detailed discussion in Chapter 8). Promotion of a woman to the top police position, Director-General, has never happened, the promotion of a woman to role of local police chief has taken place only once, and appointment as district chief is extremely rare. In short, the status of women within the police force remains that of aspiration to equal treatment rather than that of truly equal partners in a gender-neutral organization.

Promotion is officially based on the principles of merit systems that have developed over many decades. Promotion from Inspector Rank Four to Rank One is guided in principle by the NPA's regulations, but in reality there are numerous factors unrelated to these official guidelines that come into play in major ways. As a government organization, politics as well as complex human relationships are two such major factors beyond any official documents. In addition, two additional factors seem to be associated with the pace of promotion (Yang 1999). First, the location of the job is related to the pace of promotion; those who work within or near the headquarters of the NPA and/or the major cities of Taiwan are more likely to be noticed and promoted than those who work in the more remote areas, such as Penghu Island. Second, the kind of job held within a police bureau is associated to the pace of the promotion experienced; those who work as detectives and as internal affairs officers (督察) are more likely to be promoted than others.

The evaluation process for promotion is sometimes clearly unfair. At times, the process has been described as not competing on merit, but competing for lack of scandals. It is alleged that some ambitious officers have sent anonymous letters/emails (*heihan*, 黑函, "black mails") to the supervisors of their potential competitors in order to sabotage them. Theoretically, these mailings go nowhere because they are anonymous, but it is said that they tend to create a bad impression anyway in the eyes of the leaders. In a proportional stratified sampling survey, more than half of current officers are not satisfied with the way promotion is conducted (Qiu 2005). The level of dissatisfaction within the police is quite high, and it is mainly directed toward the top police administration. The promotion process is certainly another source for the police cynicism documented among the police force.

Patronage has never been totally eliminated in Taiwan's police force, but it has been kept pretty low. Seniority based on the year of graduation, either from the TPC or from the CPU, is important in the police subculture. Since age is common to all individuals, the year one graduated demarcates one's seniority. The newcomers have to show their respect to their senior officers, both in gesture and in tone.

Before the repeal of martial law, the Central Police Academy largely monopolized the market for MA degrees for police officers. Presently, there are alternative reputable masters' programs at non-police universities, such as National

Taipei University and National Chong Cheng University, although the advantage of being a CPU alumnus does loom large.

Basically, the American police dream of *twenty-years-patrol-officer-turned police chief* is impossible in Taiwan. Graduates of the CPU have a far greater chance of getting promoted than TPC graduates. It is also possible to get a master's degree in other universities to become the police chief. Since the democratic transition, many police functions carried out by the police have been assigned to other government agencies, and the police have become increasingly focused on professionalization in line with international standards

At the level of local county/city police chiefs (26 in total), their appointments have some additional hurdles. In 1999, the *Local Autonomy Statute* (地方自治法) was passed by the Legislative Yuan. It empowers the localities with the veto power in the appointment of local police chiefs. The local police departments are now considered part of the local government, and city mayors and county magistrates are responsible for the evaluation of police performance in their jurisdictions. The appointment of chief of police is also subject to the approval of the city mayors and county magistrates. The NPA produces a list of potential names as police chiefs, and city and county administrators pick a name from the list. In this way, the centralized police structure is largely intact while the opinions of the local regimes are respected (see Chapter 3).

Summary

The democratic transition in Taiwan has resulted in police officers becoming legally and functionally more similar to their counterparts in the United States. While American police practices are extremely decentralized (Bayley 1991; Manning 1997), Taiwanese police have been centralized and standardized from the outset, with a relatively recent modification involving decentralization to the municipality/county levels of government. Over time, Taiwan has developed its own unique systems of police education and police organization. Under this system, there is relatively little differentiation between training and education, producing a large number of police officers with associate degrees, bachelor's, master's, and even PhD degrees. With the possibility of entering the police college or university through special civil services examinations, it makes little sense to maintain two separate police educational institutions. The emphasis on the earning of academic degrees mirrors Taiwanese society at large, in that educational degrees are broadly considered to be desirable and there is a burgeoning number of PhDs in nearly all professions, with politics and police included. While emphasizing the use of the examination process is not an issue, overemphasizing its results and not according adequate consideration to other qualifications may lead to problematic outcomes. In addition, a strong connection between academic degree and career upward mobility may encourage officers to expand their knowledge while neglecting basic skills and police professionalism. Thus, the overemphasizing of the achievement of academic degrees may lead to the best choices for the top police administrators being overlooked. After all, policing is a profession, not an academic discipline in the sense of criminology or criminal justice.

As public–police relations have deteriorated somewhat over the years as the democratization process has progressed (see Chapter 10), it is perhaps time to consider appointing a civilian police chief to run the NPA. It is possible that such persons might be more inclined to develop new insights as they approach policing from a different angle. In common law societies, such as the US and Canada, it is normal for a civilian without a police background to run national-level police agencies. This is seen as the best way of breaking down the barriers of communication between the police and the people they serve – addressing the "them versus us" mentality common to law enforcement. It is also consistent with the principles of democratic policing of transparency and civil supremacy. Perhaps, most important of all, it may increase public confidence in the police – the true foundation of democratic policing.

6 Police culture

Police culture is a complex concept that has been defined in a variety of ways by different researchers. Research has identified and examined two major types of police culture: *occupational* and *organizational*. Most previous studies have focused on the former, and most have failed to delineate the important differences between the two (Worden 1995a). We will deal with both types of police culture in this chapter.

Police occupational culture refers to the typical values, norms, perspectives, and craft rules that are commonly found and socially transmitted among police officers in an attempt to cope with the strains and problems they confront frequently in their daily work (Paoline 2001). Research suggests that occupational culture originates from and is defined mainly by frontline workers (i.e., patrol officers). Early research tended to document the existence of a homogeneous occupational culture of the police (Niederhoffer 1969; Skolnick 1966; Van Maanen 1974). Police officers everywhere were depicted as possessing a common set of characteristics, such as authoritative in bearing, sensitivity to criticism, cynicism, suspiciousness, solidarity seeking, secrecy, conservatism, display of machismo, and prejudice against minorities. More recent studies have discovered that there are significant variations in this occupational culture, often even within the same police department (Brown 1988; Muir 1977; White 1972). For instance, researchers have reported that there are often two cultures within larger police departments, with "management officers" being mainly concerned with the issues of financial and social accountability, rational decision making, bureaucratic efficiency, affirmative action, and the principle of merit promotion, whereas "street officers" typically resist any changes made in these areas and look back fondly to "the good old days" when less close supervision and less strictness in accountability characterized their normal work environment (Reuss-Ianni and Ianni 1983).

Police occupational culture is chiefly a reflection of the nature of police work itself (i.e., unpredictability, rule-intensive routines, episodic danger, and authority to use force) as well as the socialization process (such as peer influence, personal street experiences, role-orientation development, and so on), which occurs after officers join the police force (Van Maanen 1974). The development of police occupational culture thus is a dynamic process, starting at the police academy, being reshaped and reinforced during field training officer (FTO) programs, and

74 *Critical issues*

constantly evolving through daily interactions with important reference groups (e.g., fellow officers, supervisors, and citizens).

Police organizational culture is an aggregate feature defined as shared meaning, shared understanding, and shared decision making within a police department. More specifically, an agency's organizational culture can be identified by examining formal and informal departmental missions, strategies, policies and procedures, and styles of administration and policing. The development of police organizational culture is influenced primarily by two groups – namely, police administrators and external sovereigns. The latter group includes city council members, mayors, politicians, the press, powerful individual citizens, interest groups, and police unions. The power struggles and/or ongoing negotiations between the internal and external players tend to contribute to variation in police organizational culture. The pioneering research on police organizational culture is Wilson's (1968) seminal work conducted over four decades ago, but still read for its insight even today. Wilson found that variation in organizational culture is evident in distinctive styles of policing, including the "watchman," the "legalistic," and the "service" styles of police departments in the American setting (see the tests of the thesis by Zhao *et al.* 2006, 2010, 2013). Scholars from other countries have made use of these same concepts in identifying different police organizational cultures in their own national settings (e.g., Ferreira 1996).

The study of police culture in Taiwan is essential to this book for at least three reasons. First, as the police force is a universal organization in contemporary societies, it is interesting to learn what aspect of the police culture is local, or in our case, "oriental," and what aspect of the police culture is more or less universal in nature.

Second, police culture is the key to understanding and theorizing about policing. Indeed, police culture has become the principal lens through which various aspects of policing have been analyzed, including police discretion, use of force, corruption, institutional sexism and racism, police–community relations, and adoption of, versus resistance to, police reform. Police occupational culture emerges mainly from officers' routine interactions with important internal and external groups, such as peers, supervisors, top managers, citizens, politicians, the media, and the courts (Crank 2004). In other words, police occupational culture is primarily a reflection and result of both officers' reactions to and influences on these various groups affecting their work. Understanding police culture in Taiwan allows police researchers and administrators to gain a deeper insight into the nature of daily police work, the players who matter in shaping that culture, factors that affect police work, and the social and political context of the police profession.

Third, police culture is instrumental in promoting/forestalling police reform. It has been widely viewed as a major barrier to police reform because it generally tends to discourage changes in customary and traditionalized practices (Goldsmith 1990; Sparrow *et al.* 1990). Therefore, efforts to change the ways in which police operate must be geared toward the effective transformation of police culture (Chan 1997). The examination of police culture in Taiwan provides important baseline information on changes that could enhance the effectiveness of desired police reform.

This chapter is divided into four sections. The first two sections discuss police occupational culture, with one section focusing on officers' occupational outlooks and the other section stressing their operational behavior. The third part of this chapter deals with major aspects and factors contributing to the development of organizational culture, with a brief discussion of the relationship between police occupational culture and police organizational culture. The final section summarizes the main points and findings discussed in the previous sections.

Occupational outlooks

Police occupational attitudes represent a complex phenomenon that entails "a constellation of beliefs, sentiments, and behavioral tendencies concerning some object" (Worden 1995b: 51). Fortunately, a substantial number of studies have been conducted to investigate various aspects of police occupational outlooks in Taiwan. Similar to early research conducted in the US, studies published before 2000 tend to depict a set of cultural characteristics frequently displayed by police officers across the world. In two studies of the police culture in Taiwan, Wu (1985, 1990), for instance, outlined six distinct categories of cultural traits – namely, beliefs, cognitions, values, norms, objects of affection, and attitudes. Under the categories of beliefs and attitudes, officers were portrayed as holding a firm belief in the importance of the police maintaining social order, having a strong sense of honor and responsibility, and showing a tendency toward quick judgment, keen observation, and suspiciousness.

Another line of research on police culture has emerged in Taiwan which looks specifically at police attitudes toward such dimensions as training, the prestige of the police profession, promotion and career development, salary and compensation, cynicism and stress, perceptions of fellow workers and supervisors, and attitudes toward community policing. Some common findings include:

1   While most officers feel that their training in the police university or college prepared them well for handling real street situations, approximately one third of the police reported that basic training for the police is "inadequate" (Chen 1981; Chen 1988).
2   Only half of the officers believed that they were respected in society and that officers' self-perceived social status declined over the years (Chen 1981; Cheng 1993; Luo 1980).
3   Officers expressed widespread dissatisfaction with the promotion process, and about 40 percent of officers would consider leaving the profession if good alternative opportunities arose (Chen 1981; Chen 1994).
4   The majority of officers stated that they were not adequately compensated, but such concern appeared to be receding (Chen 1994; Luo 1980).
5   Lower rank officers and urban police were more cynical than their higher rank and rural counterparts (Hou *et al.* 1983); work-related stress was pervasive among officers (Tsao 1983; Yang 1995).

6 While most officers reported that they maintained good relationships with co-workers, their evaluations of supervisors' leadership varied greatly, ranging from a 32 percent to an 80 percent satisfactory rate (Chen 1988; Qiu 1991).
7 Officers who supported community policing programs were more likely to believe that programs associated with this approach to policing have a positive effect on various types of crime (Lee et al. 1998).

Interestingly, these findings reveal a degree of congruence with the results from early studies of Western police forces showing such notions as the inadequacy of academy training, a limited opportunity for promotion, a high degree of stress and cynicism, and frequent experience of non-supportive and overly demanding supervisors (Brown 1988; Niederhoffer 1969; Skolnick 1966; Van Maanen 1974).

Although these studies provided valuable insights into Taiwanese officers' job-related attitudes and echo the argument that the "study of police culture must tap some of the meanings and feelings that police work holds for officers" (Crank 1998: 16), they suffer some noteworthy theoretical and methodological limitations. First, none of them have attempted to develop and/or test any theoretical model or framework of police occupational outlooks. In fact, almost all these studies were either descriptive in nature, reporting most common frequency distributions, or performed no more than basic bivariate statistical analyses. Regression analysis that takes relevant explanatory and control variables into consideration has been consistently absent, hindering theoretical advancement and empirical testing in this area of the literature.

A second and related point is that, although elements of police occupational culture have been described in considerable detail, little is known about the sources of variation in police cultural traits among officers. While studies conducted in Western societies have found that police officers are not a monolithic group of individuals regarding their occupational attitudes and behavior (Brown 1988; Muir 1977), researchers have paid very little attention to the possibility of, and the factors that may have contributed to, cultural differences among Taiwanese officers.

Third, some descriptions of police occupational culture are obviously outdated because dramatic social and political transformations taking place in Taiwan between 1980 and 2000 have greatly influenced many aspects in policing, including police culture. For example, McBeath's (1979) analysis showed that most police recruits favored the continuation of one party rule rather than the advent of multi-party competition. One would suspect that officers might be reluctant to truthfully reveal their political beliefs during GMD's authoritarian rule of Taiwan. Like McBeath, Wu (1985) portrayed officers as having a high degree of loyalty to the long-term ruling party (i.e., GMD), a tendency which is highly questionable today given that the police have become a more diverse group in terms of their political party orientations (see Chapter 4). Finally, none of these studies have assessed officers' attitudes from an international, comparative perspective. We thus do not know whether Taiwanese officers' occupational outlooks are congruent or incongruent with those of their counterparts elsewhere in the world. A lack of such comparison limits our knowledge of alternative possibilities or strategies and reduces the likelihood of achieving successful reform toward democratic policing (Bayley 1999).

Some of these concerns have been addressed by more recent research on officers' occupational attitudes. In a series of studies, Sun and Chu assessed attitudinal differences among Taiwanese officers and between Taiwanese and the US officers (Chu and Sun 2006, 2007; Sun and Chu 2006, 2008a,b,c, 2009, 2010). Their analyses found similar gender and geographic area (urban versus rural) distinctions in officers' professional attitudes. For example, Taiwanese female officers showed stronger support for aggressive enforcement, less favorable attitudes toward peer groups, and weaker concern about promotion as an important issue than their male colleagues (Sun and Chu 2008a). Female officers were also found to be more likely than male officers to be in favor of a combination of male and female officers over female officers alone for handling battered women, and to prefer male over female officers and a combination of male and female officers for handling domestic violence offenders (Sun and Chu 2010). Compared to their urban counterparts, rural officers were more inclined to display higher levels of group cohesion and favor citizen co-operation (Sun and Chu 2009). These studies confirm that Taiwanese officers are not homogeneous in their job-related attitudes, a fact which has become much more apparent since the late 1990s. Unfortunately, the absence of comparable data before 1990s makes the evolution (or resilience) of police culture during drastic social changes less evident.

Sun and Chu's research also demonstrates that Taiwanese police supervisors' and officers' attitudes are distinguishable from their comparable American counterparts. Looking at police officers in general, Taiwanese officers tended to have a broader role orientation, more positive attitudes toward aggressive patrol and community building, and more negative attitudes toward legal restrictions, selective enforcement, and citizen support (Sun and Chu 2006, 2008b). Comparisons of female officers in the two countries found that Taiwanese female officers were more likely than the US female officers to have a broad role orientation, to support aggressive patrol, to be resentful of rules and legal restrictions, to disapprove of selective enforcement, to be critical of citizens, to consider promotion to be an important issue in their career, and to have friends in their work units (Chu and Sun 2006; Sun and Chu 2008c). Focusing on police supervisors (i.e., officers at the rank of sergeant and above) specifically, Taiwanese supervisors were found to have a broad role orientation, positive attitudes toward aggressive law enforcement and legal restrictions, and negative attitudes toward citizens compared to American supervisors (Chu and Sun 2007). Collectively, these findings indicate that while police officers worldwide may share some common attitudinal propensities, the degree to which officers ascribe to various cultural traits varies across societies.

One area that concerns many police officers is how their performance is evaluated by their own agency. Hou's (2007) study revealed that officers who liked their work, who had good relationships with supervisors, and who received support and respect from the public were more likely to have positive attitudes toward police performance evaluation policy. In contrast, officers who reported that police work was frustrating and risky and their family members cared about their work were more likely to have negative attitudes toward the performance evaluation policy in place in their agency. Another important area is that of job satisfaction. Wu (2010) found that officers work values reflecting collective interest and diligence were positively related to job satisfaction, but unexpectedly, that work pressure was not predictive of job satisfaction. These studies clearly indicate that aspects of police occupational outlooks are not stand-alone dimensions, but rather highly intertwined with one another.

Several interesting observations pertinent to the policing of a democratic Taiwan are worth mentioning. First, rank-and-file officers often express a feeling of powerless, which may be caused by such sources as the loss of administrative sanction power, an increase in judicial and local control, and the pervasiveness of media and public scrutiny. Many officers would agree with the observation that "they are a disadvantaged group with guns" (警察是帶槍的弱勢群體) (Cai 2003). This emotion may well reflect the difficult task of transforming what was once a bureaucracy "above" the citizenry into a service-oriented democratic agency. The concept of an officer as a superior (*guan*, 官) is deeply rooted in the Chinese culture. For all the years during the Japanese colonial rule and during the period of martial law, Taiwan's police officers possessed largely unchecked power over ordinary citizens. When the democratic transition was initiated, many officers needed to be re-trained in order to adapt more fully to the new situation. While American police were also found to have a high degree of cynicism (Niederhoffer 1969), a firm confidence in the need and ability to maintain civilian control over the police occupies a central core element of their belief system (Worden 1995a). In comparison, police cynicism in Taiwan has made "cops as grumblers" who complain in public about their work environment, even though few police officers would actually choose to quit the law enforcement profession. Such frustration crystalizes the social dynamic characteristic of a newly formed democracy with a traditional culture and long-held values still playing an important role in society.

Second, while Taiwanese police officers tend to feel less powerful in interactions with the citizenry than their US counterparts, they nonetheless show a strong sense of "police-know-what-they-do" when asked about self-confidence. In the US, the story is quite different, as Crank (1998: 2) observed: "The problem, of course, is that we really have few ideas and little agreement about what really works, and even less about what it is that the police should be doing." Similarly, Bayley (1994) argued that the best secret about the police is that they cannot prevent crime. It seems clear that the pessimistic US law enforcement sentiment toward the effectiveness of various police strategies and tactics is not shared by either Taiwanese scholars or Taiwanese police officers. The dominant sentiment is close to "I know it all" for Taiwan scholars, and "I can prevent crime" for Taiwan police officers.

Third, officers in Taiwan remain locally connected and are friendly, inasmuch as many police officers live in their *paichusuo* (PCS) or field stations. They tend to carouse with business people, network with local political figures, mediate conflicts between neighbors, and socialize regularly with community residents.

The cozy atmosphere surrounding them may make them look like a person in heaven, while in reality they constantly "maneuver in troubled waters," trying not to get their shoes wet. That is, they constantly attempt to keep social harmony and to avoid bad publicity and the taint of corruption while working long hours.

Operational behavior

A second area of police occupational culture concerns officers' operational styles or field behavior in carrying out their tasks. Police behavior has consistently been one of the major subjects in policing literature over the past four decades. Some early researchers treated US police as rather monolithic in their inquiries into police behavior (e.g., Skolnick 1966; Van Maanen 1974; Wesley 1970). Police operational behavior was portrayed as officers depending upon each other for assistance and protection and maintaining authority and autonomy in handling situations principally because of the periodic danger and unpredictability embedded in their work environment (Worden 1995b). Officers also are inclined to rely upon situationally-justified use of force (Bittner 1980) or legitimate violence empowered by the state to perform their work in some circumstances (Klockars 1985; Wesley 1970). Unfortunately, such police use of aggressive enforcement has not been evenly distributed across society, with minority and poor populations being the primary targets of vigorous police enforcement actions (Bayley and Mendelsohn 1969).

While police officers may share some behavioral tendencies, scholars who developed typologies of police officers found that they are not particularly homogeneous in their street-level enforcement behavior (Brown 1988; Muir 1977; White 1972). Using Muir's and Brown's typologies as an example, professional officers act differently from non-professional officers in handling problematic situations such as interpersonal conflicts and traffic stops. They tend to study the situation thoroughly and, after careful and deliberate assessment, apply the law only when the purpose of assisting people can be justified (Brown 1988). This line of inquiry provided rich insights into variations in officers' field behavior.

Prior to the 1990s, studies on US police behavior focused primarily on four types of activities: arrest, use of force, detection, and service (Riksheim and Chermak 1993; Sherman 1980). Among them, officers' discretionary decisions to arrest and use coercive force represented the focal concern in most studies, whereas service or non-coercive behavior received relatively scant attention. Researchers have long noted the key role of threat and use of violence in American police's occupational culture (Wesley 1970). Arrest and use of force occupy the central stage of research on police behavior; this is not surprising because of the distinctiveness of the police role in society resting on their general authority to use coercive force if necessary (Bittner 1980; Klockars 1985; Reiss 1971).

An emphasis on coercive behavior remained largely unchanged in studies published since 1990, although an increasing amount of attention has been paid to police non-coercive actions. Several common findings related to frequency, type of force, and common scenarios have emerged from research on police use of

80 *Critical issues*

force, including: (1) coercive behavior is a rare event, occurring only in about 1–2 percent of police-citizen encounters; (2) use of force typically occurs at the lower end of the force continuum, normally involving grabbing, pushing, or shoving; and (3) coercive action is most likely to be applied when the police are trying to make an arrest and the suspect is resisting (Adams 1999). Despite its rare occurrence, force or coercion remains a defining characteristic of the police culture.

Theoretical explanations of police coercive behavior have been tested vis-a-vis *situational factors* (e.g., citizens' background characteristics, demeanor, seriousness of offense, and strength of evidence), *officers' characteristics* (e.g., officers' demographics, training, assignment, and occupational attitudes), *organizational considerations* (e.g., departmental philosophies, strategies, and leadership and supervisory styles), and *neighborhood context* (e.g., crime rate, concentrated disadvantaged, and racial composition). The most consistent predictors of officer coercive behavior fall in the category of situational variables, with stronger evidence, more serious crime, and citizen hostile attitudes being linked to high levels of police coercion.

A less investigated area of police behavior is the non-coercive or supportive actions exercised by patrol officers. Unlike coercive actions, which stress the exercise of authority or influence over citizens to contain violence and control disorder, supportive actions emphasize the provision of emotional or psychological support to enhance citizen compliance and satisfaction. They represent informal actions that have traditionally received little recognition as goals for police.

Supportive actions tend to enhance the legitimacy of police interventions, especially in conflicts involving intimates who often view police responses as an intrusion into their private matters. Basically, such supportive police actions as walk-by checks on businesses and "meet and greet" contacts with citizens subsequently increase citizen compliance with the law (Sun 2003). Studies have shown that officers engaged in a wide range of such actions such as helping citizens to file a formal complaint, to make use of accessible legal processes to solve a problem, to seek the help of other service agencies, to seek help of family members and friends, to invite a call to the police if the problem recurs, to provide physical assistance to citizens on their own initiative, to secure timely information for citizens on their own initiative, to comfort or reassure citizens, and to show respect to citizens in their dealings with the police (Sun and Payne 2004).

Taiwan police exhibit certain behavior tendencies quite similar to those of their Western counterparts. For example, Wu's (1985, 1990) early studies showed that police officers tend to have a high degree of solidarity, a strong sense of camaraderie, and an inclination to be distrustful of citizens. Further, officers frequently attend wedding parties, funerals, and other social gatherings in major part to maintain police–community relations and secondarily to enhance their crime-solving capability. Officers on the average are sociable and display strong interpersonal communication skills in dealing with people with diverse backgrounds. Rapid social and economic developments also have created many opportunities for private personal gains, leading to police misconduct and sometimes corrupt behavior (see Chapter 7 for a detailed discussion of this issue). Such descriptions seem to remain largely valid based on limited evidence from later research (e.g., Ong 2004). As mentioned above, however, this line of investigation tends to employ relatively elementary statistical approaches, shedding only limited light on factors that influence police field practice.

Martin's (2007) ethnographic study illustrated how street-level officers balanced the traditional legal culture of sentiment, reason, and law (*qing, li, fa*, 情理法) in performing their daily work. Although the transformation from an authoritarian to democratic style of policing seemed to suggest a higher priority of law (or the rule of law) over sentiment (or the rule of man), patrol officers' decision making involved a careful calculation attempting to reach a delicate balance of the three. A form of police culture was gradually established when

> Taiwanese street patrolmen carefully modulate their interventions so as to avoid aggravating social forces that exceed their powers of control, and they must do this because their actions are embedded within the reproduction of a social "order" that is constituted in a balance between contradictory foundations of power and authority.
>
> (Martin 2007: 676)

Martin brought up an interesting concept, that of "obscurity," to depict how officers sometimes preferred to settle or reconcile conflicts at mainly a private space (e.g., at a field station) to avoid causing further repercussions. For Martin, police activities did not change much during the transition from authoritarian to democratic policing, showing the resilience of Chinese culture on the conduct of the police. Indeed, his work accurately pointed out the importance of broader social expectations and cultural sensibilities in shaping the evolution of police occupational culture. Police use of force is a great example of this line of argument.

The death of a police officer is a real drama for officers in the US. Manning (1997) begins his work on the police with the death and funeral of Officer Gail Cobb, whereas Crank (1998) ends his work on police culture with the image of a police funeral. The coercion-centered theme and death orientation in policing are demonstrably less applicable in Taiwan. Very little systematic research has been done on this phenomenon in Taiwan for several clear reasons. First, weapon ownership is not permitted except for public safety and military forces. Violent or even deadly confrontations between the police and public are far less common in Taiwan compared to the US. The "we versus they" (officers versus citizens/suspects) mentality and the notion of "don't trust a guy until you have him checked out" play a less vital role in influencing officers' expectations of police–citizen encounters in Taiwan as opposed to their counterparts in the West.

Second, and perhaps the more important reason, is that while the NPA has been tracking and recording police use of weapons for decades, such data were seldom made available to researchers. Research on police use of deadly or non-deadly force is consequently sketchy, with a limited number of studies touching on general policies and regulations regarding the use of weapons. We thus don't know much about the general patterns of police use of force in Taiwan and the various factors likely influencing engagement in such behavior by the police remain unknown.

In one of the rare studies on the use of lethal weapons by the police, Shi's (2009) interviews of seven officers who were involved in the deadly shooting of a citizen during a pursuit revealed that these officers years' of experience ranged from 14 to 29 years and it was the first time for all but one officer to fire their weapon during their entire career. All officers believed that they were very familiar with the rules regulating the use of weapons, and they were all found to have used their weapons properly during the encounter in question. All of the officers felt tremendous pressure after the incident due to potential civil lawsuits and liability for the compensation of citizens unlawfully injured by police action.

Similar to the situations in the case of US police officers, the Taiwan police must deal with a special category of offenses commonly known as victimless crimes or vice – principally gambling, prostitution, excessive alcohol consumption, pornography, and drug abuse and addiction. Since the enforcement of these offenses has had a profound impact on police integrity and corruption, we will discuss these issues more fully under the heading of police misconduct in the next chapter.

Organizational cultures

We noted earlier that police organizational culture can be determined by assessing formal and informal departmental missions, strategies, policies and procedures, and styles of administration and policing. Wilson's (1968) work showed that police departments varied with respect to their core mission, control of discretion, and use of criminal justice sanctions. The *watchman* style of departments focused on order maintenance. Officers enjoyed a high degree of discretion in doing their work, and they seldom invoked formal sanctions against citizens unless it was felt to be necessary after non-coercive measures were attempted and proved ineffective. The *legalistic* departments in contrast stressed full enforcement of law and subsequently were more likely to utilize formal sanctions against the non-compliant citizens. Officers were discouraged from making use of discretion in carrying out tasks. Lastly, the *service* style of agencies concentrated on responses to community needs. The degree of control of discretion and the frequency of use of criminal justice process to handle incidents fell in between the watchman and legalistic departments.

The growth in the adoption of community policing also shed light on the degree of variation existing in police organizational culture because community police initiatives varied greatly in philosophy, strategy, administrative change attempted, and program scope across law enforcement departments. For example, in community policing in Indianapolis, Indiana, the police department emphasized traditional "aggressive enforcement" strategies (e.g., traffic stops, field interrogation, drug law enforcement, and arrests) to enhance quality of life in the neighborhoods, while community policing in St. Petersburg, Florida, the police department stressed the utilization of the Goldstein's "problem solving" model to improve police services and enhance citizen satisfaction with the police (Sun 2003). Similarly, the extent of inclusion of female officers into police departments reveals variation in organizational culture, with women in misogynist agencies being more likely to be mistreated while those working in inclusive agencies being more likely to be treated fairly and interacted with in a friendly manner (Kingshott 2009).

Previous research conducted in various countries has linked police organizational culture to officers' attitudes and behavior. For example, in the US, police organizational culture was found to have an influence on officers' decision making (Sever 2008), patrol practices (Hassell 2006), and police misconduct (Armacost 2004). In Europe, British officers' perceptions of organizational justice was associated with more favorable attitudes toward community residents (Myhill and Bradford 2013), and the organizational factors of openness to innovation and management support tended to improve Slovenian officers' job satisfaction (Nalla et al. 2011).

In Taiwan, a small number of studies have investigated the primary dimensions of police organizational culture. For example, some scholars report that police organizational culture in Taiwan tends to be centered on formalism, rigorous performance evaluation, promotion, internal operational inspections, and authoritarianism (Lin 1999; Wu 1993). A senior police administrator posited that police organizational culture was centered upon four vital dimensions, those being discipline, leadership style, administrative decisions made by NPA staff, and the dynamics of promotion in ranks and issuance of assignments (Wu 1993). Lee (2000) proposed that a positive police organizational culture for Taiwanese police would be one that stresses the value of democracy, human rights, equality, and justice. The origins of these central themes are argued to be the traditional culture of government officials and police organizational structure.

While some research has been conducted to examine Taiwan police organizational culture, various unanswered questions persist. For example, similarities and differences in police organizational culture have rarely been discussed or tested empirically. In fact, none of the studies conducted thus far have examined possible differences in organizational culture across police departments in Taiwan, and none has explored the relationship between police occupational and organizational cultures. Additionally, most empirical studies have failed to test for the presence of multiple cultures within and across individual agencies. The lack of research on these issues may be attributed chiefly to a centralized system of police in Taiwan. While local control of the police has grown during recent years, Taiwan police are still by-and-large a centralized force featuring standardized training, uniform operational guidelines, similar equipment, a single promotion process, and an award and discipline process governed by the NPA.

While variation in organizational culture may be somewhat limited within Taiwan, Taiwanese police departments collectively display some characteristics that clearly distinguish them from their Western counterparts. Perhaps the best way to understand these differences in police organizational culture in Taiwan is to study the lowest formal organizational unit in the police hierarchy, those being *paichusuo* (PCS) or field stations. Largely non-existent in Western societies, a PCS system has been in place for over a century and arguably represents the backbone of Taiwan policing. A PCS is a self-sustaining, community-based unit that undertakes various missions and tasks required by the NPA and local police chiefs. There are 1,600 field stations in Taiwan (Huang and Sun 2014). It is similar to the Japanese *koban* (Bayley 1991), but it is generally somewhat larger in size. Such structural and operational features have led to the development of "the PCS culture," one which is characterized by the core elements of community membership, nearly unbearable workload, and shared honor/disgrace depending on outcomes and practices of each PCS.

First, the PCS culture emphasizes the police being an integral element of the local community. Although the idea that "the police are the public and the public are the police" is advocated by many US departments in their community policing initiatives, the integration of American police forces into local neighborhoods and the development of a true sense of belonging to the community remain largely rhetorical goals rather than an accomplished fact. Through the PCS, the Taiwanese police are deployed much closer to the community than their US counterparts (Sun and Chu 2008b). Very few urban American officers actually live in the neighborhoods they police, and they seldom if ever socialize with local residents after work; in contrast, the PCS serves as a second home (and even a primary residence for young and unmarried officers) for the Taiwanese police. Throughout the country, the police are heavily involved in community activities on and off duty. PCS officers are often invited by their neighborhood residents to attend social events, such as wedding receptions and birthday parties, during their off duty time; this is largely unheard of among American officers. These events are not purely social gatherings but also represent valuable mechanisms for community networking, information collection, and even problem solving. The relationship between PCS officers and community residents is reciprocal rather than unilateral. Being a genuine member of the community is viewed as a must (and widely accepted obligation), rather than merely an option among PCS officers.

Second, the urban PCS culture entails an extremely heavy workload, which to some officers is seen as nearly unbearable. American patrol officers normally work an 8–12 hour shift, rarely engage in civic affairs, and are seldom called back to duty after completing their shifts. PCS officers are literally responsible for more than 100 different tasks and work 12–16 hours for 5 or 6 days a week. Awkward shift assignments often take a toll on officers' physical health and family life. The job responsibilities of the PCS commanding officer are particularly demanding. He (in a few cases, she) has to be a true street-corner-level politician; he/she must have superlative interpersonal skills to manage an average group of 10–20 officers who have diverse police experiences, maintain harmonious relationships with many local residents, business owners, public officials, and political party representatives who periodically bring public concerns to the station. The PCS leader might be willing to follow most of the requests made from the district stations and shield his subordinates from administrative "bull-shit." The commanding officer (normally a lieutenant) and the deputy commanding officer (normally a sergeant) of a PCS work almost 24 hours a day, 6 or 7 days a week. They sleep and eat, along with patrol officers, in the station and also participate in motorized or foot patrol with two or three patrol officers on a daily basis. For young graduates of the Central Police University, the PCS commanding position is required experience for career advancement. For graduates of the Police College, the PCS is surely their first assignment. The PCS, especially those in urban areas, are clearly not a secure heaven for officers, but rather constitute a grueling test of their training and endurance. Unfortunately police officers have few alternatives to such workplace arrangement for much of their careers.

Finally, the PCS culture stresses shared honor and disgrace. A culture of "performance first" (績效掛帥) is deeply rooted in the entire police force (Wu 1999). Quota systems for officers and the PCS are routinely used to assess officers' individual and PCSs' collective performance. It is important for officers to achieve their quotas and avoid being the under-performers that reduce the evaluation of the whole PCS. Furthermore, a crooked officer would bring shame to the entire station. PCS commanding officers are held strictly accountable for the behavior of all of their subordinates. If an officer were involved in corrupt or illegal behaviors, the PCS commanders would be disciplined by being transferred to a low status desk job or a remote station (Chu and Sun 2007). Similar to members of a symbiotic community, PCS officers depend on each other for survival. They work, live, and share joy and sorrow together.

In brief, for most new recruits the PCS is the venue where they learn the ins and outs of street-level policing, they experience the daunting and sometimes unreasonable demands emanating from the top leadership of the police, they come to appreciate the importance of solidarity and support among co-workers, and they come to understand the need to socialize with community residents. The PCS is a tight-knit organization with a high degree of shared understandings and responsibilities. Officers in the PCS are the first line of police response. They are the first on the crime scene or at any emergency. While patrol forms the backbone of American policing, the PCS is the backbone of Taiwanese policing. It would be interesting to assess organizational culture from the lens of street-level leaders and examine how variation in their leadership styles may influence occupational attitudes and the behavior of patrol officers.

Summary

Police culture is a miniaturized version of its larger societal culture, and it can be conceptually divided into two broad aspects – occupational culture and organizational culture. Police occupational culture refers to the typical values, norms, perspectives, and craft rules that are commonly found among police officers, whereas police organizational culture is most evident in aggregate features such as formal and informal departmental missions, strategies, policies and procedures, and styles of administration and policing practiced. Indeed, similar to the portrait of police which emerges from the study of US police (Reuss-Ianni and Ianni 1983), Taiwanese police officers frequently look back fondly to "the good old days" when less close supervision and fewer demands for accountability characterized their work environment.

Police occupational culture can be identified by assessing officers' work-related outlooks and behavior. Early studies depicted a set of negative perceptual or attitudinal characteristics displayed by many Taiwanese police officers, such as the sense that their academy training was less than optimal, there is very limited opportunity for promotion, a high degree of stress is associated with their work, uncooperative and disrespectful citizens abound, and non-supportive and demanding supervisors are commonplace. All of these negative sentiments combine to lead to a good deal of cynicism being present among police ranks in Taiwan. Later studies revealed that Taiwanese officers are far from a homogeneous group in their occupational attitudes, but rather there are substantial differences among them. Taiwanese officers are also found to display occupational outlooks that are quite different from their American counterparts in many respects.

Research on police operational behavior in Taiwan has shown that officers maintain a strong bond with their fellow officers, tend to be somewhat distrustful of citizens, are nevertheless very active in attending social gatherings, have developed excellent social skills in dealing with people with diverse backgrounds, are inclined to grumble a lot, and are fearful of misconduct and occasional corruption in the ranks. Although the rule of law is sacrosanct in authoritarian and democratic styles of policing alike, contemporary officers' street-level decisions involve thoughtful considerations of maintaining a delicate balance among *qing, li, fa* (sentiment, reason, and law). Police use of force is a less defining feature in Taiwanese officers' field activity since deadly confrontations between the police and the public are exceedingly rare events. Police work is much less drama, and more mundane routines. In addition, officers tend to be performance-oriented despite expressing feelings of powerlessness and despite being cynical. In a rapidly changing society, the police culture in Taiwan is adapting, albeit slowly, to its new economic, political, and social reality.

Police organizational culture in Taiwan has been portrayed as emphasizing formalism, rigorous performance evaluation, promotion through competitive examinations and political connections, frequent internal inspections, and authoritarianism in management styles. The development of these central themes is attributed to a combination of the traditional culture of governance and police organizational structure. Due to the use of a centralized police system, important questions about the similarities and differences in organizational culture across police agencies and the relationship between organizational culture and occupational culture remain largely unanswered. Future research on Taiwan police organizational culture should pay particular attention to the lowest level of organization unit in the hierarchical structure – the PCS. The PCS culture can be characterized by community membership, unbearable workload, and shared honor and disgrace. It serves as a fundamental aspect of policing in Taiwan and deserves far more study than it has received to date.

7 Police misconduct and corruption
Déjà vu experience?

According to the 2001 citizen survey conducted in Asian countries, people in Taiwan gave the lowest score on police integrity on all indicators in the survey dealing with police performance (Eastern Survey Center 2001). One-in-four respondents considered police taking bribes to be a serious or very serious problem in Taiwan. Almost 10 percent of Taiwanese survey respondents admitted that members of their family or they themselves have bribed a police officer on occasion. In addition, survey results indicated that females, youth, and people with higher educational levels tend to hold a more negative view on police integrity than males, older people, and persons of more modest education.

A similar pattern has been found consistently in more recent assessments of the Taiwan police. For example, Jou and colleagues (2011) found that while residents in three cities and two counties held generally positive views of police politeness, friendliness, and fairness, more than 60 percent of survey respondents believed that most police officers were likely to engage in misconduct and illegal behavior. Apparently, people in Taiwan are highly concerned with problems related to police misconduct and corruption.

The concept of police misconduct (or police deviance) refers to undesirable non-criminal behavior committed by police during the course of normal work (Walker and Katz 2002). It often involves behaviors which violate organizational rules, but are not necessarily unlawful. The difficulty with the concept of police misconduct is that the boundary between such deviance and crime is rather thin, and often is blurred in practice. For example, giving and taking gratuities in the form of *hongbao* or red envelopes (紅包) during seasonal holidays, weddings, and baptisms in Taiwan is a longstanding social custom. However, police officers who work in urban neighborhoods with hospitality businesses (or special businesses), such as night clubs, often receive gratuities more generous than mere tokens of appreciation, which could constitute bribes if they are prohibited by department policy or law.

Past research has focused more heavily on police corruption than on police misconduct (Shih 2010). Corruption is a kind of occupational crime, involving misuse of authority in a manner designed to produce personal gain for self or particular others (Goldstein 1975, 1977). Corruption can be classified into three categories – namely, individual corruption, pervasive unorganized corruption, and pervasive organized corruption (Sherman 1978). It is believed that corruption often begins with police deviance and misconduct. Once that boundary is blurred, the development of a subculture for neutralizing corruption often follows (Ayling and Shearing 2008; Grabosky and Ayling 2007). Once corruption becomes tolerated, it is likely to evolve into pervasive organizational behavior gradually over time.

As is the case in Western societies, police misconduct in Taiwan consists of a wide array of improper and illegal actions, ranging from ill-advised conduct to deviant behavior, on to corruption, and then on to serious criminal behaviors (Shih 2010; Tsai 1982). Within the police force, these various types of behaviors are all referred to as police "*fengji*" (風紀, disciplinary) problems.

During the period of authoritarian rule prior to 1987, Taiwan had a strong central state with a weak society (Jou *et al*. 2010; Moody 1992). One of the characteristics of a strong state was its highly moralistic stance in attempting to guide the entire society. A separation of the public sphere from the private sphere was lacking; such a demarcation is clearly in place in the Western world. Historically, similar to their Japanese counterparts (Bayley 1991), Taiwanese officers served as moral role models in the community. Police officers were held to a high moral standard. Even after the democratic transition, the moral tendency in this post-Confucian society lingers in the public services. In April 2012, the National Police Agency, for example, entered into the private sphere of officers by regulating extra-marital affairs involving the police. Married police officers often receive formal administrative punishment for having affairs outside their marriage. Despite its moralistic stance, however, the police maintain no official statistics available to researchers on the prevalence of police unfavorable behaviors such as alcohol abuse, gambling, prostitution, or extra-marital affairs. In this regard, the Taiwanese government, like governments all over the world (Zhang *et al*. 2009), is reluctant to collect, retain and conduct research with such systematic data.

Under democratic regimes, police officers continue to reinforce the law within the culturally accepted milieu. Most studies of Taiwanese society have found that a variety of "parochial" and "particularistic" institutions are structurally central to virtually all political and economic organizations in the country. However, the democratic transition has made the contrast between the parochial and particularistic realm and the public sector dictums of socio-political virtue increasingly incongruous. The ubiquity of informal relationship networks means that large sectors of the social order penetrate the boundaries of the police in Taiwan. Taiwanese police thus work in an environment that is quite different from that of the police in the West; the police in democratic nations generally have a rather clear separation between the public and the private spheres of their lives.

In this chapter we discuss the issues of police misconduct and corruption in Taiwan. It is argued here that the current level of police integrity in Taiwan is no worse or no better than it was during its authoritarian past. Misconduct and corruption, however, are broadly perceived as more serious problems today because the prior principal evil of authoritarian rule has been successfully removed and greater transparency in governance has been demanded and brought into being. The news media are actively exposing and chasing after news concerning political scandals, with police scandals included, elevating in the public mind a broadly shared sense of frequently corrupt politics in general.

We begin our discussion with a description of the various interactions between the police and underground societies to illustrate the complexity of the working environment of the police. We then discuss police misconduct in the Taiwanese context. We introduce several forms of police misconduct, and examine various motivations and means used to earn extra income by Taiwanese police. We use law enforcement examples in the areas of electronic gambling machines, organized prostitution, and gravel truck operations to further illustrate the general patterns and content of police misconduct and corruption in Taiwan. Finally, we explore the approaches taken to control misconduct and corruption in Taiwan policing.

Policing underground societies

Police misconduct is a broad term. As is the case with the concept of beauty, the definition of police misconduct is often "in the eye of the beholder." The police are ineluctably part of the intricate political, economic, legal, and cultural institutions of a country, and their conduct cannot be understood apart from an examination of the effects upon police of those distinctive institutions. Still, some forms of police behavior are almost universally condemned as wrongful, such as police corruption or the intentional misuse of police powers by officers. Other forms of police conduct generate heated debate and controversy as people with different perspectives judge police actions differently, such as approving or disapproving the use of deadly force in violent confrontations with rioters, showing favoritism to informers, and monitoring the off-duty morality of officers. In Taiwan, the blurred distinction between legitimacy and illegitimacy and between the "*baidao*" (白道, legal way) and "*heidao*" (黑道, clandestine way) is complicated by a culture in transition to democracy.

Following the GMD government's retreat to Taiwan in 1949, some criminal gangs with mainland roots also relocated to Taiwan. There had been an informal working relationship between the GMD government security agencies and these underground societies prior to taking refuge on Formosa. It was in 1984, after the *Incident of Jiang Nan* (江南案), that the government took action to sever all such ties. With the advent of the democratization process, many gangsters began their own transition and directed their energy and resources toward the political and business arenas (Chin 2003; Sheu 2010). The emergence of a set of political-economic alliances referred to locally as "black gold" (or *heijin* 黑金) arose, representing a collaboration between elements in politics, business, and organized crime. Elections everywhere are expensive and democratic politics often works to the advantage of the rich and those who can provide money to politicians in a timely manner. Taiwan is no exception to this rule. Many politicians run for office with the support of underground societies; moreover, individuals with an established background of underground societies are frequently elected to public offices as local officials or selected as political representatives. Given this situation, the fight against gangsters becomes convoluted, if not entirely impossible, on the part of the police in many areas of Taiwan.

90 *Critical issues*

In considering the complexities of underground societies and their effective policing, we also must understand the operational culture of police beats (*Jingqinqu*, JQQ) or police precincts in Taiwan. It is a system resembling the *baojia* (保甲), which has a long tradition in China (see Dutton 1992). It is "a key nodal institution in mediating the interface between central political authority and local social order" (Martin 2007: 672). Although the national police organization is indeed highly centralized, police beats are decentralized in their administration. Police beats consist of a couple of urban blocks, usually containing about 300–500 households; they are typically assigned to an individual beat officer for several years. This officer is held personally responsible for maintaining the area's census records and supplying any necessary surveillance about local affairs. This group of localized officers is called the "administrative police" (*xingzheng jingcha*, 行政警察) in contrast with the other major kind of centralized officers referred to as the "security police" (*bao-an jingcha*, 保安警察). During the period of the Japanese colonization (1895–1945), administrative police officers even had the power to adjudicate immediately any offense punishable by detention or fine (Wang 2000), and during the martial law period (see Chapter 2) they were armed with the power of the *Law for Punishment of Police Offenses* until that particular statute was ruled unconstitutional in 1980 and replaced by the more circumspect *Social Order Maintenance Act* in 1991. Presently, whenever spatially fixed criminal activities such as illegal gambling establishments or prostitution joints are discovered or revealed by non-beat or other unit officers, the beat officer and his/her supervisor are penalized for failing to prevent and, if prevention was not attained, detect such illegal activities.

The home of *xingzheng jingcha* or beat police officers, the *paichusuo* (PCS), is the basic unit of the police organization in Taiwan (see Chapter 6). As is the case with their Japanese counterparts (Bayley 1991), the Taiwanese police penetrate their society deeply and are interacting with local residents on a daily basis. The beat officer knows many families, interacts with local business owners, and develops relationships with politically important residents in their community. The PCS is a second home for many police officers, who in nearly all cases become involved in community activities on duty and off duty alike. The police culture emphasizes the importance of being an integral element of the local community. The integration of police officers into community life is truly remarkable. Police officers are frequently invited by local residents in their respective neighborhoods to attend major social events, such as wedding receptions and birthday parties, events which serve the functions of not only a social gathering, but they also offer opportunities for the police to accomplish community networking, information collection, and even problem solving. Therefore, regardless of the socio-economic and political backgrounds of local residents, being a part of these social activities is viewed as an absolute necessity rather than an option for PCS officers. Through these social interactions, the distinction between legitimacy and illegitimacy and between the *baidao* and *heidao* often becomes blurred. For most police officers in the West, they would back away from a relationship when they sense that a gift given is a prelude to an obligation (Grabosky and Ayling 2007). For officers in Taiwan, many of the gifts are seen as a mixture of voluntary and obligatory conduct, and the importance attached to the creation of a harmonious relationship in a post-Confucian society makes the rejection of such gifts more difficult.

Situated between the rule of law and strong local relationship networks, police officers have to learn "smoothing the way" (*baiping*, 擺平) by marshaling the connections required for a given project and for getting things done (*gaoding*, 搞定). Clientele networks are ubiquitous in Taiwan. Many businesses, especially questionable ones, are eager to be associated with government officials, legislators, or high ranking police officers. It is also a rather open secret that gangster "friends" can often get many things sorted out at lower cost. The triads keep order in the rough areas and regularly provide the police with information on other types of crime (Maguire 1997). To understand the phenomenon of police corruption, we must understand the contours of their working environment (Klockars *et al.* 2004). For example, on May 28, 2010, a gangster by the name of Weng Qinan (翁其楠) was murdered in cold blood.

> The murder shocked the nation's police system after it was discovered that four Taichung police officers were playing *mahjong* and drinking tea as the gunman walked into Weng's office and shot him. Police have since established that as many as 10 police officers had been in Weng's office at one point, suggesting ties between Taichung police and gangsters.
>
> (R. Chang 2010)

When the reporter interviewed a former investigator, he stated that it was part of a detective's job to keep in touch with local gangsters in order to obtain useful information.

Local control in governance is a hallmark of democracy. The police are fully aware that absolute prohibitions of victimless crime, such as gambling and prostitution, are at once unrealistic and undesirable in many prospects. The enforcement of these laws at times has served as a symbolic gesture for the police upper administration, and has been used to fulfill the performance demands for the rank-and-file officers. The hierarchical structure of the government tends to compel the rank-and-file officers to enforce the vice laws with a moralistic zeal, which is a particularly problematic practice in regulating gamblers, prostitutes, peddlers, and gangsters. In balancing sentiment (*qing*, 情), reason (*li*, 理), and law (*fa*, 法) within the Taiwanese context, the prevailing local sentiment often overrides the national law (Martin 2007). An example is the case of Zhang Tongrong (張通榮), Mayor of Keelung City, who ordered the police to release a woman who "allegedly assaulted and injured a female officer while under the influence of alcohol" in September 2012 (CNA 2013). Both the woman and the mayor were later charged with obstruction of official duties.

After the democratic transition, a shift in the police mission took effect toward greater service provision: beat officers are de rigueur to maintain outreach programs with their local constituency in a quasi-informal capacity. Police officers, who are supposed to be on the figurative front line against organized crime, are perceived as having become co-opted at best, or corrupt at worst. On the surface, they monitor those dangerous individuals and groups (gangsters, hoodlums, and hooligans) as well as keep watch over high-risk places (night clubs, game shops, bars), while in fact they often provide them with protection from vigorous enforcement of Taiwan's vice laws.

The infusion of underground influence into local politics is indeed a serious problem, but the solution most certainly is not simply moral condemnation. Cai (1998), a member of the Legislative Yuan, wrote a book on the issue of black gold. In this book he noted the prevalence of political figures who have the support of underground societies or are themselves members of underground societies. In addition, he listed numerous instances of the underground-society-members-turned-politicians' wild and arrogant behaviors. Upon reading this book, Taiwan would appear to be a badly corrupted society governed by unprincipled politicians. In a democratic country, societal power, whether it be legitimate political power or underground societies' power, should be controlled by the rule of law. The majority, if not all, of the cases in Cai's book are eligible to be investigated by the police, and prosecuted in the criminal courts. The reluctance of the major forces in the criminal justice system to invoke the legal system is in part a reflection of the continued impact of Confucian ethics and in part a lack of moral courage on the part of many of the country's leaders.

Police misconduct in the Taiwanese context

Punch (2000) categorizes police misbehaviors into misconduct, straightforward corruption, strategic corruption, predatory corruption, noble-cause corruption, police crime, and state-related police crime. In Taiwan, most media revelations of police scandals fell into the categories of strategic corruption, straightforward corruption, and police crime. Strategic corruption entails the active collaboration between police and organized criminal organizations to form a stable and long-term system of pay-offs. It often relates to the commission of victimless crimes, such as the operation of electronic gambling machines and prostitution. Straightforward corruption involves passively receiving some reward for doing or not doing something. In the US, the Knapp Commission (1972) classified corrupt police officers in the New York Police Department into two categories: "meat eaters" and "grass eaters." Meat eaters were those officers who aggressively demanded bribes or pay-offs and threatened legal action if the favors were not received, whereas grass eaters were those who passively accepted what came their way without overtly asking or demanding anything. Straightforward corruption is similar to the "grass eaters" scenario identified by the Knapp Commission. In Taiwan, it is often subtly transformed into generous gratuities, public relation expenses, and similar benefits. The lack of research literature on minor misconduct, however, seriously hinders our understanding of the behavior of "grass eaters" in a corrupt police organization.

About three decades ago, more than sixty percent of Taiwanese police officers surveyed stated that low salary was directly related to disciplinary problems in their work (Lin 1978). The situation has changed a good deal since then because police salaries are now generally better than those of other public servants. Low salary, therefore, can no longer be the main reason for police misconduct. Instead, the desire for personal enrichment on the part of a few officers more likely is the case.

As noted earlier, the police officers' job is typically carried out within an extremely complex set of social networks. As is the case in Western societies, much of what police officers do is characterized by the use of discretion; police officers are permitted to choose between different courses of action or inaction based on their professional judgment. Police officers often work without much direct supervision, and frequently make low-visibility decisions that are not amenable to subsequent review and control. The considerable extent to which police discretion exists contributes to a climate conducive to police misconduct.

Some research on police in Taiwan suggests that post-authoritarian Taiwan has witnessed the advent of Black Gold Politics (Chin 2003). This entails the pursuit of financial interest (i.e., gold) through hidden (or black) networks of collusion and conspiracy submerged within the conventional routines of everyday governmental interaction, including the police. Police work does indeed expose officers to many temptations, large and small in nature. Even for officers with otherwise normal scruples, some may take advantage of some favors of illegal income simply to pay off the mortgage ahead of time. Other officers may become corrupt because of their personal or family involvement with criminal activities, such as drugs and gambling. Still others, in order to influence their assignments and promotion, may bribe their supervisors or other police personnel for favorable decisions.

Some police officers are accustomed to use their discretionary powers to exchange benefits for themselves and for the organization. After the decentralization reform, some police departments suffered serious financial difficulty, causing not only the cutting of benefits (such as overtime pay) but also the allocation of very tight budgets. Many such police precincts do indeed have questionable businesses in their jurisdictions, which are understandably willing to make "contributions" to the local police. A more formal system of privately-sponsored rewards is funneled into a few police local organizations to facilitate their operation through non-profit organizations such as Associations of Police Friends. Again, more often than not the distinction between the *baidao* and *heidao* is highly blurred.

Making extra money at the police agency level is said to be related to the performance agenda (Wu 1999); covering the cost of investigating crimes or fulfilling their arrest quota often requires resources that are not readily available from the department. The current policies and procedures to regulate reimbursable expenses are rather rigid, and some officers choose to offset their expenses incurred by using other means rather than going through the red-tape-laden process of official reimbursement. It is especially true for the rank-and-file officers. Also, the very great emphasis placed on arrest quotas pushes some officers to go astray. For example, Peng (2008) describes how the police often use informants to initiate arrests of prostitutes. The informants are given money to buy sexual favors. Since there is no punishment due for brothel customers, the informants are willing to get free sex and do the police a favor in the bargain. Lower-rank street walkers and prostitutes are often targeted by police for achieving their arrest quotas.

There are several other common ways the police could make extra income. First, there are many kinds of monetary rewards provided under the existing performance assessment regime. Some police officers might falsely declare their expenses to get extra money. Others would claim the informant's stipend or cash reward without handing over the money due. Because these are all low visibility acts, police internal corruption is less likely to make to the headlines of the news media.

The second common way of police making extra money is to give or sell information maintained in governmental databases or internal information about police operations and law enforcement priorities. It is not uncommon that the police leak information to private enterprises, including security companies, which need such information for employee background checks or client services. The "eating of a case" (*chi-an*, 吃案) is another type of police misconduct with a smell of corruption (Martin 2007). Before the implementation of *Computer-Processed Personal Data Protection Law* in 1995, leaking and even selling information to unauthorized users was a rather commonplace occurrence. A police officer was found selling information, including personal traffic, criminal, resident, and entry and exit records, to a retired police employee over the period 1998 to 2002 (Shieu 2007).

Several kinds of misuse of information by the police in exchange for goods, services, or money entail so-called kickbacks. For example, there was a scandal involving police passing information on the crime scene to certain funeral service providers so that they can reach family members of crime victims for offering their services (Z. R. Huang 2012). In another example, officers were found to be receiving money from tow truck companies for referring them to the location of stolen cars (The Control Yuan 2009: 12).

Finally, police officers may be directly or indirectly involved in local businesses. Business owners in the "eight classified businesses" (karaoke places, bars, restaurants, dance halls, bathhouses and spa houses, barber shops, massage parlors, and coffee shops) sometimes offer free business shares or *gan-gu* (乾股) to police officers and/or their close relatives in exchange for special services such as information provision or protection services. The exchange, of course, is not an outright business transaction, but is wrapped within the idiom of *qing* (情) or particularistic relationships defining a space of intimacy explicitly insulated from the formalized space of public interactions. In such an atmosphere, the line between the legal and illegal and between the acceptable and corruption is highly blurred.

As police officers in Taiwan are usually assigned to a beat or *qinchu* for a period of three or four years, they become quite familiar with owners and managers who run "the eight classified businesses" who are usually eager to make friends with police officers. The officer often gets discount purchases and is even offered free meals and recreation services. Sometimes these offers are extended to police officers' friends. Monetary payments may also be regularly made to officers for their protection.

Unlike in the United States, lethal weapon incidents are extremely rare in Taiwan and police abuse of substances is infrequent. As is the case in Western countries, many instances of police misconduct are shielded and protected by the "blue curtain of silence" (Walker and Katz 2002), or the conspiracy of silence among police (Goldstein 1977: 202). Scandals associated with police corruption jeopardize organizational stability and leadership continuity (Cao and Huang 2000; Sherman 1978; Zhang et al. 2009). Hence there is usually a desire on the part of the police to "circle the wagons" and be protective of accused officers.

Electronic gambling machines, prostitution and the gravel truck industry

Unenforceable laws have frequently been cited as one major contributing factor of police corruption (Goldstein 1977). In Taiwan, most high-profile police collective corruption cases are related to underground businesses such as gambling and prostitution. Implementing the laws against gambling, prostitution, and drug abuse is often problematic because these activities all involve considerable profits and officers have great discretion in enforcement.

According to Chu's (2004) analysis, over 20 percent of police corruption cases in Taiwan have been related to electronic gambling and game machines since 2000. Gambling is prohibited in the criminal code. No casino of any kind is allowed in Taiwan. In addition to the criminal code, since 2000 special legislation exists to regulate electronic gambling/game arcade business. The promulgation of the *Electronic Game Arcade Business Regulation Act* was occasioned chiefly by a high-profile police corruption case in 1995. More than 200 police officers were prosecuted on that case, and most of them were found guilty for taking bribes from an electronic game arcade tycoon by the name of Zhou Renshen (周人蔘). Since some of the electronic gaming joints provide gambling machines, the regulation of such business had long been controversial. Although the laws prohibit any design or device of gambling in electronic game machines, violations of these laws have been under-enforced. The government's decision to ban certain kinds of electronic gambling machines in 1990 led to a burst of police corruption cases involving bribery. However, electronic gambling machines continue to be one of the primary sources of police corruption.

In addition, another main source of police corruption is found in the underground sex industry, which constitutes nearly one third of all prosecuted cases (Chu 2004). Despite repeated manifestations of abolitionist inclinations, the central governments, GMD and DPP alike, have never been able to fashion the means to carry out their policy of controlling prostitution and of suppressing the human trafficking related to this activity (Jou et al. 2010). Periodic crackdowns are more symbolic than real, and sure enough the sordid business re-emerges soon after the crackdown lifts.

As is the case in Western countries, providing protection to legal and illegal businesses is a long-established way to make extra money for the Taiwan police. In this regard, new ways of making money out of prostitution have been developed. The notorious prostitute hostage case (擄妓勒贖) in Taipei is one such example. Along with an improved and more open relationship between Taiwan and the mainland, an increasing number of Chinese women were smuggled into

96 *Critical issues*

Taiwan by local human trafficking organizations. Some Chinese women also entered Taiwan through fake marriages. The police know that these organizations have invested a great amount of money in importing these women. Instead of enforcing the law and arresting these illegal immigrants, some police detained these women and demanded lucrative ransom payments from criminal organizations. Such police behavior should be categorized as criminal, and as entailing both extortion and shakedowns (Stoddard 1979). Basically, the police restrain these women in the name of law, and aggressively demand a bribe in exchange of not following through on the required criminal investigation.

The notorious gravel truck industry is another classic example of police corruption. For many years the gravel truck industry was able to speed and operate overloaded trucks all over Taiwan, and in the process these trucks were acting in violation of environmental laws, paying no road taxation, and taking innocent lives (Kuo 1994). As a by-product of the nation's construction boom, the gravel truck industry made tremendous illicit profits from illegal gravel quarrying on riverbeds and selling their loads to construction companies. Drivers with worn out brakes driving overloaded trucks play a sort of Russian roulette, charging through dangerous intersections while saving their brakes for the next, possibly greater, hazard ahead. The problem came to the public's attention after the collapse of the Gaoping Bridge on August 27, 2000, an event which was attributed to the loss of riverbed gravel due to illegal gravel quarrying. It is widely believed that the gravel industry, some police authorities, and politicians rode a merry-go-round bribe scheme for many years. In some places, police also made up false documents, such as fake records with weigh-station companies, to earn extra bribe money. In 2002, Taipei City councillors accused the Taipei Traffic Police of collaborating with weigh-station companies (S. Huang 2002). In 2007, twenty-two police officers were prosecuted in Taipei County; three of them were convicted and sentenced from one to twelve years, and the others were awaiting trial (Shih 2010).

When the corrupt police officers are involved with the protection of illegal activities, such as electronic gambling machines, prostitution, and gravel stealing, their behaviors become indistinct from those of criminal organizations. They are no longer engaged in police misconduct, but rather are committing police criminal offenses.

Controlling police misconduct and corruption

During the last half of the twentieth century, the police in Taiwan have made noticeable progress in many aspects. However, the problem of misconduct and corruption continues to plague the police and tarnish the image of the police force. Two major factors contribute to a less than fully successful anti-corruption effort in Taiwan.

First, the inertia of established practice in the past authoritarian regime left a high level of tolerance of police corruption within the police organization. Second, as a relatively new democracy has come into being in Taiwan the police have not fully adapted to the unstable political atmosphere that is part and parcel of democratic politics. Beneath the smooth transitions of political regimes, a new police culture appropriate to democratic policing has been quietly emerging, often by fits and starts. The good aspect of this new culture is that the police force has become considerably more professional. One unexpected consequence of democratization is that there are far more opportunistic administrators within the police organization who are using their connections with the political parties to advance their own professional careers. This has often made the implementation of anti-corruption measures a partisan political issue, not simply an issue of police integrity.

Lundman (1980) proposed one of the most complete sociological theories of how to control police misconduct. His theory, labelled the organizational product thesis (Cao *et al.* 2000), maintains that since most police misconduct is a product of organizational deviance, it is organizational climates rather than individual officers' behavior that need to be controlled. Building upon the works of Bittner (1980), Goldstein (1977), Reiss (1971), and Sherman (1978), Lundman (1980: 141) argued that "police misconduct is organizational deviance when actions violate external expectations for what the department should do. Simultaneously, the actions must be in conformity with internal operating norms, and supported by socialization, peers, and the administrative personnel of the department." While emphasizing organizational characteristics and outside control of police misconduct, Lundman (1980) does not ignore the potential for competent police administrators and organizational regulations to reduce police misconduct. The test of his theory in the United States shows that police departments with formalized field training officer programs tend to have lower rates of police misconduct, and in-service training programs effectively reduce the rate of citizen complaints (Cao *et al.* 2000).

Any successful control of misconduct and any measure of anti-corruption adopted, however, has to be consistent with the legal culture of Taiwan. Kennedy (2003) notes in this regard, "the legal system and law of a nation owe far more to culture and history than they do to some *a priori* logic." Martin (2007) posits that Taiwan tends to reproduce a social order organized around an alternative set of cultural values. Democratization of politics in Taiwan has brought with it the principles of a liberal "thick" version of the rule of law concept (Cooney 2004). Often, the thick version of the rule of law is in conflict with the long tradition of compromises and harmony which are the ready grounds for misconduct and corruption. The control of police misconduct must be understood in the context of this cultural milieu wherein "A cultural space of legitimacy in which the solidification of the rule of law within state institutions is kept within boundaries of a social sensibility that does not take law as the last word" (Martin 2007: 694).

The documented resilience of police corruption has coincided with the substantial liberation of Taiwanese media in 1988 when the police also began to promote their image as a crime fighter profession (L. Huang 2003). The media has turned its "magnifying glass" on police misconduct, failure, and under-performance and has become a major source shaping the contemporary police image (Jou *et al.* 2011). The police are alternatively described as a "disadvantaged group with guns" at best, and "hoodlums with guns" at worst.

98 *Critical issues*

In addition, as mentioned in Chapter 6, "performance first" is deeply embedded in police organizational culture (Wu 1999). The performance indicators set by the NPA and used to evaluate local departments are in turn adopted by local political authorities to evaluate police precincts in their communities. Since the performance evaluation system emphasizes aggregate statistics, such as the number of arrests made and tickets issued, the misbehaviors of officers who have performed well are usually ignored. Many police corruption cases were committed by these otherwise productive figures in the ranks. Moreover, with the promulgation of the *Statute of Province and County Self Governance* (省縣自治法, 1994–9), the *Statute of Municipal City Self Governance* (直轄市自治法 1994–9), and the *Local Government Act 2010* (地方制度法), local police now operate under the joint pressures of providing an exceptional service to the public and being more responsive to local demands. It is widely believed that much of the problematic behavior documented among the police arises from police work pressure and the occupational environment within which the police operate (Weng 2003).

It is indeed ironic that the police claim that they base their actions upon the law when more than half of the public believe that police are corrupt. It seems that Wilson's observation (1968) of the US police also aptly applies to the police in Taiwan: the police as a subtle bureaucratic compromise between corruption and service patterned by local political culture. For any further changing of the culture of policing in Taiwan, the close relationship between the NPA and the Central Police University needs to be severed because it tends to dominate the police agenda without proposing a comprehensive alternative strategy. A major public sector reform is needed to break the culture of mutual protectionism and the domination of "old boy networks" (Chu 2013). The police education leaders should strengthen the courses offered on police integrity and police ethics, and the police administration should work in partnership with external bodies, such as the Investigation Bureau and Agency against Corruption, to make certain that any criminal behaviors of the police are dutifully prosecuted. In addition, an independent outside supervisory body should be formed to process citizen complaints against the police and investigate police misconduct. Corrupt police officers have to be held accountable to the public they serve, to the laws of the land they enforce, and to the oaths of their office to which they swore loyalty.

Summary

The perception of police misconduct is widespread in Taiwan. It is partially related to the nature of a democratic regime, one emphasizing accountability and transparency. The majority of police misconduct cases on record have involved conventional corrupt behaviors. Similar to those forms of malfeasance found in other societies, such behaviors include kickbacks, shakedowns, the protection of questionable activities, the fix, and internal pay-offs. It is evident that the "few rotten apples theory" is not sufficient to explain repeated corruption scandals among the police. Enhancing police integrity by firmly controlling police "*fengji*" problems is an organizational and administrative responsibility that goes well beyond the culling out of "bad apples" among police officers. Both pervasive unorganized corruption and pervasive organized corruption have happened in Taiwan much too frequently. The Eastern culture that places emphasis on *guanxi* (關係) or the human relationships (Bian and Zhang 2013) adds a further layer of complexity to the problem of police misconduct and corruption in Taiwan.

Punch (2000: 301) correctly notes that "a clean police is a crucial barometer of a healthy society." An effective strategy for combating corruption must combine a stable political regime with strong incentives among political elites for upright conduct (Grigor'ev and Ovchinnikov 2009). The ingredients for a clean police force must include both proactive preventives and reactive sanction-based strategies. For the former, the partisan competition and decentralization of the state have weakened rather than strengthened the rule of law in Taiwan in unanticipated ways (Martin 2007; Moody 1992). The standing of the police is not high in the public eye, and the strong scrutiny given to the police by the news media further tarnishes the police image on a regular basis. The NPA would be wise to undertake new major initiatives to control police misconduct more effectively.

As to the reactive approach to deter police corruption, several recent corruption cases led some critics to argue that corruption is "going from bad to worse," and neither the *Act on Property Declaration by Public Servants* nor the *Political Donations Act* have had a positive effect on the discovery of corruption cases (Chiu 2013). The sentencing of former Executive Yuan secretary-general Lin Yishi (林益世) and of Ex-President Chen Shuibian, however, confirms that while these statutes may have many loopholes, they nonetheless are the primary instruments for regulating misconduct and corruption among public officials. Although the culture of service and occasional gratuity collection remains strong and the "mafia-like" political culture of abusing power continues to characterize policing in some settings, many new police officers with a deep sense of integrity are staying away from the old culture of pretending to enforce the rule of law while doing shady business. Some officers are even willing to pay out of their own pocket to make peace and show that they can still "get things done" instead of abusing their publicly entrusted power.

The extent of police misconduct in a post-Confucian society such as Taiwan is largely a secret for the general public. It has never been a secret among police officers who live and work in the same PCS. More research is needed to document the relationship between police misconduct and the broader occupational and organizational culture. Promoting the integrity and self-esteem of police officers definitely deserves more attention than they have been accorded up to now. One preliminary step would be to collect reliable statistics on police misconduct and corruption so that the phenomena could be systematic scrutinized. The well-documented widespread perception of police corruption has been at the heart of citizen distrust of the police – a topic that we will examine in considerable detail in Chapter 10. We will discuss the issues related to female police officers in the next chapter.

Part III
Emerging challenges

8 Female officers on the move

The democratic transition and the consolidation of democratic practices have had a dramatic impact on both the political structures and the police force in Taiwan. These noteworthy changes, nevertheless, have had relatively slight effect on the country's culture, especially with respect to the deeply imbedded patriarchal and masculine culture of the police. Gender equality in society at large, and the employment of women in the police profession in particular, remain problematic. Although some progress has been made toward the integration of women into the police ranks over the past decade, female officers continue to face noticeable hurdles due to their gender (Huang and Cao 2008). Indeed, changing the law is relatively quick and easy, but changing the post-Confucian culture is a much more daunting and much slower process. The resilience of the East Asian culture is discussed in regard to the training and education of police officers in Chapter 5, in regard to the management of frontline officers in Chapter 6, and in regard to the complex relationship between *baidao* and *heidao* in Chapter 7.

In this chapter, we explore the culture barriers faced by Taiwan's female police officers. We argue that the police administration should be blamed only partially for its failure to achieve the full integration of policewomen into the ranks; the ultimate culprit in this matter is the deeply patriarchal culture of Confucianism. We begin with a historical review of female police officers in Taiwan, dividing the key developments observed into three eras in the post-1945 period. After this historical review, we move to a discussion of the research literature on gender and policing. Finally, we address some contemporary barriers being faced by female police officers in Taiwan today.

From clerks in the office to co-workers on the street: the historical development of female officers

As a male-dominated profession, the police everywhere have a "macho" culture that values the traits of aggressiveness, decisiveness, display of authority, and toughness (Heidensohn 2003). Such a culture runs counter to the traditional images of women as being responsive to the social expectations of being caring, nurturing, having consideration for feelings and sentimentality. These commonplace social expectations lead many people to feel that women are not suitable for

104 Emerging challenges

police work. In spite of such cultural resistance, both outside and inside police ranks, the number of female police officers in Taiwan reached an all-time high in 2012 – 4,094 policewomen in total (see Figure 8.1). In percentage terms, the presence of women has doubled over the past 12 years, going from 3.2 percent in 2001 to 6.4 percent in 2012.

This overall rate of inclusion, however, remains low compared to most democratic societies which have reached the 10 percent mark and beyond in female inclusion in their police forces (Prenzler and Sinclair 2013). In the United States, for example, approximately 20 percent of Federal sworn law enforcement officers were women in 2008, and in 2007 women accounted for almost 15 percent of total sworn law enforcement officers in large local police departments and 13 percent in sheriff's offices (Langton 2010). The rate is even higher in England and Wales where 25 percent of police officers are women (Prenzler and Sinclair 2013).

Very little has been recorded about the early development of women police officers in Taiwan. In a deeply and persistently patrimonial society, the issue of women in the police force was nearly totally ignored. With the growing awareness of the global women's liberation movement, the issue of women police officers at long last reached the agenda of Taiwan's police administration at the dawning of the new century. It would appear from the scant literature available on the subject that the process of incorporation of female police officers can be divided into three distinct historical eras featuring: (1) gender segregation; (2) disadvantaged group experience; and (3) persisting inequality and institutional indifference.

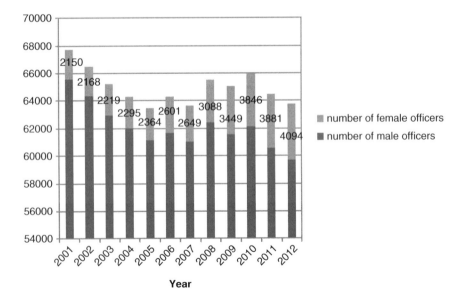

Figure 8.1 Number of male and female police officers in Taiwan (2001–12).

Source: National Police Agency (2012b).

The gender segregation era: women officers as social workers and clerks (1947–69)

After World War II, the first instance of the active recruitment of female officers took place in 1947 when the Taiwan Police School began to accept women police cadets (Cheng 2008). The first 61 graduates started their police career in 1949 after completing 2 years of academy training and in-service summer internships. Since then, the recruitment of female officers became routine, but was strictly limited in number and in the function they would serve within the police force. Female trainees were required to remain single for three years, and they were obligated to serve for at least five years after graduation (Ministry of Foreign Affairs 1976).

Once commissioned and at work, police women typically were excluded from patrol duties and their functions were limited and segregated from those of their male colleagues. The first *Women's Police Squad* was established in Taipei City in 1952, and the first Division Chief was a woman officer by the name of Chen Quanmei (陳泉湄). There was a consensus at the time that the commanding officer of the women's unit should be female.

Special welfare-related and similarly gendered tasks were assigned to such Women's Police Squads. For example, they were assigned to the tasks of rehabilitating prostitutes, leading women's activities, preventing females from gambling, and a variety of clerical work. While gender segregation in regard to work assignments was a norm, women officers' salary and benefits were comparable to those of their male counterparts. At that time, the concept of gender equality was not popular (or was effectively suppressed if it did crop up), and female complaints about their unequal status were virtually unheard of. Partially because of the war preparation mentality and patriotic sentiment, a police career was not as attractive to women as it is today.

The "pink ghetto" era: women as a disadvantaged group (1970–99)

From 1970 to 2000, the worldwide women's liberation movement finally reached the shores of Taiwan. With improved economic conditions and an increased level of education, calls for gender equity and for the inclusion of more female police officers began to emerge. Gradually, these calls for reform produced a series of social and institutional changes toward gender equity in Taiwan. There were three driving forces behind the reforms. First, the rapid industrialization process brought many more women into the labor force. Second, female officers were believed to be able to "soften" the image of the police and to reduce the authoritarian image attributed to traditional policing practices in the past. This point was particularly important since the country had entered a period of slowly accelerating evolution toward democracy, and social protests in the 1985–95 period were pretty much a part of daily life. Third, the ruling party (GMD) sought to draw more support from female voters by putting forth some measures of gender equity in its policy programs.

106 *Emerging challenges*

As a result, the Central Police Academy, which was empowered to train police administrators, recruited its first cohort of female cadets in 1974. In the same year, Taipei Women's Police Squad increased its female officers to 61. In 1981, that unit was granted an independent budget. A year later, the first experiment featuring a female officer team performing a wider range of police duties was put into action. In 1988, the Taipei police formed a female investigation task force to assist female crime victims. In 1991, a six-month experiment of female officers working in *paichusuo* (field stations, PCS) was introduced. Unfortunately, these initiatives involving female detectives and working in a PCS did not become routinized and failed to open more doors for female officers. Despite these preliminary efforts to expand the role of women, female officers' assignments remained predominately clerical and ancillary in nature over this 30-year period.

The suspension of martial law in 1987 triggered a limited push for greater gender equality (Chung 2008). From 1952 to the lifting of martial law, the police force was led by former military generals, and female officers were supposed to support the war against the communist China as female representatives (see Chapter 2). Their role was limited to this task. In the late 1990s, the passage of the *Three Anti-Violence Act* (防暴三法) marginally expanded the role of female officers, who were directed to help victims of domestic violence in addition to protecting women and children. Lacking the opportunity to serve as field patrol officers and as detectives, female officers were systematically left behind in terms of career advancement. Although their assignments within the police force began to expand, the new assignments continued to be those of largely dead-end jobs because they were by no means the mainstream tasks recognized and rewarded by the management in a police organization. Finally, realizing that police organizational policies and practices dealing with recruitment and selection, training and assignment, performance evaluation and promotion have gendered police work to the disadvantage of women, some female officers described themselves as working in "pink-ghettos" (Chen 1997).

Persistent inequality and institutional indifference era: women as unwanted members in PCS (2000 to present)

After becoming the President of the country in 2000, Chen Shuibian announced that he would increase the number of female officers and expand their role in police departments. The DPP and women's right groups worked together to promote a gender equality agenda in police organizations. The *Act of Gender Equality in Employment* (AGEE, 性別工作平等法) was enacted in 2002. In the same year, the Women's Police Squad was renamed the *Women and Children's Squad* to stress the nature of work assignments instead of the officers' gender. Male officers were encouraged to work side-by-side with female colleagues on preventing and reducing violence against women and children. The Ministry of Interior launched the first generation of programs associated with the "gender agenda" in 2004; those programs aimed to increase the number of female officers substantially, and to expand their representation in all police departments across the country.

Even though these changes toward gender equity are noteworthy, the third phase is labeled as "persistent inequality and institutional indifference" because the police administration not only has continued to discriminate against female officers, but it has become demonstrably indifferent to its own principle of gender equity. Article Seven of the AGEE states that "employers shall not discriminate against applicants or employees because of their gender or sexual orientation in the course of recruitment, screening tests, hiring, placement, assignment, evaluation and promotion." This article has an exclusionary clause, however, which states that "if the nature of work (is) only suitable to a specific gender, the above-mentioned restriction shall not apply." In response to the AGEE, the National Police Agency (NPA) launched a seven-year "Policy for Females in Police Occupation" (2004–10), which heightened expectation among women officers that progress toward gender equity would be forthcoming.

The Ma Yingjiu's government came into power in 2008 and has continued the unfinished task of promoting gender equity. In 2012, the NPA renamed the "Policy for Females in Police Occupation" to the "Police Gender Policy" as a part of a gender-equity mainstream effort enacted by the Executive Yuan. In order to integrate this new "Police Gender Policy" into the overall police agenda, a gender equality task force was formed. After so many years, female officers have finally begun to broaden their roles from clerks in the office and working in "pink ghettos" to that of co-workers on the street with other officers.

Despite some outward signs of progress, female officers, however, are still routinely excluded from policy making and decision making in the nation's local police forces; their representation in the police force's supervisory and managerial ranks remains low, a situation similar to those found in the UK and the US (Berman 2013; Martin 1989). Although female officers compose 8.6 percent of all with supervisory ranks (equal or higher than Police Inspector Rank Four), a ratio higher than their national average (6.4 percent), women are much less likely than men to hold command positions. Progressive gender equity policy is not easily translated into practice; the resistance currently faced by policewomen is perhaps less visible than it was in the past, but it is no less insidious.

Indeed, as viewed from the outside, more female officers are seen on the street working side-by-side with male colleagues than in the past. Nevertheless, in certain key areas, the current "Police Gender Policy" fails to promote the status of policewomen or to enhance equality between genders, contrary to the goals of the AGEE. For example, to "manage" the number of female officers coming on board, the number of women admitted to both the Central Police University and Taiwan Police College remains restricted. In 2004, in order to increase police manpower in a relatively short term, new police employees were recruited directly from a national examination – namely, the so-called *grassroot special examination*. In 2006, this examination became open to anyone in the public who had yet to be trained in either the Central Police University or Taiwan Police College. In 2010, gender quotas were 18 and 10 percent for females to enrol in the Central Police University and at Taiwan Police College,

108 *Emerging challenges*

respectively (Chen 2007). As a consequence, female applicants had to perform at a higher level than men in entrance examinations to be accepted by both training institutions (see Figures 8.2 and 8.3).

As shown in Figure 8.2, between 2003 and 2010, the lowest selection rate for male applicants of the Central Police University was about the same as the highest selection rate for females, while in every year a male applicant had at least twice as much chance as a female applicant to be admitted. The situation was even worse if a female applicant was attempting to gain admission to the Taiwan Police College (see Figure 8.3).

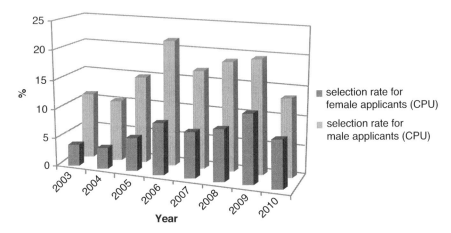

Figure 8.2 The selection rate for female and male applicants to Central Police University.
Source: Ministry of Interior (2010).

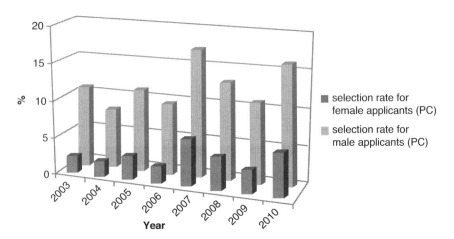

Figure 8.3 The selection rate for female and male applicants to Taiwan Police College.
Source: Ministry of Interior (2010).

In another area of active police recruitment, the Ministry of Interior and the Examination Yuan developed a system of "two tracks" (Huang 2010). The two tracks system distinguishes two approaches of becoming a police officer getting enrolled in the police educational system (featuring gender quotas) and then taking the national civil service examination, or taking the national examination first (without gender quotas) followed by training in the police educational system. Under the two-track recruitment system, a system of sex discrimination in the selection process is openly on display. Since more than 90 percent of the new recruits use the first approach (training first and examination later), female applicants are systematically kept out of the occupation, and this disadvantage will persist for a long time to come (see also Chapter 5).

Female officers continue to endure a token status in a profession dominated by men, lacking equal footing with their male colleagues in the number present and in the significance of work assigned to them; worst of all, they are severely disadvantaged in promotion. While the gender quota policy limits women's opportunity to become police officers, police departments have started desegregating job assignments, which ironically might not necessarily favor female officers. For example, the Women and Children's Squad used to provide a safe environment for female officers and offer an opportunity among the limited administrative posts for women. In the name of "gender equality" gender-segregated units (i.e., women's squads) are no longer permitted in police forces. As a result, male officers began to take over the posts associated with the last administrative stronghold reserved for women. In addition, the NPA rules provide that the deployment of female officers in PCS should remain a 1:9 gender ratio, meaning that no more than two female officers should be deployed to a PCS with twenty officers. The combination of unprepared male colleagues and female officers' rookie status might easily form a hostile work environment for women. Most police departments are yet to be transformed from a gender-segregated environment into a gender-friendly work environment, with police officers embracing women colleagues as one of their true equals.

In a survey of police officers, more than 85 percent of the female officers in Taipei agreed that gender discrimination is a general phenomenon in police departments (Huang 2005). The glass ceiling phenomenon is a real problem for female officers with regard to their career advancement. In a male-dominated work environment, gender segregation was a temporary solution that might have been a useful form of protection for female workers. In the long run, the true challenge for the police force, however, is to develop a genuine gender equality infrastructure wherein female officers, once moving from clerks in the office to co-workers on the street, can work side-by-side comfortably with male police officers as their equals; their counterparts in the US and the UK can serve as examples of how democratic policing has led to a more advanced stage of gender equity within the once male-dominant profession.

Female officers in the literature

The experience of policewomen in Taiwan is not entirely unique. Their sisters all over the world share somewhat similar experiences (Chan *et al.* 2010).

The domination of a masculine order in policing is often justified in terms of the mythic vision of police as crime fighters. The obvious male/female biological differences lead to the sexual division of labor, it is argued by the defenders of the idea of a male-exclusive police profession. The social artifact of the manly man or the womanly woman (Bourdieu 2001: 23) traps both men and women: "women either accept their biological inferiority or attempt to overcome it by becoming the manly policewomen, while men risk their lives to prove 'they have balls'" to their colleagues and broader society.

The empirical literature on female police officers and their performance, however, reveals a different reality of fitness to serve in the police officer role. In a classic evaluation of policewomen on patrol in the St. Louis County Police Department, Missouri, Sherman (1975) compared 16 pairs of female and male officers. The results illustrated that the women were equally as effective as the men in performing patrol work duties. Some differences were indeed noted; women were less aggressive, made fewer arrests, and engaged in fewer "preventive" activities such as motor vehicle and pedestrian stops. In another study conducted more recently, Parsons and Jesilow (2001) noted that the attitudes and behavior of female police officers differed very little from those of their male counterparts. Paoline and Terrill (2004) found little difference in the use of coercion by male and female officers. Poteyeva and Sun's (2009) meta-analysis of empirical evidence suggested that officer gender has only a weak effect on officers' attitudes toward community policing, the elements of the community and the neighborhood residents, job satisfaction, and domestic violence. Gender distinctions have been reported by some researchers, however. For example, Novak *et al.* (2011) found that male and female officers do tend to make different discretionary decisions when it comes to the decision to arrest. Sun (2007) found that female officers were more likely than male officers to provide support to citizens involved in domestic violence, although they did not differ in exercising control actions toward citizens.

Gender differences manifest themselves when officers are being observed by others within the police organization. This is likely because female police officers must learn to navigate the male-dominant environment carefully; they need to know when to defer to powerful male peers, yet prove themselves as capable officers to their supervisors. This has to be accomplished while maintaining the appearance of competency in the eyes of suspects. Male officers do not have this same set of constraints, and generally behave similarly regardless of whether they are acting independently or are being observed by supervisors. Some key tenets of community policing are thought of as "non-masculine" by police traditionalists in part because they fly in the face of the image of the adventurous crime fighter. Female behavior tends to be consistent with these tenets of community policing when it takes place in the presence of fellow officers, but then takes on the more masculine role when being evaluated by a supervisor.

In Taiwan before the 1980s, the combination of a patrimonial society and a governmental mandate for military readiness acted to make the issue of incorporating women into the police force largely irrelevant. The few women officers were severely underrepresented and their voices were virtually absent from the policing literature. Scholars associated with the officially sanctioned police training institutions were largely silent about the issue of women in policing.

Over the following decades, a limited literature on the subject has emerged in Taiwan. In evaluating the performance and job satisfaction of female officers, Liu (2003) and Shang (2003), using rather rudimentary statistics, reported that female officers feel a great extent of work pressure and a low degree of job satisfaction. Having approached the topic from a male perspective, these studies suffer some noticeable limitations. For example, in Shang's (2003) study, one survey question for female officers is "I can work with my superior officers." The underlying assumption of the question is that female officers do not hold any supervisory positions. In addition, despite the fact that neither of the above studies ever really compared male and female officers in their work performance and experience, they alleged that any problems experienced by female officers were a result of their gender rather than a consequence of the police occupational culture. Female officers were blamed for lower dedication to the police profession without considering the structural barriers and family responsibilities that greatly distracted female officers. Yeh (2004) even averred that female officers do not want "real equality." Liu (2003: 138) bluntly asserted that "if female officers want to win more social support, the only way is to change their own attitudes, to make self-examination, to discipline themselves, and to respect the values of police work."

These statements echo findings from early studies of policewomen in the US, suggesting that women displayed supposedly undesirable traits for the police profession. The principal underlying messages in these studies would seem to be twofold: one message suggests that female officers are inferior in character to their male counterparts; the other is one of blaming female officers for not showing sufficient support for their law enforcement organizations. The common problem of these studies is that their authors failed to address the "wider structural, engendered inequalities and occupational cultural processes" at play for women police officers (Holdaway and Parker 1998: 40). These broader contextual factors often could have a profound influence on female officers' professional experience. Nor did they ever try to address the discriminatory mechanisms affecting an officer's assignments and their prospects for promotion and career advancement.

In offering some counter-evidence, Huang's (2005) study of 189 female officers in the Taipei City Police Department found that many female officers are motivated to gain promotion and are willing to make personal sacrifice for their agencies. Policewomen's willingness to sacrifice their personal life to pursue career development, however, is conditional based on their marital and family status. Not surprisingly, married female officers with young children were more reluctant to accept the position change that would accompany promotion. It is wrong, however, to interpret this reservation as women being "less ambitious" compared with their male fellow officers; unlike female officers, male officers share little family responsibility in a patriarchal society. The heavy household responsibility is a huge burden on the shoulders of policewomen because women

112 Emerging challenges

in Taiwan are expected to take on the majority of responsibilities of caring for the young and elderly and for carrying out daily chores at home (Wang 2008).

The problems faced by female police officers also reflect the existing widespread unequal labor arrangement/distribution within the large society. The facts that work assignments are unevenly distributed and that human resources are not efficiently distributed in the police organizations have been largely neglected. High work pressure and low job satisfaction are a common experience among all officers, male and female officers alike. The differences, however, might be that male officers complain less about the demands of their work because their relative absence from family duties is broadly accepted in Taiwanese society. Female officers' relative lack of enthusiasm for promotion also may be attributed to the fact of the absence of female role models in the police organization.

The findings reported in the study of female officers reveal the presence of a root problem of police departments in Taiwan. Male officers are also burdened by long work hours and little managerial support, but they tend to remain silent because they are highly concerned with their career advancement and are afraid of jeopardizing their chances of promotion (Loa 2012). Instead of complaining overtly, many male officers tend to complain privately and often encourage their wives to join citizen rallies against overwork.

How police organizations might cause different experiences for male and female officers is an interesting subject. Many scholars study female officers from a gender equality framework. They investigate the reality and meaning of being a police officer for women, including their motivations, work conduct, and sources of job satisfaction or frustration. Lin (1997) interviewed 39 female and male police officers to serve as a basis for describing the life of Taiwanese policewomen. She found that women and men shared a similar sense of frustration from the slow pace of institutional evolution toward democratic policing and the passive work culture, and likewise abhorred the hostile attitudes toward the police on the part of the public. Nevertheless, policewomen are more likely to enjoy helping the citizens and the feedback received from the public than their male counterparts. In contrast, male officers gain satisfaction from solving a case. Lin (1997) therefore concluded that the discriminatory work distribution in a police organization largely replicates the gendered work distribution in society.

Another stream of research focuses on the workplace conduct of female officers by exploring the "suitability" of women in frontline assignments (C. Lai 2010; M. Lai 2010; Sun and Chu 2010; Tsai 2011). These studies identify some differences between female and male officers. Some of these researchers are themselves police officers, male and female, who conclude that the male and female differences found justify the work division and gender ratio policy, especially as it pertains to PCS (C. Lai 2010; M. Lai 2010; Tsai 2011).

Chu and Sun (2010) studied the responses to domestic violence of female and male officers, finding that male officers show more tolerance of the actions of offenders engaged in domestic violence than do female officers. In addition, there is no gender difference in terms of attitudes toward proactive approaches for preventing and handling domestic violence. They concluded from their study it is managerial support rather than officers' gender, that counts the most for the promotion of a positive influence on officers' proactive response to domestic violence.

Importantly, Chu and Sun (2010) posited that their findings suggest that female officers might be better candidates for handling domestic violence cases than their male counterparts. Given that responding to domestic violence incidents has become a main task for frontline officers in Taiwan, their research findings suggest that more female officers should be serving in the PCS. Indeed, by deploying more female officers into local police stations, better service to domestic violence victims can be anticipated. This change in police staffing, in turn, may enhance crime victims' willingness to report domestic violence to the police.

We will explore this issue of gender, minority populations, and policing practices more fully in Chapter 9. To sum it up, the extant research literature on Taiwan female officers seldom captures the real and persisting obstacles working in a male-dominated occupation. Most of the previous studies have preconditioned their framework on the assumption that policewomen should more fully "fit in" to a police organization without questioning the legitimacy of the prevailing job distribution process or resource and reward allocation policies in place.

Barriers facing female officers

Taiwan is a relatively safe society and citizens generally obey the police because they have respect for the uniform which symbolizes legitimate state power. The use of force by the police is rare, taking up only a tiny fraction of police time. Police officers spend the vast bulk of their time building relationships with residents within the local communities they serve. Female officers are trained exactly the same way as their male counterparts at both the TPC and the CPU. Most policewomen see themselves as fully competent police officers who are significantly underrepresented in police administrative and other supervising posts.

The effort to advance the professional status of policewomen has been ongoing for decades, with limited success being achieved. It is ironic to find that under current "gender-equity mainstream" policy, it is actually taking back the resources previously set aside for female officers instead of providing more. Xie Fen-Fen (謝芬芬) was at once the first and the last female county/city-level police chief, serving in the Yi-lan County Police Department from 2003 to 2007. Around the country, only a handful of female officers currently serve as PCS commanding officers or district commanders within a city/county bureau. The likelihood of promotion does not seem to have grown after the extent of gender segregation at work was greatly reduced. The work environment for policewomen remains harsh since most female officers are asked to match the effort of their male counterparts at work without equal opportunity to promote. Admittedly, there are a few policewomen who make use of the traditional stereotype of being a weaker gender and demand for special treatment in their work, but they should not be regarded as representative and the majority of policewomen are working as equal partners with their male counterparts. Under the current patriarchal environment, an incompetent female officer is easier to be picked up as the black sheep while an incompetent male officer is often tolerated and less noticeable.

The police are an occupation dominated by men, mostly because policing was viewed as a risky job requiring ample physical strength. Traditionally, policing was not a very attractive occupation to young people, not to mention young women. Before 1990, many young people enrolled in TPC and CPU chiefly because these educational institutions were tuition-free and cadets received a monthly stipend. This policy makes policing attractive to young people from modest socio-economic backgrounds who otherwise could not afford college tuition and/or needed to support their family while acquiring their education (Gao 1999).

Since then, police salaries have exceeded the average pay for young graduates from regular universities and colleges. Police salaries are also higher than those of other public servants. Careers in the police gained in popularity initially because of the short-term premier Hao Bochun's action to significantly raise police salaries in the early 1990s. With the tension between Taiwan and China gradually receding, policing has become an increasingly attractive profession to many young people. More and more young men and women have chosen to pursue a police career, and as a consequence the entrance examination has become fiercely competitive. In addition to the ever-present family influence of a police-connected parent or close relative, more and more people seek to join the police force because of the job stability and the decent salaries paid to novice officers.

Traditionally, being a school teacher is the primary choice for a young woman who seeks employment in the public service in Taiwan. With the increased number of unemployed teachers resulting from a declining birth rate, more female college graduates with teaching qualifications are shifting their focus toward a police career. Despite the cold reaction from many male colleagues and despite substantial job barriers and high performance standards, a police career still appears attractive as a job featuring the proverbial "iron bowl" – that is, it is a position in which once one is recruited, one is nearly certain to make it through to retirement with good pension benefits. In addition, the average difference in earnings between women and men in the police is smaller than that found in the vast majority of private sector jobs. The fact that more and more young women are aiming at a police career likely says more about the harsh job market in Taiwan than the beneficial impact of the women's liberation movement.

Several longstanding impediments facing women in policing are still present nowadays. First, the quota system remains in place. In responding to the gender-equity mainstreaming policy, the Ministry of Interior and the Examination Yuan jointly developed the double-track system, controlling the gender quotas of both academy entrants and new trainees, a fact which has limited the greater inclusion of women in the police force. In countries such as the US and UK, affirmative action policies have been in place to encourage police departments to recruit more female officers as an action intended to correct the long-term problem of *de jure* discrimination and prior institutional exclusion. In the US, police departments with affirmative action policies (either voluntary or court-ordered) recruited more female applicants than those without such a policy (Martin 1989). In the UK, the

Home Office urges the police forces to continue to recruit more female officers until they make up 35 percent of all police officers (Berman 2013, Brown *et al.* 2006). In Taiwan, even though the police force encounters a serious shortage of manpower, the NPA still shows no intention to further increase the proportion of female officers to any substantial extent.

Second, resistance to policewomen continues to come from senior male police colleagues, often resulting in a hostile work environment for some female officers. Since the average police officer is male in his middle age, most officers joined the police force when the prime qualifications for a police officer were "undivided loyalty, unquestioning obedience, a solid physique, and a powerful fist" (Ministry of Foreign Affairs 1998). About half of the male officers have only senior high school educational attainment, meaning that most of the frontline female officers are younger with higher educational achievement. In 2010, 39 percent of female officers were younger than 29 years old, compared with 12 percent of male officers in the same age group. Forty-eight percent of male officers were between 40 to 49 years old while only 30 percent of females fell into that age group. The male officers in their forties might well entertain inappropriate role expectations of their women colleagues due to their lack of prior working experiences with women colleagues. They are also more likely to be influenced by the traditional patriarchal views of the broader culture, leading them to hold less equalitarian attitudes toward female colleagues.

Third, the widespread incidence of sexual harassment adds to their uneasiness at work and increases the turnover rate among women officers. Sexual harassment is recognized as a common problem in police organizations around the world (Brown 1998; Collins 2004; Heidensohn 2003). In an extension of Western scholars' conceptual framework into Taiwan, Huang and Cao (2008) conducted one of the rare studies on the topic. They examined two types of sexual harassment experienced by Taipei female officers: hostile work environment and *quid pro quo* harassment. Hostile work environment refers to a broad range of verbal and non-verbal behaviors conveying insulting, hostile, and degrading attitudes about women, including the telling of sexually explicit jokes in the workplace (MacKinnon 1979; Whaley and Tucker 1998). In contrast, *quid pro quo* harassment refers to various behaviors ranging from unwanted or non-reciprocal physical gestures to coercively or threateningly demanded sexual favors. In their survey of 189 Taipei female officers, they found that nearly half of respondents encountered at least one incident of hostile work environment, and 15 percent experienced *quid pro quo* harassment incidents. Those survey respondents who sensed sexism in the police organization are more likely to report experiencing a hostile work environment. The greater the job desegregation accomplished by the woman officer, the more likely she is to be exposed to a hostile work environment. Their analysis supported the work environment model which suggests that sexism, job barriers, and work absences are better predictors of sexual harassment than demographic factors (Huang and Cao 2008). Using the same data set, Hsieh (2007) points out that female police officers who suffer from sexual harassment are more inclined either to transfer to other units or even leave police organizations.

116 *Emerging challenges*

To be a female police officer in a patriarchal society is indeed demanding. Officer Pi-Ya Lew commented on women as officers after five years' experience (Ministry of Foreign Affairs 1976) thus: ". . . there is nothing significant about a female cop. What's significant is the work itself. The job may be special compared with other professions, but we are not special at all."

What was said more than thirty years ago by Officer Lew remains true today. Being female carries the negative symbolic capital in a patriarchal society. Female officers are viewed as "females," not as "police officers."

For some people, resistance to the integration of women into policing is based on the supposed fear that citizens may defy a female's authority, but the real worry underlying the resistance among the police force is the threat to the self-image of male officers and the public image of the police as crime fighters (Martin 1980). Admittedly, a few women officers make use of the stereotype of being "weaker" partners and demand special treatment in their work, but the majority of women officers are working as equal partners with their male counterparts. With respect to women achieving appointment to the administrative positions, physicality as a reason to exclude from further promotion becomes less tenable; in practice, female officers are confronted with a different kind of demand for masculinity where traits associated with managerial masculinity dominate (Silvestri 2007).

Even though the barriers confronting women seeking to join the police continue to exist, the enthusiasm for becoming a female police officer nonetheless remains strong. The *status quo* of gender inequality is difficult to challenge. The police administration would be well advised to modify its discriminatory policy toward women and open its doors to recruitment, favorable assignment, and promotion in rank to female officers. The police in Taiwan can be described as truly democratic only when it fully integrates females into the law enforcement labor force and into the administrative and supervisory ranks.

Summary

Taiwan has undergone significant political changes in the direction of democratic governance in the past few decades. The extent of change in its patriarchal culture, including the police culture, however, lags behind the pace of political change. The practice of open discrimination against women seeking entrance into the police force exemplifies well this lag in the process of favourable change. Both major political parties support the principle of gender equality, but they both maintain the same quota policy to keep many women out of the police force. In addition, a similar quota remains in place to keep the number of female officers entering PCS. Consistent with the non-litigation preferences of Confucian culture (Huang and Cao 2008), no advocacy group has launched a constitutional challenge to these practices. Women have not yet been fully integrated into the police force in Taiwan.

Former Minister for Justice and Customs of Australia, Vanstone (2001: 126), once observed the following: "As long as women remain under-represented in law enforcement, the service provided will not accurately reflect the composition of society." The representation of female officers in the police is not merely an issue of equal employment, but also it is an issue of the gendered nature of public services (Zhao *et al.* 2001). The democratic transition and democratic consolidation of the past two decades have significantly increased the number of female officers, but their number remains distant from the level of parity and their promotion to the top positions remains remote. Policewomen still face numerous institutional and organizational hurdles due to their gender. Sexual harassment is one of these persistent barriers, and promotion to command and supervisory positions is another. Other issues, such as those of gay and lesbian cops, have yet to make their debut.

Judging from the fact that the police administration has neither abolished the gender quota nor increased the availability of female administrative positions, the value orientation of the police administration is still highly patriarchal. The continued resistance to the full integration of women in policing is not surprising, given that the integration of women into police forces has also been opposed, resisted, and undermined elsewhere in the world. With equal employment opportunity policy and the promises emanating from both major political parties, we are somewhat confident that the professional situation for policewomen will improve in the future. In the next chapter, we will shift our gears by examining a few recurring challenges to the job of being a police officer, paying particular attention to the police handling of socially disadvantaged groups such as victims of domestic violence, foreign workers, and mainland immigrants.

9 Policing socially disadvantaged groups
Criminalization or victimization?

In Chapter 1 we argue that the twin principles of democracy are liberty and equality for all. Applying the principle of equality to democratic policing means that the police must provide equal treatment of all citizens regardless of their race/ethnicity and socio-economic statuses (Cao 2011; Ren *et al*. 2005). The problem of equal treatment of all citizens is quite prominent in immigrant societies, such as the US and Canada. This does not mean, however, that it is not an issue in a largely homogenous society such as Taiwan. Although conflicts between the dominant group and other ethnic groups and/or newcomers are less noticeable because the scale of conflicts tends to be small, they are equally, if not more, intense and insidious. To varying degrees, the problems of racism and class prejudice exist in all post-Confucian societies, Taiwan included. The issue of equal protection from the police, however, has attracted little attention from police scholars in Taiwan. As Taiwan evolves into a democracy and continues to become more global in its commerce and communications, equal protection of socially disadvantaged groups emerges as a vital issue for the nation's law enforcement. In recent decades, Taiwan has quietly become more diversified in its populace, and fair and equal treatment-based policing has surfaced as an agenda item for the police.

The delivery of policing, both in the form of application of "force" and delivery of "service," should not be "greatly inferior for some social groups than others" (Bowling and Philips 2003: 528). Unlike their counterparts in North America and Europe, the Taiwan police have not been involved in any major racial conflicts. As a traditional heathen Confucian society, the culture is deeply ethnocentric: China is the equivalent of civilization itself. The Taiwanese culture has deeply entrenched within it the Confucian division of the population into the gentry (*junzi*, 君子) and the inferior (*xiaoren*, 小人) (Wu and Cao 2014). Between the Han – the dominant ethnic group – and the rest of the other non-Han ethnic groups, there are various pejorative names for "uncivilized" minority groups, such as *fan* (番), *yi* (夷), *man* (蠻) etc. The principle of equality for all is not the dominant philosophical theme found in Confucianism. Many forms of institutional racism and sexism, such as the gender discrimination we discussed in the previous chapter, are embedded in the culture and are seldom challenged.

In this chapter we first identify the socially disadvantaged groups in question. A brief discussion of the history of governing aboriginal peoples follows to illustrate the complicated and understudied relationship between the government, the police being its representatives, and the aboriginal peoples. The approach taken to the policing of the aboriginal peoples is largely replicated in the policing of other socially disadvantaged groups, such as immigrants and the victims of domestic violence. Members of these groups are not only more likely than other citizens to be victimized, but they are also more likely to be criminalized and stigmatized in the process of having contact with Taiwan's criminal justice systems. We call here for more reform measures and initiatives that a more demographically diverse police force would likely embrace; the true meaning of democratic policing entails a deep commitment to fair and equal policing for all citizens, socially privileged and marginalized alike.

The socially disadvantaged groups

Socially disadvantaged groups are those who suffer from ethnic prejudice or cultural bias because of their identity as members of a targeted group. Social disadvantages then stem from circumstances beyond group members' control – such as gender, ethnicity, nationality, and physical or psychological disabilities. These traits hinder the fulfillment of marginalized group members' social advancement due to the discrimination. These people are often neglected and mistreated in a society in good part because of a lack of political representation and the lack of political power.

Taiwan has been described as a highly homogenous society, with over 95 percent of its population claiming Han ancestry (Ministry of Foreign Affairs 2012). The majority Hans are from Fukien and Hakka. Among the 95 percent Han ethnic group, not all are created equal politically. They are divided in the political arena as *waishengren* (外省人) or "post-1949 mainlander Chinese" and *benshengren* (本省人) or "pre-1949 native Taiwanese." Albeit small in number (roughly 20 percent of the population), the relative newcomers (i.e., the post-1949 mainlanders) were in total control of the political life on the island before the 1980s. The absence of equal rights in political participation created strong resentment toward the GMD government among the pre-1949 populace. The then GMD leader Chiang Jing-kuo was aware of the problem and started cultivating some resident elites and including some of them into his tight ruling circle. Although the post-martial law era of politics has allowed local Taiwanese equal opportunities to fulfill their political dreams, the long-time pre- and post-1949 division was purposefully chosen by the DPP as the most important distinguishing line to form its party base and mobilize political support for its political agenda. As a counter-measure, Chiang Jing-kuo and his successor Li Denghui adopted the slogan of *"new Taiwanese"* (*xintaiwanren*, 新台灣人), suggesting that people who care about the interests of Taiwan and have made contributions to the society should be viewed as true Taiwanese even though they were born on the mainland or somewhere else. During the eight years of Chen Shuibian's administration (2000–8), this decisive political theme was repeatedly used successfully to achieve DDP's political purposes. The current president Ma Yingjiu, however, reassumes the GMD's long-term policy of "new Taiwanese" in an effort to unify the entire population behind his regime (Da Guang 2011).

There are 14 distinguishable indigenous peoples with a total number over half a million (530,756) as of July 2013 (Monthly Bulletin of Interior Statistics 2013). The 14 indigenous tribes in Taiwan are the Amis, Atayal, Paiwan, Bunun, Tsou, Rukai, Puyuma, Saisiyat, Yami, Thao, Kamalan, Truku, Sakizaya, and Seediq. They are all non-Han, and can be classified as Austronesian people who likely began arriving in Taiwan in 4000 BC (Fetzer and Soper 2011: 99). Pushed back into the mountain areas by the immigrant groups of Han who began their domination during the Ming Dynasty (1368–1644), the aboriginal peoples in Taiwan, as is the case with other aboriginal groups around the world, are the most disadvantaged ethnic minority communities who suffer from "political exploitation, economic extortion, and cultural chauvinism" by whomever happens to be in power (Fetzer and Soper 2011: 95–9). As a group, they were traditionally called mountaineers (*shandiren*, 山地人), a word carrying a derogatory connotation of "uncivilized people" while the more progressive label is *yuanzhumin* (原住民). Despite rhetoric to the contrary on the part of some Han group spokespersons, all Han groups – Fukien, Hakka, native Taiwanese, and mainlander Chinese – have been guilty of bigotry against the aboriginal peoples in Taiwan.

Apart from the aboriginal population, Taiwan has gradually become a demographically diverse society as an unexpected consequence of its "economic miracle" beginning in the 1970s. Coinciding with the democratic transition and cross-Straits visitation initiated in the 1990s, a large number of marriages have taken place between the people of Taiwan and elsewhere, involving mainly the upwardly mobile bridegrooms from Taiwan and the poor and hopeful brides from China and southeastern Asian countries (Williams and Yu 2006).

Today, Taiwan has a substantially higher rate of international marriage in comparison to the neighboring countries of South Korea, Japan, and China (Executive Yuan 2012). In June 2013, the number of registered marriage immigrants has exceeded 480,000. Among them, the majority are marriage immigrants from the People's Republic of China (64.84 percent), and Hong Kong and Macau (2.7 percent). Other nationalities among these brides include those of Vietnam (18.42 percent), Indonesia (5.8 percent), Thailand (1.74 percent), the Philippines (1.58 percent), Cambodia (0.89 percent), Japan (0.84 percent), and South Korea (0.25 percent) (National Immigration Agency 2013a). Whether naturalized or not, marriage immigrants have become a new social force which has continuously been struggling for their citizenship and rights to fair treatment. Cross-cultural marriages in Taiwan largely involve low income Taiwanese males and females from countries with a lower level of economic development (Executive Yuan 2012; Wang 2005).

International migrant workers, according to the immigration policy, must return to their country of origin after their work contract expires, and they can never become citizens of Taiwan. These workers are mainly from Southeast Asian countries such as Vietnam, Indonesia, Thailand, Cambodia, Bangladesh, India, and the Philippines.

In addition to aboriginal peoples, marriage immigrants, and foreign labor workers, socially disadvantaged groups also include victims of domestic violence as they fit with the definition of these groups. In Taiwan, domestic violence was a hidden crime until the *Domestic Violence Prevention Act* (DVPA, 家庭暴力防治法) was promulgated in 1998. Before that, the police tended to adopt a hands-off policy to domestic violence and the prevalent sayings were those such as "Law should be kept outside the door of a family" (法不入家門) and "Even an upright judge finds it hard to settle a family quarrel" (清官難斷家務事). Similar to statistics reported in other countries, more than 90 percent of domestic violence victims in Taiwan are female. Official response to domestic violence is still inadequate in some areas, making victims of such offenses members of the disadvantaged groups of marginalized residents.

Sellin's (1938: 98) culture conflict theory suggested that the conflict of conduct norms "may arise as a result of contact between norms drawn from different cultural systems or areas" and should be studied as the likely underlying cause of legal violation. He identified some conduct norms which are peculiar to the migrant groups, making cultural conflicts a pervasive phenomenon of such groups. It follows that the socially disadvantaged groups are subject to a higher risk of breaking the law.

Aboriginal governance

The movie *Seediq Bale* (2011) by director Wei Desheng (魏德聖) describes a historical battle episode between the police and the aboriginal people taking place during the period of the Japanese occupation (1895–1945). The story was based on the last major uprising of Seediq people against colonial Japanese forces, referred to as the Wushe Incident (霧社事件), in central Taiwan in 1930. The Japanese rulers, namely the local police, abolished the custom of head hunting and animal hunting and forced the men to do low-wage logging to make a living. Seediq people were also forbidden to tattoo their faces, a practice which they believed to be a requirement for them to go to the other side across the rainbow bridge after death. The conflict intensified in the late autumn of 1930 at a wedding ceremony, turning into a battle against the Japanese. The police station was the first target of the Seediq, and among the 134 Japanese killed, many were police officers (Wu 2011c). After reinforcements arrived on the scene, over 1,000 Seediq people were killed by the Japanese and their tribe nearly became extinct after the incident.

Tracing back to the period of aboriginal governance in Taiwan, Taiwanese natives were referred to as *fan*, which means barbarians, under the Qing Dynasty (1636–1912) (Wu 2011a). Accordingly, aboriginal governance was referred to as *lifan* (i.e., governing barbarians 理蕃). The Qing appointed governor adopted the policy of "divide and rule" and implemented a strict segregation policy between aboriginal peoples and Han immigrants (L. Huang 2003: 209–10). Otherwise, aboriginal peoples were left alone to manage their own internal affairs. In the early days of Japanese occupation, the Japanese government took a more suppressive policy toward the aboriginal peoples. Under the rule of Governor-General Sakuma Samata (佐久間左馬太), the police were directed to penetrate aboriginal settlements in order to extract forest resources for the economic growth of Japan (Wu 2011a). For that purpose, he created the "Bureau of Aboriginal Affairs" and reformulated the Aboriginal Control Principles which emphasized the point that the police posted in the mountains should be of "high quality." Later in July 1915, his successor closed the Bureau of Aboriginal Affairs and returned control of the aboriginal regions from the governor's administration to the jurisdiction of the police bureau of mountain areas (Wu 2011b). During the period of Japanese colonization, the Japanese police often made aboriginals work without pay. Aboriginal men were also drafted to serve the overseas wars and aboriginal women were summoned by the police to work in support of larger wars; many of these women were even forced to work as comfort women (sex slaves) in the Japanese military in Taiwan or overseas during World War II (Lai 2012).

After the GMD took over Taiwan, aboriginal peoples continued to suffer from both labor and sexual exploitation. The areas where they resided were severely underdeveloped in a booming economy. The outcry for their economic development was heard during the mid-1980s. Young aboriginal people were attracted by the modernized urban life, and they either willingly or forcefully went to major cities in search of gainful employment.

In 1986, an aboriginal youth by the name of Tang Yingshen (湯英伸) was convicted and sentenced to death for killing his employer Lin Mucai and his family (Lin 2010). He was executed in 1987 at the age of nineteen, making him the youngest convict executed in Taiwanese history. Tang was one of the many aboriginal youths who had dreamed about making a fortune by working hard and honestly in Taipei City, but unfortunately he encountered unfair employment treatment due to his aboriginal status. Many people held a deep prejudice against aboriginal peoples, believing that they were lazy and destined to become alcoholics. Tang's boss, the owner of a laundry business, took away his identification card and refused to pay his salary. Out of desperation and in a fit of rage, Tang took three lives. This event formed the base of a movie entitled *The Barefoot Angel*.

In the late 1980s, Presbyterian relief workers first noted that "aboriginal girls were sold into city brothels by a bankrupt aboriginal economy amidst a booming Taiwanese economic miracle" (Ho 2003). The Presbyterian Church set up a so-called Rainbow Project to promote the rescue of these underage aboriginal girls. Demonstration rallies were held in front of the Taipei Police Department because it was believed that the police failed to oversee the notorious red-light district which harbored many aboriginal prostitutes. On January 11, 1987 over 100 marchers gathered in front of the Taipei police headquarters to protest against the police for their ineptitude for "leaving the girls trapped in the vicious circle of trafficking and prostitution" (Ho 2003). In March of 1987, the government launched the *Straightening Project* (正風專案), an action which the police claimed freed more than 200 enslaved underage prostitutes. However, underground brothels were still open for business and aboriginal girls continued to disappear from their tribes. Chiu (1993) pointed out that the real culprit of the ineptitude of the police and politicians in controlling the aboriginal underage prostitute problem was the corrupt relationship between the police and some sex industry operators. The Police District Chiefs of the Taipei City Police Department joined the NGO-organized Anti-Child-Prostitution Jog on November 14, 1993. Ironically, on the one hand, the police showed their partnership with the NGO to rescue underage prostitutes, and on the other hand, the police accused the NGO of exaggerating the number of underage prostitutes involved in the illicit sex trade.

Along with the democratization process after the suspension of martial law, aboriginal peoples began to express their opinions in the political arena and to fight for their own identity and rights during the 1980s (J. Chang 2011). The aboriginal social movement's activities resulted in a few clashes with the police during protests. For example, violent confrontations with the police took place on November 15, 2003, when about 1,000 aboriginal people convened in front of the Executive Yuan to protest the government's failure to rebuild some roads in mountainous areas ravaged by flooding (CNA 2004).

The tension between the aboriginals and the police continued after the establishment of the Forest and Nature Conservation Police Unit in 2003, a police unit which was formed to enforce the Wildlife Conservation Act. In an effort to reduce the danger of potential conflict, the police administration actively recruited aboriginal police officers into the unit, ending with about 80 percent of the members of this special unit being persons of aboriginal origins. Despite this effort to incorporate sensitivity to aboriginal concerns in the police, many of the tribes are still reluctant to accept the fact that the Forest and Nature Conservation Police Unit can enforce the law in their lands so that the natural resources can be protected. To many of these people these protections jeopardize their traditional right of hunting in their areas.

On December 31, 2007, more than 60 Pinuyumayan tribesmen were chased by the armed forest police when they hunted in Mountain Chihpen as a celebration of the tribe's annual hunting festival (CNA 2008). These tribesmen claimed that some of them were subjected to rough body searches. In a statement issued by the forest police unit, the police officers said that they only took enforcement action because the tribesmen went beyond their reservation areas. Another clash with the police took place on January 28, 2011 when about 200 Amis people protested against what they felt was the unjust and uncompensated theft of their land.

Since the 1980s, the police administration has been criticized for the lack of integrity in their effort to address the problem of underage aboriginal prostitutes. More recently, it has been criticized for not making a sincere effort to recruit aboriginals into the police force. The aboriginal population was 2.3 percent in 2011, but only 1.1 percent of the examinees passing special police examination were aboriginal peoples in 2010. If this proportion does not change, the underrepresentation of the aborigines in the police force will not be eliminated. In response to a proposal by the aboriginal Legislator Kong Wenji (孔文吉), the National Police Agency announced a new plan to recruit more aboriginal peoples into the police force (Chuang 2010). The new program holds that if the aboriginal officer candidate passes the "certificate of indigenous culture and language" examination, they could obtain extra credits (3.75 percent) on the entrance examination for the Central Police University. The measure does increase the opportunity for aboriginal applicants to gain admittance into the Central Police University.

Yesterday's criminals, today's victims? Policing immigrants

From the 1990s to the present, a new disadvantaged group has come to the attention of the media as the target of exploitation and slavery – namely, trafficked women and foreign migrant workers. Their fates as marginalized subpopulations in an otherwise prosperous nation are similar to that of the aboriginal peoples, and the police have paid little attention to their dilemmas of existence in Taiwanese society.

Traditionally, law enforcement's principal tactics against illegal immigrants have involved interception, detention, and deportation. Those being smuggled had never been viewed by the police as "victims of crime." The police experienced a major policy shift in the area mainly because of the Miaoli Diubao Incident (苗栗丟包事件) involving smuggled persons being dumped into the sea. In 2003, twelve women from the PRC were forced to jump into the sea by a snakehead (smuggler) who was panicked during a police investigation, resulting in the drowning deaths of six of the women. The snakehead was sentenced to the death penalty and executed in 2005. The prosecutor's office in Miaoli, however, rejected the victim families' petition for criminal victimization compensation on the basis that these women were considered to "be responsible for their victimization by involvement in criminal activities."

In its Trafficking in Persons Report 2006, the US State Department placed Taiwan on its Tier II watch list because of "its failure to show evidence of increasing efforts over the past year to address trafficking . . . particularly to address the serious level of forced labor and sexual servitude among legally migrating Southeast Asian contract workers and brides." It further stated that "Taiwan authorities do not fully comply with the minimum standards for the elimination of trafficking." The report not only criticized the fact that foreign workers are not protected by Taiwan's labor law, but also accused Taiwan of permitting poor treatment and forced labor of foreign brides (US Department of State 2006).

The above report specifically points out that many earlier marriage immigrants could have fallen into the category of trafficked victims. These women were powerless and vulnerable to abuse, and they were largely without the capacity to develop their own voice to make their plight be known to people in Taiwan (C. Chang 2003). As a result, they deserve to be classified as the innocent victims of human trafficking and should be treated separately from their profit-seeking smugglers.

Due to strong domestic and international criticisms, the Taiwanese authorities have strengthened not only their enforcement efforts on snakeheads, but also the protections extended to human trafficking victims. The NPA launched two special projects in 2006, one being the "repressing snake project" and the other being the "anti-slavery project." The former is enforced by the Office of Foreign Affairs Police, while the latter is enforced by the Crime Investigation Police. Both projects are targeted at organized human trafficking networks led by criminals, such as illegal brokers or snakeheads, separating the victims of being smuggled from the culprits – the smugglers. The so called "being smuggled" thus are regarded as "human trafficking victims"; mainly women and youths, many of those who were yesterday's targets of criminal control have become today's targets of protection.

Although there are indeed many stories of happy cross-nationality marriages, the media tends to focus on those cases where the women were the victims of domestic abuse and related crimes. For example, a man called Li Tai-an (李泰安) and his brother Li Shuangquan (李雙全) plotted a train crash to mask the murder of Chen Hongshen (陳氏紅琛), the Vietnamese spouse of Li Shuangquan on March 17, 2007 (R. Chang 2006). Li Shuangquan had two other foreign spouses, one of whom died from a mysterious snake bite. He committed suicide before the trial, and Li Tai-an was sentenced to life imprisonment in 2013. The fate of many foreign spouses is similar to those of the aboriginal girls who suffer chronic abuse and/or neglect without seeking any help from the police.

With the end of the Cold War (1947–91), the process of globalization has spread to Taiwan and has created a growing integrated market for the countries of Asia. The more developed regions, including Taiwan, have started to experience labor shortages and consequently have begun to develop a market for migrant workers (Lee 2005). In Taiwan, the recruitment of foreign labor workers is brokered by private companies since the government is reluctant to get into the issue of managing migrant workers. Some entrepreneurs have abused the unregulated market. A survey conducted in 2009 revealed that about 20 percent of foreign workers called the 1955 helpline and complained about their working conditions (Council of Labor Affairs 2009). Restrictive immigration policies, such as limited residence permits and strict limitation of changing employers, have produced a substantial market demand for illicit workers. In 1995, more than 17,000 foreign workers disappeared from official status without leaving the island, and presumably began to work illegally thereafter. At the end of June 2013, the total number of known runaway foreign labor reached an estimated figure of 38,354 (National Immigration Agency 2013b).

Before the establishment of the National Immigration Agency (NIA), investigating human trafficking was the sole responsibility of the police. From 1972 to 2007, border control was managed by the Immigration Bureau under the National Police Agency. When the problem of illegal workers became severe in 1995, the National Police Agency drafted a plan to apprehend 1,000 illegal foreign workers each month by offering cash reward bonuses to arresting officers (Anonymous 1995). The plan was later abandoned due to widespread criticisms from various quarters, both within the police and from outside. However, despite the abandonment of this plan, many local police precincts still have quotas on the number of illegal foreign workers to be apprehended. Although the Immigration Act was promulgated in 1999, it was not until January 2007 that the NIA officially initiated its implementation. Due to the lack of manpower in the NIA, however, the police continue to share some responsibilities on crime and victimization related to immigrants.

126 *Emerging challenges*

The police also are the main enforcement agency of submitting cases of labor and sexual exploitation for prosecution (National Immigration Agency 2013b). From January 2007 to June 2013, for example, among the 423 cases of labor exploitation submitted for prosecution, 230 cases (54.4 percent) were discovered by the police; another 442 cases of sexual exploitation were submitted to prosecution, and 318 of these cases (71.9 percent) were initiated by the police (National Immigration Agency 2013b). NGOs frequently criticize law enforcement agencies for failing to identify more victims of human trafficking. They are convinced that the real problem is much more serious than the police recognize, and that the efforts made by the police to identify and protect victims are still inadequate. In 2012, a worker from Vietnam who was unable to get the attention of the police after calling them repeatedly was found to be paralyzed after being beaten up by his abusive employers (*The China Post* 2012).

In Wang's survey of police officers in Taiwan (2010, 2011), he found that 40 percent of police respondents considered themselves as having only a vague idea about sexual exploitation and human trafficking. Over 85 percent of his respondents stated that they had only a vague idea about the punishments associated with human trafficking offenses. Wang also found that the majority of officers considered the investigation resources and manpower available to police in this area to be insufficient. Over 85 percent of police respondents felt that it is difficult to communicate with victims during human trafficking investigations. Over 80 percent of police respondents believed that it is difficult to earn the victims' trust. Above all, gathering solid evidence is the most difficult part of investigating human trafficking cases.

In talking with a number of currently serving police officers, it seems clear that they show little enthusiasm for dealing with the victims of human trafficking. Indeed, they are inclined to offer several reasons for not handling these cases. The first problem is the low rate of prosecution and conviction due to the existence of various legislative loopholes and investigation difficulties associated with human trafficking cases. For example, officers frequently complain about having to pay for the translation fees involved from their own pockets because of the strict limitations on permissible reimbursements. Second, officers often find it difficult to gain the trust of human trafficking victims because they generally are reluctant to share information and otherwise cooperate with the police. Many victims are convinced that the Taiwan police are as corrupt and as violent as the police in their own home countries. They are also told that the illegal agencies or the brokers enjoy good relationships with the police and have access to inside information from the police force. They are instructed that if they are to speak to the police and end up revealing some incriminating evidence, they would put their families and themselves in danger. In addition, they are afraid that the police might send them to the detention center or temporary shelters for months or even years without further processing their cases once they identified them as victims of human trafficking. They are also told that the criminal justice process is always lengthy and that they would normally receive no compensation at all while waiting for protective action (see also Fuchs 2011).

Although a number of police officers claim that they have been able to establish rather good relationships with some human trafficking victims, and that they frequently receive letters of appreciation from the returnees, the NGOs that work in this area allege that some of the police officers use detention as a tool to force victims' cooperation (Fuchs 2011: 24). An additional problem of policing in this area is that police officers often find it hard to guarantee the victims' safety because the location of shelters is often known by the illegal recruitment agencies.

Among the few studies on the policing of human trafficking, Farrell and colleagues (2010) found that larger law enforcement agencies were more likely to identify human trafficking as a problem than smaller agencies. Similarly, in analyzing Taiwan district court proceedings dealing with of human trafficking cases, it was found that the majority of cases were brought in by prosecution offices in larger cities; these are agencies which have more financial resources (Huang *et al.* 2013). The training and resources for human trafficking enforcement are unevenly distributed. Each agency has developed different ways of putting state-level human trafficking laws into operation, hence causing much variance in the handling of human trafficking cases across the nation. It is clear that many of these incidents remain unprocessed by the police departments in many towns and smaller cities.

It is also the case that the police are sometimes accused of using excessive force in controlling illegal workers. On September 13, 2010, TV news reported that a police officer from Chung-Cheng Precinct of Taipei Police Department "wrestled and touched down" and straddled a female foreign worker. The event caused a small scale protest in front of police field station demanding an apology and a promise of fair treatment in the future to workers from Southeast Asian countries. Meanwhile, the police were unwillingly made to work with the government's Labor section because of a lack of manpower for the inspection of workplaces (Mo 2011).

Policing violence against women

On October 27, 1993, the case of Deng Ruwen (鄧如雯), who killed her violence-prone husband (Lin A-qi, 林阿祺) after a four-year abusive marriage, shocked Taiwan. Although Lin A-qi had sexually abused Deng even before their marriage, and had violently assaulted and intimidated her and her family, including their two sons, during their marriage, the police had never taken any legal action against him. Several feminist groups supported Ms. Deng during the case proceedings and called for the systematic protection for domestic violence victims. As a result, the Legislative Yuan took action soon thereafter and passed the DVPA in 1998.

The aim of the 1998 DVPA is to develop an integrated framework of efficient and effective police and social services responses to domestic violence (Executive Yuan 2012). According to the legislation, the multi-agency system set up for combating domestic violence must include the police, education, health, welfare, household, and judicial units. These collaborating agencies play different roles in the network, with some agencies being more centrally involved than others.

128 *Emerging challenges*

For example, the police department acts as one of the key regulatory agencies in the domestic violence prevention network. At local governmental levels, the police play multiple roles in the handling of domestic violence cases. Police roles and responsibilities can be divided into three categories: (1) officers as front desk workers; (2) officers as criminal investigators; and (3) officers as third party petitioners for civil remedy.

Officers as front desk workers

As agents of authority operating 24 hours a day and seven days a week, police officers are the first to receive calls for help from victims of domestic violence. They are the first to provide protective intervention to victims. Over 40 percent of registered cases entered the domestic violence network system through police referrals (Executive Yuan 2012). In addition to referrals, other non-coercive intervention strategies that police have deployed include home visitation, evidence collection, escort to home, escort to refuge or medical care, and safety plan development. From the victim's point of view, immediate police intervention plays an important role as formal social support in an emergency setting (Jou 1994; Shen 2003). It is stressed that arrest is not the only and final solution to all domestic violence cases. A domestic violence policy which aims at increasing arrest rates without other supportive systems for both victims and suspects is indeed problematic. Any active police intervention into domestic violence should be complemented by a well-designed supportive system for the victims.

Officers as criminal investigators

Police officers also act as the main party initiating the investigation of domestic violence cases. If an incident is brought to the attention of the police, the officer decides whether or not to file a criminal case after their preliminary investigation of the complaint. First of all, if the case involves the committing of a felony, the suspect could be charged without a victim complaint. Officers are obliged to submit the case to prosecutors stating the cause(s) of violation. If a domestic violence incident involves violation of family court protection orders, it automatically falls into the category of chargeable offenses without the filing of a victim complaint. If the incident is chargeable with victim complaint, the police submit the case according to the victim's request. In practice, the majority of domestic violence incidents do not proceed to criminal charges. A recent study found that only about 13 percent of all police-registered domestic violence cases were later submitted to the prosecution office for further legal action (Wei 2010).

Officers as third party petitioners for civil remedy

Police officers can also serve as third party petitioners for protection orders in civil courts. In 2009 alone, the police enforced 15,486 protection orders (about 300 times of the number of warrantless arrests). An application for protection order can be initiated by either the victims or the police. The criminal investigation division within each district bureau is required to assign a detective to serve as the district domestic violence officer whose primary responsibilities include, among others, applying for protection orders on behalf of victims and informing officers at local stations about the nature (e.g., time and place) of the protection orders issued (Sun et al. 2012).

The police have been criticized by women's rights advocacy groups and others for how they are dealing with domestic violence cases. In spite of the availability of forceful actions, some required and some permitted, by the legislation, many officers tend to respond passively to domestic violence cases because they continue to view such incidents as private matters rather than criminal behavior. For example, feminist advocates have criticized the police for handling domestic violence more leniently than other criminal offenses. However, the empirical evidence regarding the "leniency thesis" is not consistent (Avakame and Fyfe 2001; Fyfe et al. 1997). Since the police are members of a broader criminal justice system, their discretionary behavior toward domestic violence incidents must be understood in the broader context of legislation, prior established policy and customary practices, and the implementation of the new law by the conduct of prosecution offices and the pattern of court decisions made vis-à-vis the law. On the one hand, the police might mirror the attitudes and values of the general public toward domestic violence while making decisions. On the other hand, police discretion is influenced by their prediction of case outcomes, such as the probability of successful prosecution, the likelihood of the granting of a protection order, and the willingness of victims to cooperate (Worrall, Ross, and McCord 2006). In other words, the police in Taiwan, as with their counterparts elsewhere, tend to calculate the odds of successful case proceeding and decide the next step in order to reduce uncertainty in their workload.

It is noteworthy that the proportion of immigrant females among registered intimate partner violence victims has increased three-fold from 5.2 percent to 15.0 percent between 2001 and 2009 (Huang et al. 2010a). Huang and her colleagues analyzed 1,605 intimate partner violence incidents involving female victims in two northern Taiwan counties. They divided victims into four groups – non-aboriginal natives, aboriginal natives, southeastern Asians, and mainlanders. They found that immigrant females (mainlanders and southeastern Asians) were more likely to call for help when violence occurred than other domestic violence victims. Marriage immigrants also expressed more needs during their contact with the police, particularly the need for emergency relocation. Generally speaking, immigrant victims were less likely to apply for protection orders or place charges to prevent retaliation by their abusers.

Using the same dataset, Huang and Lin (2010) found that, compared to the aboriginal and mainlander Chinese victims, foreign victims were significantly less likely to receive police-initiated emergency protection order petitions, suggesting that victim disadvantages owing to non-Chinese status and language barriers were likely to be taken into consideration by the police (see also McFarlane et al. 2002; Perilla et al. Norris 1994). Previous research also pointed out that foreign victims, who seldom speak Mandarin, either are unaware of the protection order system or lack social support for their actions against the offending partners (Chen et al. 2003). In addition, the fact that more than 90 percent of police officers are male is certainly not helpful for this situation. Although policies to strengthen formal responses to female immigrant victims have been put into place, the effectiveness of these measures has not been systematically evaluated.

Research on the experience of the Taiwan police with marriage immigrants suggests that police responses might also not be adequate to this disadvantaged group. While native victims of domestic violence might be able to turn to family and relatives for other forms of social support, immigrant female victims are more likely to come back to the police because they have few other places to seek help. History teaches that these victims are more likely to suffer re-victimization than other victim groups.

A recent comparative study shows that college students in Taipei demonstrate the highest levels of support for aggressive law enforcement interventions into domestic violence by the police in comparison to comparable students in both Hong Kong and Beijing (Sun et al. 2012). Given that Taiwan is the only jurisdiction among the three to have a domestic violence prevention law, it would appear that substantial public support for a more forceful approach to victim protection is present if the Taiwanese police were to adopt a more proactive stance.

Shelley (2011) described women and girls as the main victims of the growing problem of human trafficking as a form of transnational crime. They are frequently trafficked for prostitution, for domestic servitude, and for other forms of labor exploitation. Taiwan is experiencing this set of problems along with other nations. Foreign women are more vulnerable to deportation because of their low economic status and weak political standing in their original countries. In Taiwan as is the case elsewhere around the world, the women victims are likely to be blamed for contributing to their own victimization through illegal migration. Since prostitution is illegal in Taiwan, those women who are trafficked for the sex industry are easily categorized derogatively as whores and foreigners, viewed as "unworthy lawbreakers" by both the media and criminal justice practitioners.

Summary

The democratic transition has revived Taiwanese society, and in the process brought some old wounds to the surface. The division between natives versus mainlanders is one of these old wounds. The unfair treatment of aboriginal peoples is another. Since the 1990s, new challenges to the police, such as foreign migrant workers, cross-border marriages, and violence against spouses have emerged as major challenges in policing. While the literature on these issues remains limited, existing studies suggest that the relationship between the police and aboriginal peoples has not improved to any noteworthy extent. Basically, the police continue to be viewed as an outside force, not sympathetic to the interests of the aboriginal communities. In some ways the culture of the police tends to lag behind the process of political change. The shaming and blaming of socially disadvantaged groups is frequently witnessed during police encounters with aboriginal peoples, with foreign migrant workers, with marriage immigrants, and with female victims of domestic abuse. In realizing the democratic ideal of equal policing for all, the police administration needs to act more proactively by allying closely with representative NGOs, acting as the advocates for vulnerable victims, and more forcefully protecting the rights and freedom of all individuals living and working in Taiwan.

Many of the issues discussed in this chapter are, of course, beyond the limited power of police administration. To some degrees, all democratic societies are facing these same difficult challenges with increased globalization and fading jurisdictional borders. These issues represent the truly universal challenges in the policing of democratic countries. Nevertheless, as an arm of a progressive and democratic regime who is partially responsible for redistribution of life chances, the police can be a palliative force if it wishes to act as such (Manning 2010). The police administration in Taiwan could do considerably more to ease many of the existing tensions in the policing of marginalized groups in society. Cultural awareness and sensitivity should be raised in the recruitment process, in the police academy, and in in-service police training programs. In the short run, it is hoped that the police administration pays attention to the issue of bi- or multi-lingual ability of officers, and actively encourages both officers and police applicants to expand their language ability. Police officers are encouraged to attend to civilities and observe procedural justice. In the long run, diversity in the police force should increase to reflect the actual composition of the contemporary Taiwanese society.

10 Confidence in the police

In Chapter 2, we noted that the interaction between an increasingly liberated and independent mass media and politics played a role in weakening authoritarian rule in Taiwan beginning in the late 1970s. Once the mass media was free of political censorship, their social role became quite prominent during the democratic transition. Huge market pressures and widely accepted media logic added a new dynamic dimension in Taiwanese politics. On the one hand, the free media pushed the political parties toward moderation on some of the most sensitive and divisive issues (e.g., independence versus unification), and thus helped a smooth democratic transition (Clark 2001). On the other hand, they actively sought out sensationalistic news content on government officials to attract audience attention. Negative and sometime grossly exaggerated reports of police misbehavior serve this purpose (Wu *et al.* 2012). Even without any scandals, action-oriented police news and police dramas are first-rate media materials (Manning 1997).

From the very beginning of the democratic transition, public opinion poll results by television stations, newspapers, and the Internet in more recent times, have become one of the more dominant social forces in Taiwan. Virtually all major aspects of political life, including the police, have been reflected in these polls. Although a plethora of survey studies have been conducted to assess public attitudes toward the police in Western societies, this particular line of research remains relatively unexplored in Taiwan. Some studies were atheoretical and largely descriptive in nature, elucidating the general prevailing patterns and trends in public evaluations of the police without much discussion of their likely underpinnings and causal mechanisms (e.g., see C. Huang 2002, 2003, 2004; Tsai and Yang 1999; Yang *et al.* 2010). Some scholars have tested the explanatory power of variables along theoretical frameworks, greatly expanding our understanding of factors influencing public attitudes toward the police in Taiwan (e.g., Cao and Dai 2006; Y. Huang 2012; Lai *et al.* 2010; Sun *et al.* 2013a; Wu *et al.* 2012).

Past research has utilized a large number of concepts to depict public opinions on the police. In this chapter we focus our discussion on trust or confidence in the police, both because these concepts are the key indicators of the legitimacy of governance and because they have been fairly well articulated and tested (Sun *et al.* 2013b). We examine three issues related to public trust in or confidence in the police. First, we discuss the nature of public opinion in relation to the police work. Second, we review some findings about confidence in the police in Taiwan. Finally, we put the rating of the police in Taiwan within the broader global perspective.

Police legitimacy and performance

Lipset (1959) and Almond and Verba (1963) posit that mass democratic support arising from cultural values reflecting a civic society orientation to politics is critical in facilitating democratic transition and consolidation. Democratization is a dynamic process which requires the abandonment of many undemocratic habits and customary ways of making collective decisions. Taiwan faces many challenges in democratic regime consolidation, such as a deeply-entrenched traditional culture, sub-ethnic cleavages, ongoing geo-strategic vulnerability, and an abundance of non-majoritarian electoral institutions. Public opinion is a major way for a responsive democratic government to understand what citizens prefer in the way of public policy, and determine what the public wants to be the priority concerns of its government at the local and national levels.

Scholars have long characterized a successful functioning democracy as *a way of life*. It is not just a set of political institutions running in a vacuum without connection to the prevailing values of the society. Whether citizens will embrace the values that are fundamental to its operation is thus crucial to the success of a democratic polity. The value of political tolerance, for example, is one of the major tenets of democracy that is difficult to maintain during the period of democratic transition when diverse opinions, radical and extreme opinions included, came to the surface. Fortunately, Taiwan did well in this regard. From survey data, it is clear that the majority of Taiwanese residents show a willingness to extend rights of citizenship to others in the polity on the most salient issues that divide them (Wang and Chang 2006). The more one subscribes to the value of democracy as the correct political system for Taiwan, the more tolerant one is of the civil liberties of the "harmful" target groups; conversely, the greater the perceived threats from Beijing's claims to the island and from the Taiwan independence movement, the more intolerant one is of the civil liberties of those advocating the stance (Marsh 2005).

The police are the most visible institution of social control in all contemporary societies, democratic and autocratic alike (Lai *et al.* 2010). They represent the technological and organizational answer to the Hobbesian question of social order, the *deus ex machina*. The maintenance of public order by peaceful means is the preferred style of democratic policing, and this preference for enhancing the level of voluntary compliance over reliance on the use of force to compel obedience is regarded as one of the cultural traits of modern civilization (Grabosky 2008; Manning 1997). The police in Taiwan have indeed changed from a control-oriented agency during the marital law years to a decidedly professional institution today that emphasizes a need to strike a delicate balance between maintaining public order and protecting the rights of individuals (Sun and Chu 2006; Yang *et al.* 2012).

In a democratic society, the study of public opinion toward the police is important for at least three reasons. First, confidence in the police concerns one of the fundamental issues of the police: *legitimacy*, which is usually defined in terms of public acceptance of the role and conduct of the police as being right and proper. As such, it is vital to obtain periodic public evaluation of the police. Studies have shown that both objective legitimacy and perceived legitimacy are important (Tyler 2002). It is not enough to focus solely on the quality of police performance, since the police may execute their job duties constitutionally and still find themselves without public support (Ren *et al.* 2005). The public is the consumer of police services in a democracy and the police receive their mandates from the citizenry (Manning 1997). Hsieh (2000) introduced this perspective in his article on how to improve the service functions of the Taiwanese police. He advocated client orientations as the new direction that the police should take, emphasizing the necessity for the police to understand the needs of the public.

Second, positive images of the police are necessary for the police to function effectively in a democracy (Cao *et al.*1998; Manning 1997). The police are the society's solution to the problem of crime in theory whereas in reality they only deliver authoritative interventions in crisis situations and symbolic justice after behavioral norms have been violated. Police work relies on citizens' cooperation in reporting crimes, providing information, and ultimately in supporting the provision of funding to the police. Cooperation from the public greatly enhances police work, making it more effective and less costly.

Finally, confidence in the police has additional value in the era of community policing. It may serve as one important alternative measure of police effectiveness (Hebenton *et al.* 2010; Ren *et al.* 2005). The traditional approach to the evaluation of police effectiveness places too much emphasis on response time and crime clearance rates. While these outcomes are indeed important, they are not enough. Ultimately, police effectiveness should be reflected in the citizens' satisfaction with and/or confidence in their police. Consistent with the first point, there is no reason why police administrators should forego the use of public opinion as one of the indicators of police performance. Indeed, both the European Union and China make use of confidence in the police as one of the indicators of public safety and crime (Hebenton *et al.* 2010). In Taiwan, the Research Development and Evaluation Commission accepted Hebenton *et al.*'s proposal for evaluating police performance, which includes measures of confidence in the capability, integrity, and fairness of the police, and integrated those elements into a broader set of performance measures (Hebenton *et al.* 2010). The key issue now is to figure out how to overcome the cultural inertia of opposing change and implement these measures. Relatedly, the study of public opinion may not only yield important insights into citizens' confidence in the police, but also into the correlates of that confidence (Zhao *et al.* 1999). The police, as a key provider of public services, need feedback from the citizens on how to improve their services. Surveys on citizen confidence in the police generally contain some specific information which can be used to improve the quality and content of police services.

Trust in and confidence in the government of which the police are a part are important in a Confucian society like Taiwan. With or without the process of democracy, they are considered fundamental. In the often violent cycle of replacing dynasties, one of the justifications for change is that the previous dynasty has lost the mandate of heaven and the trust of the ordinary people. Although the reading of the public mood was not scientific, trust was, nonetheless greatly valued as a moral good in social life (Tao 2010). The importance of trust is illustrated in conversations between Confucius and one of his students: "For a government, trust is regarded as one of three foundations, with the other two being weapons and food supply." Pressured on which to give up first in dire circumstances, Confucius advices his student to give up the weapons first and the food next. Confucius concludes that all governments will go to the dustbin eventually, but the governments established on trust will endure the longest.[1]

The study of cross-national public opinions toward the police has additional values for scholars and police practitioners alike. Unfortunately, in the US and in Taiwan as well, such studies are frequently considered to be an exotic frill by many researchers and police professionals (Bayley 1996; Chu and Sun 2007). The comparative study of confidence in the police has not received enough attention from the academics of Taiwan. It is, however, important for at least three reasons (Cao and Dai 2006).

First, such studies advance the broader recognition of Taiwan as a unique society among the nations of the world. Comparative public opinion may serve as a figurative barometer of a culture's contemporary sentiment, either reflecting the universality of public mood or the presence of differentiation. The results of multi-societal citizen surveys may reveal certain persistent cultural variations that distinguish one society from another. Moreover, the deeply grounded cultural values may foreshadow any possible changes in attitudes toward the police over time. Second, greater comprehension of international public opinion may help us appreciate the cultures and practices of legal authorities in different societies, and shed further light on why crime occurs and how its control is attempted in those societies. Finally, public opinion will help us evaluate the extent of the public's acceptance of any policing practices and strategies borrowed from other nations. In a global village of democracies, the principles that govern policing bear a number of "family resemblances" (Bayley 1985). Under globalized conditions, particular policing strategies – zero-tolerance, problem-oriented policing, etc. – resonate across territorial boundaries in ways that open up "local" policing practices to increased scrutiny. However, policing practices are inevitably local in application, and local residents' opinions ultimately decide the final appropriateness of a particular police program or strategy.

In the literature on public opinion toward the police, two competing theoretical traditions contend as the most appropriate approach to the assessment of confidence in the police. These two traditions offer very different perspectives on the prospects for developing sufficient confidence in the police to allow them to function effectively. One tradition is grounded on *cultural theories* which hypothesize that confidence in the police is exogenous. Confidence in the police is hypothesized to originate outside the political sphere in long-standing and deeply seeded beliefs about people that are rooted in cultural norms and communicated through early-life socialization. From this perspective, confidence in the police is an extension of interpersonal trust, learned early in life and, much later, projected onto political institutions at-large, thereby conditioning police performance capabilities (Almond and Verba 1963; Inglehart 1997; also see Skogan 2009).

The other tradition is grounded on *institution-centered approaches*. These theories, in contrast, hypothesize that confidence in the police is principally endogenous. Institutional confidence is the reflection of the expected utility of institutions performing satisfactorily (Cao *et al.*1996; Coleman 1990; Lipset 1959; Wu *et al.* 2012); confidence is a consequence, not a cause, of police performance. Confidence in the police is rationally based; it hinges on citizen evaluations of police performance. Police who perform well breed confidence; untrustworthy police generate skepticism and distrust. This is not to deny the reality of early-life cultural influences. On the contrary, insofar as the police persist and perform relatively consistently over successive generations, socialization and police performance should exert very similar and reinforcing effects on confidence in the police. In post-authoritarian societies, however, the replacement of undemocratic by democratic police necessarily introduces fundamental institutional discontinuities. The police whose performance is being evaluated today are different from the police into which individuals have been socialized through their lives. In this context, the institutional hypothesis is that if socialization and performance influences confidence, more proximate performance evaluation will override the earlier influence exerted by cultural norms and socialization experiences. Most of research studies reviewed in this chapter take this general approach.

Citizen evaluations of the police

Police work is complex everywhere. In Taiwan, democratic transition replaced the police as the *discretionary granter* of services status with that of an *obligated provider* of services. This assumption of democratic policing has made police work more complicated than before. Levels of police professionalism have increased dramatically with a focus on multiple job responsibilities, legal education, and expanded practical training for Taiwanese police personnel (see Chapter 4). Police discretion is an ongoing issue because structurally and genealogically the police and the law remain distinct modalities of political power, achieving the ideal of their full integration continues to be one of the unresolved dilemmas of modern governance (Skolnick 1966). Martin (2007) observed the ubiquity of informal order-keeping institutions in Taiwan. He averred that large sectors of the social order are being maintained outside any ostensible monopoly by the state on the use of legitimate force. With the culture's inclination of settling disputes informally, police officers have to keep a reasonable balance of *qing, li, fa* (sentiment, reason, and law or 情理法) in carrying out democratic policing.

Scientific surveys of citizen perceptions of the police have gained considerable prominence in emerging democracies in recent years (Davis *et al.* 2004; Hsieh 2000; Mishler and Rose 2001; Zhuang 2001). As we argued previously, confidence in the police links ordinary citizens to the police who serve them, thereby enhancing both the legitimacy of the police and the effectiveness of democratic government. Confidence in the police is especially critical for new democracies because of the legacy of being tied to authoritarian regime in the past; because of this historical legacy confidence also is likely to be in relatively short supply. In Taiwan, academic attention in criminology and criminal justice, however, remains seriously underdeveloped with regard to research on public confidence in the police.

Although democracy is a pre-condition for a *more accurate* expression of public opinion (Cao et al. 2012; LaFree, 2003; Lai et al. 2010) as well as for the more accurate collection of crime data (Cao 1999), in itself democracy does not assure a favorable public opinion towards particular social and political institutions in a nation, including the police. The transition from elite dominance to a mass-driven political environment and to a strong civil society is never smooth and without setbacks and dramatic breakthroughs. In fact, many old wounds might resurface and new conflicts might emerge during democratic transition. Taiwan is a living example of both. The 2/28 Incident resurfaced soon after the lifting of martial law. The various ethnic cleavages, which were suppressed but re-emerged to unite the opposition in the initial stage of democratic transition, began to divide the society bitterly during the democratic consolidation in the new century. The political charge that the GMD was an outside party was only partially true. The mainlanders were indeed overrepresented in the top political echelon under martial law. However, even then between 70 to 80 percent of the GMD members were Taiwan natives (Tien 1989). After the democratic transition, there is no doubt that the GMD is a much more integrated political party than the DPP.

In regard to Taiwanese public opinion on the police, the results of surveys conducted with a variety of questions in the new century indicate that citizens' satisfaction with the police registered around the 50 percent range in the new century. For example, Huang (2004) reported that 48.34 percent of respondents were satisfied with the level of police professionalism exhibited by the Taiwanese police. Moreover, 53 percent of those who had reported a crime to the police in the past 12 months were satisfied with how the police handled their cases. Fifty-seven percent believed that covering up a crime is not a serious problem. These results are more or less "official" because these survey projects were funded by the NPA and conducted by scholars at the Central Police University. Data collected by others show similar but somewhat lower levels of public confidence in the police.

Direct comparison of survey results, however, is impossible, unfortunately, because of the differences in questionnaire item wording and in the response categories in each survey. A few other independent polls and surveys deserve attention. The public poll data confirmed the trend of a declining level of public confidence – that is, public confidence in the police was higher during the 1990s. For example, a poll conducted in 1998 (Poll Center of TVBS 1998) showed that 55 percent of the public expressed their confidence in the police. Since then, the confidence level has declined. In 2004, the opinion poll indicated that only 45 percent of the residents were confident in the police (Poll Center of TVBS 2004). Another opinion poll, conducted by the research institute of the police at the Central Police University in 2001, indicates that 46 percent of the residents were satisfied with the police (Cao and Dai 2006).

Similarly, data from the *World Values Surveys* show that in the summer of 1995 the percentage of Taiwanese who said that they had confidence in the police was 51.4 percent. By contrast, the percentage was only 38 percent in 2006 according to the *World Value Surveys* (Lai *et al.* 2010). There was a 13 percent drop in the level of confidence in the police. By 2006, Taiwan had a new ruling party – the DPP led by President Chen Shuibian – for six years. Data drawn from the *Asian Barometer Survey* also revealed that fewer than half of the Taiwan respondents trusted the police "quite a lot" or "a great deal" (Wu *et al.* 2012). In another study, only 40 percent of the respondents reported that they were either highly satisfied or satisfied with police performance in the area of maintaining law and order (Yang *et al.* 2010).

In all fairness, the decreased confidence in or satisfaction with the police documented in these surveys and polls may have been prompted less by significantly declining quality in police services than by the public's increased dissatisfaction with political institutions in general as democratic values become integrated into daily life. Confidence in the police is only a part of a larger attitudinal complex relating to public institutions (Stack and Cao 1998). This observation is supported by Sun and colleagues' (2013a) recent work, showing that public evaluations of the performance of the central government, local government, and the judiciary, respectively, were all positively related to public trust in the police. It appears that citizens' evaluations of the performance of government and non-police political institutions are not stand-alone sentiments, but rather are highly intertwined with their assessments of the police (Wu *et al.* 2012).

Sherman (2005) observed that the rise in equalitarian culture increases the demand for government officials to show more respect to citizens. When that demand goes unmet, public opinion toward the police and/or criminal justice tends to suffer. Traditional Taiwanese society reflected a Confucian collective culture wherein the relationship between individuals and the state is hierarchical rather than reciprocal, one in which the obligations of obedience to and respect for authority were strong, and where the culture rests upon cooperation and the informal resolution of disputes. In situations where one person's interests clash in important ways with those of another, the culture opts for non-confrontational approaches to resolving the conflict and stresses the virtue of being willing to sacrifice one's own interest for the harmony of society as whole. Moving away from its cultural roots, the current Taiwanese political culture adapting to democratic politics is highly individualistic; the public in this "low power distance society" (Hosftede 2001) tends to blame the politicians for everything that goes wrong.

In addition, the decline in confidence may be a reflection of the contentious presidential election in 2004. The adverse public mood might target the DPP more than the police. Taiwan in the new century was in the period of democratic consolidation, which may be defined as a process by which the rules, institutions, constraints of democracy become "the only game in town" (Paolino and Meernik 2008). Using survey data collected from residents in three cities and two counties in 2010, Y. Huang (2012) found that political party orientation influenced public assessments of the police with pan-green (pro-DPP) respondents displaying more negative evaluations than the pan-blue (pro-GMD) respondents. As Lipset (1959) and Almond and Verba (1963) correctly noted, mass democratic support and the development of trust-related cultural values are critical in facilitating democratic consolidation. Taiwan faces many challenges in democratic institutional consolidation, and the decline of public confidence in the police is perhaps one of the most important of these challenges.

Some studies suggest that the relationship between confidence in the police and democracy (Cao et al. 2012), and between police effectiveness and democracy (Sung 2006) are not linear but rather are curve-linear in nature. That is, confidence in the police is high in nations with long-term stable democracy such as Finland and similarly is high in countries with long-term stable authoritarian regimes such as China. The relatively low evaluation of the police, therefore, is a natural by-product of a society that is moving from a "high power distance society" of the authoritarian and Confucian past to a "low power distance society" of democracy where the public is expected to have input into government decision making and citizens can influence the way they are governed (Hosftede 2001).

Recent studies have identified the linkages between a number of theoretically relevant variables and public evaluations of the police. For example, Sun and his co-researchers (2013a) found that variables derived from both the instrumental model (e.g., concerns about safety) and the expressive model (e.g., trust in neighbors and perceived quality of life) were significantly related to Taiwanese trust in their police. In addition, satisfaction with government performance and media influence were also predictive of police trustworthiness. Wu and colleagues (2012) compared the explanatory power of three theories – the social structural thesis, the institutional performance thesis, and the cultural thesis – in accounting for public trust in the police in Taiwan. They found that the performance thesis received the strongest support. Similar findings were reported by other researchers as well. Cao and Dai (2006) found that trusting other political institutions, personal happiness and parents with children are a few factors that tend to increase confidence, while formal education is inversely related to confidence in the police. Lai et al. (2010) confirmed that only happiness enhanced confidence in the police. They also reported that interest in politics is likewise related to having confidence in the police in Taiwan.

Comparison with other societies in the world

Little attention among Taiwanese academics has been paid to cross-regional/national public opinions on the police. This is so despite the fact that the use of comparative and cross-cultural approaches has a long history in the social sciences, and the field of comparative/international research on criminal justice systems has grown steadily elsewhere in the world in recent years (Davis et al. 2004; Winterdyk and Cao 2004).

There are basically two types of comparative studies featured in this area of research. The first type entails the comparison of two or more nations in detail with the intention to explain why these nations differ as they do. The second type of study involves ranking the nations in some noteworthy aspect, such as the level of confidence in the police, with relatively little effort to explain why these nations differ among themselves as they do.

The first type of study of comparative confidence in the police is difficult for two reasons (Cao and Dai 2006; Lai *et al.* 2010). First, we should avoid comparing apples with oranges. To compare public opinion in an authoritarian society with that in a democratic country is a challenging task. In an authoritarian society with non-democratic policing, public opinion is likely to be inaccurate because some people are alienated from the political decision-making process and because some are afraid of government persecution. The repression of political dissent is a requirement of high policing; opinions articulated under these conditions are not likely to be truly reflective of public sentiment.

Second, it is easier to account for similarities between societies than to explain differences between countries. Two nations have noticeably different social systems vis-a-vis culture, politics, and/or religion. Because of these differences, the nature of data collected and its associated interpretations require extreme caution. When the results from two societies vary in some noticeable aspects, it is a challenge for researchers to disentangle the causes of these differences. Specifically, such difference can be a result of political regimes, or religious traditions, or cultural environments, or language nuances, to name just a few. These variations may result in the different extent to which there is acceptance of technological diffusion and there is an understanding of the translated messages featured in the surveys of two or more countries' citizens. When a difference is found, it is more difficult to pin down which aspect plays a deciding role. Most studies, for example, attribute differences to culture, but culture is a loaded term and it embraces every aspect of life. Cultural norms, values, and ideologies can directly influence national variations, but which particular norm, which specific value or which aspect of ideology is it that separates the two nations under comparison is often impossible to identify. Nations vary in the strength of norms that motivate, allow, or even prescribe certain behavior. They also differ in having integrated systems of norms and values that promote social cohesion and social order. It is sometimes the former and other times it is the latter that cause a cross-societal difference.

With these caveats in mind, two studies (Lai *et al.* 2010; Wu *et al.* 2012) took up the challenging task of comparing Taiwan and China and two other studies (Cao and Dai 2006; Hajek *et al.* 2008) and attempted to rank Taiwanese confidence in the police among sample countries. Lai and his colleagues argue that it is more manageable to compare the two societies of Taiwan and China since they originated from a similar political ideology, and they share a common culture, the same written language, and identical religious traditions. They were, in fact, one nation before 1949. Currently, the most prominent difference between Taiwan and China is regime nature and, to a lesser degree, the level of economic development. By comparing nations with similar culture and/or religion, it is generally an easier task to pin down the reasons for the difference to a few plausible alternatives.

Lai *et al.* (2010) found that citizens in China have a higher level of confidence in the police according to the data extracted from the *2006 World Values*

Surveys. This is not surprising because it is consistent with the finding of Cao and Dai using data extracted from the earlier wave of the *1995 World Values Surveys* and Wu *et al*. (2012) using the *2003 Asian Barometer Survey* (ABS) data. Lai *et al*. offered possible three reasons for their findings. First, it is possible that some respondents in China are afraid of expressing their own opinions for fear of repercussion. China remains an authoritarian state with high policing. Even after three decades of economic reform, even after the loosening of many control-oriented regulations, and even though Chinese are indeed freer than in any historical period since 1949, the basic authoritarian political system has remained unchanged. Political dissidents, such as Liu Xiaobo or Wei Jingsheng, are either jailed or exiled. Attitudes toward the police or toward the communist leadership are broadly viewed as highly sensitive topics. Wu *et al*. (2012) nevertheless argued that the higher levels of Chinese trust seem to result more from some broader social and cultural sources than from heightened political fear or intimidation. Specifically, Chinese respondents displayed higher levels of satisfaction with the macroeconomic conditions of their country and the responsiveness of their government, and endorsed the traditional hierarchical values of deference to authority more strongly than did the Taiwanese.

Second, the level of confidence in the police may be a reflection of the progress that a government has made in the process of democratization (Cao and Hou 2001). Democratic transition in many nations has been far from smooth (Zhao and Cao 2010), and it was especially painful for people who got used to the orderly society such as predominates in Taiwan. The sense of normlessness and sudden increased cleavages among different ethnic groups were widespread in Taiwan, and public opinions become an outlet for its citizens, driving down the confidence level even further.

Finally, in an authoritarian regime such as that of China, public opinion could be heavily influenced and manipulated by the government-controlled news media which is always highly selective in what residents are permitted to watch and read (Cao, 2007). In other words, Chinese public opinion is likely to be shaped heavily by the government's oversight, while the Taiwanese are subject to a wider range of sources of information, including many prominent private media (Wu *et al*. 2012). Although more open than ever before in the PRC's 60 years' history, negative news, such as the support of killing police officers, would rarely appear in any news media in China. Popular voices, such as that of Han Han and that of Li Chengpeng, are frequently blocked from transmission. The criminal justice system denies or limits constitutional rights to its citizens, but criminal justice agencies, such as the police and courts, are fully empowered, and legal procedures are portrayed to be swift and efficient. This practice of exclusively positive image reporting and the seemingly effective control of crime may inflate public confidence in the police due in major part to misinformation.

Lai *et al*. (2010) concluded that the conflation of the above three factors can explain why the levels of confidence in legal authorities are higher in China than in Taiwan. The regime impact can also be seen clearly in other authoritarian and communist countries such as Vietnam. According to the *World Values Survey*, the police in Vietnam command the highest ranking in the entire world. Lai *et al.* (2010) speculate that the more authoritarian a regime is, the more support of the police the citizen survey results will show. However, in spite of different political systems, Chinese and Taiwanese share one common predictor of the confidence in their legal authorities – namely, level of interest in politics had an impact on confidence in the police in both countries. Residents across the Taiwan Strait who are interested in politics have more confidence in their respective legal authorities. Wu and her colleagues (2012) found variables derived from the government performance thesis exerted significant effects on public trust in the police in both Taiwan and China.

Cao and Hou (2001) cautioned that cross-sectional survey data are time-dependent and time-sensitive. The contextual and time-dependent nature of cross-sectional data, thus, limits its generalizability and ultimately its utility in hypothesis testing. Longitudinal data studies can ameliorate this particular problem (Cao and Stack 2005). Furthermore, in exploring the sources of confidence in the police some surveys contained only the single item measure of confidence in the police. Although the single item of the global attitude has been found to be highly correlated with a variety of specific attitudes toward the police in the US (Garcia and Cao 2005), the unidimentional item of global attitude may not fully capture the complex nature of public attitudes toward the police.

Broadening our comparison to other Asian societies, it is found that data from *2005 World Values Surveys* indicated that Japanese residents' confidence in legal authorities was higher than those of both Taiwan and South Korea (Cao and Dai 2006). Among the three democratic countries in Asia, Japan, as the longest and most stable democracy, has the highest level of confidence in the police, followed by South Korea and then Taiwan. Note that in 1995, the level of confidence in the police was higher in Taiwan than in South Korea (Cao and Dai 2006). Democratization is a variable process of change. Although Taiwan beat Korea in democratic transition in many respects, it apparently has not outdone it in economics during the democratic consolidation since 2000.

While the detailed studies described above are necessary to enhance our collective understanding, not all studies have the intention to pin down the exact reason for observed differences. Many times researchers are simply interested in whether there is a difference or in the relative ranking of a country on one aspect or respect to one phenomenon. For the second type of comparison, Hajek *et al.* (2008) reported that the United States enjoyed the highest police ranking, followed by China and Taiwan, quite consistent with the results of Cao and Dai (2006), Lai *et al.* (2010) and Wu *et al.* (2012). Although Taiwan seemed to have the lowest level of confidence compared with the above nations, the 38 percent confidence level was pretty admirable compared to other newly democratic societies in Eastern Europe. Mishler and Rose (2001) found that the average level of confidence in the police among ten newly democratized nations was only 28 percent. These nations were Belarus, Bulgaria, the Czech Republic, Hungary, Poland, Romania, Russia, Slovakia, Slovenia, and Ukraine.

In general, this yet limited literature on public opinions toward the police in comparative perspective remains narrowly focused, with a single indicator of confidence or trust being used (Cao and Dai 2006; Cao *et al.* 2012; Hajek *et al.* 2008; Huang 2004; Lai *et al.* 2010; Wu *et al.* 2012). While often insightful, a single-indicator measure is not only inadequate in capturing the complexity of public assessments of the police but too easily gives rise to generating simplistic and even misleading conclusions about the dynamics underlying public attitudes toward the police. Recent research in Western countries has highlighted the complexity and multidimensional character of public attitudes toward the police. In the US, trust in the police, for instance, can be delineated along at least four distinct dimensions, including priorities, respectfulness, dependability, and competency (Stoutland 2001). In the UK, trust in the police was operationalized through three pivotal areas of effectiveness (e.g., "tackle drug dealing"), fairness ("treat people with respect"), and community engagement ("listen to the concerns of local residents") (Jackson and Bradford 2010: 245). In addition, conceptual and analytical distinctions can be made between motive-based trust and outcome-based trust (Tyler and Huo 2002), and further between global satisfaction and specific satisfaction (Garcia and Cao 2006; Wu *et al.* 2011). Sun and his colleagues' (2013a) recent work found that procedure-based trust and outcome-based trust in the police are not distinguishable among Taiwanese respondents as they are elsewhere in the world. Academics in Taiwan could use these types of items on confidence in the police and collect data in Taiwan to further test whether or not these models apply in Taiwan.

Summary

Public opinion is an important area to study the police in a democracy. Traditionally, it is considered vital for any government in Confucian East Asian nations to gain and maintain the trust of its people. It is particularly important because oftentimes democratic politics in Taiwan "is more a play of opinion than of interests" (Moody 1988: 90). As a linkage between state and civil society, the police peacefully completed the transformation from high policing to low policing, or from authoritarian policing to democratic policing. The public evaluation of the police seems to correspond with the progress the police have made toward serving popular interests and needs, particularly in comparison to the democratizing countries of Central and Eastern Europe. Although findings from recent surveys sound somewhat alarming, in that these polls and surveys suggest that a significant decline in public confidence in the police has taken place during the democratic consolidation. More likely than not, this decline is largely beyond the control of the police because confidence in the police is only a part of a larger attitudinal complex toward various aspects of political life and public institutions (Stack and Cao 1998).

The lower evaluation of the police is not so much related to the effectiveness of the police, which is well demonstrated in the homicide data; the rates of homicide have continued to decline since 1998 (Hebenton and Jou 2014). More likely, it is related to the public perception of police corruption (see Chapter 7), it is a reflection of widespread suspicion of all government integrity, the police

144 *Emerging challenges*

included (Sung 2009; Yu *et al.* 2008), and it is a part of moral crises of democracy worldwide (Maier 1994). This flagging of confidence has resulted in the reduced willingness of the people to report crime to the police (see Chapter 4). It is clear that police administrators in Taiwan must do a better job of containing cynicism within the police force and overcome the cultural inertia by opening themselves up for greater public scrutiny. Policing, after all, is a means for coping with uncertainty and reducing distrust (Manning 2010). The administration would be wise to forge an alliance with scholars and the attentive public in civil society, do a better job of substantiating their services to the public, and build on the strengths of traditional Taiwanese society. In this way, the police can help heal the ethnic cleavages created and reinforced by politicians, and rebuild public confidence in all political and social institutions in Taiwan, including the police. Police administrators must continue to emphasize the clientele-oriented and/or community-oriented policing philosophy. Only through sincere, energetic, compassionate, valuable services delivered with frequent formal and informal communication with the public, can the Taiwanese police officers truly win the hearts and minds of the public (Hsieh 2000).

Note

1 In Chinese, 子贡问政, 子曰: 足食, 足兵, 民信之矣。子贡曰: 必不得已而去, 于斯三者何先? 曰: 去兵。子贡曰: 必不得已而去, 于斯二者何先? 曰: 去食。自古皆有死, 民无信不立 (*Confucian Analects* 12.7).

11 Coda

Taiwan's conundrum

Our story of the democratic transition in the Taiwan's police has come to an end. After the arrival of democratically elected government, the initial euphoria has given way to considerable cynicism among the law enforcement community. Police work has become more demanding in the democratic environment where a police officer has to strike a delicate balance between order and liberty, and between the rule of law and prevailing local sentiments.

Although this book presents a case study of Taiwan's police, it has also concerned itself with larger issues of democracy as the police reflect the society that creates it. That society, moreover, is a part of the ever changeable cross-currents of global affairs. Before we return to the topic of the challenge of the police, we will discuss briefly the question of why Chiang Ching-Kuo changed from a ruthless authoritarian paramount into a benevolent leader toward democratization of Taiwan – a question that continues to bewilder researchers (Weller 1999).

Chiang Ching-Kuo's legacy

Many books discussing the democratic transition in Taiwan fail to understand the vicissitudes of ex-President Chiang Ching-Kuo's attitude toward democratization. They either believe that his change was not important (Fulda 2002; Li 1987), or exaggerate his personal influence (Chao and Myers 1998), or regard his change as a myth (Weller 1999). The problem with these analyses is that they are all overly parochial, tending to see Taiwan via Taiwan. In other words, they all fail to place Taiwan on the larger canvas of East Asia and the world beyond.

Taiwan itself is an island, but Taiwanese society is never an island. Taiwan remains dependent upon changes in American and Chinese geopolitics (Fu 1992). It is, however, a prominent "vortex player" in international politics (Copper 2005: 27). To understand how Chiang changed from a socialist acolyte before 1950 to a ruthless autocrat between 1950 and 1978, and then to a pro-democratic reform leader after 1978, we must appreciate his domestic and international milieu. What kind of the world was Chiang faced with in the late 1970s and the early 1980s? Listed here are some of the most important events happening diachronically between 1977 until his death in 1988.

146 *Emerging challenges*

In 1977 and 1978, the general public in China was allowed greater freedom to criticize the government, to the surprise of many China-watchers. This resulted in the Democracy Wall Movement, which paved the way for Deng Xiaoping's return to the power center. Once at the top, Deng Xiaoping announced his new open-door economic policy and his market-oriented reform of the stagnating planned economy.

In December 15, 1978, the US and China announced the normalization of diplomatic affairs and Taiwan closed its embassy in Washington, DC.

In March, 1979, Wei Jingsheng (魏京生) and some 30 other Democracy Wall activists were rounded up by Chinese authorities. Seven months later, Wei was sentenced to a prison term of 15 years. Pro-democratic voices were by-and-large quenched in China.

On October 26, 1979, President Park Chung-hee of South Korea was assassinated. Park was criticized as a ruthless military dictator. The coup d'état of December Twelfth by General Chun Doo-hwan soon followed. After the coup d'état, General Chun forced the cabinet to broaden martial law to the whole nation.

In December 1979, the Formosa Incident (美麗島事件) occurred. The incident revealed the dark rule of the GMD and further strained its relationship with the democratic world.

On May 17, 1980, Chun Doo-hwan assumed the presidency, triggering nation-wide protests. In response, Chun sent special forces to suppress the Gwangju Democratization Movement.

In December 1980, Taiwan's first-ever competitive election was held. Opposition candidates gave speeches that literally flabbergasted their audiences.

In January of 1981, President Marcos of the Philippines lifted the 12-year imposition of martial law and held the first presidential election six months later.

On September 30, 1981, China abandoned Mao's long-time threat of taking over Taiwan by force and formulated a nine-point proposal for the peaceful unification of Taiwan and China.

On August 26, 1983, opposition leader Benigno Aquino, Jr was assassinated at the Manila International Airport upon his return to the Philippines. The assassination of Aquino would later prove to be the catalyst that led to Marcos' overthrow.

From October to December 1983, conservative factions within the Chinese Communist Party launched the Anti-Spiritual Pollution Campaign (清除精神污染) in an effort to curb Western-inspired liberal democratic ideas among the Chinese populace.

On September 26, 1984, China and British signed the Sino-British Joint Declaration on the Future of Hong Kong, a striking victory for the unification of China.

On October 15, 1984, Henry Liu or Jiang Nan was shot to death in the garage of his home in Daly City, California. Later it was alleged that his killers received orders from the Taiwanese government intelligence office. The assassination became a major political scandal.

In 1985, Mikhail Gorbachev came into power in the Soviet Union and began his reform with *perestroika* and *glasnost*. Taiwan's underground trade with the mainland China reached one half billion US dollars.

On February 25, 1986, the "People Power Movement" drove President Marcos of the Philippines into exile and installed Corazon Aquino as the new president.

In December 1986, a group of students organized public protests across over a dozen cities in support of political and economic liberalization in China. Deng Xiaoping directed Hu Yaobang (胡耀邦) to dismiss Fang Lizhi (方励之), Wang Ruowang (王若望), and Liu Binyan (刘宾雁) from the Communist Party in order to silence them, but Hu Yaobang refused.

In January 1987, after two weeks of student protests demanding greater Western-style freedoms, a clique of the Chinese Communist Party (CCP) elders and senior military officials forced Hu Yaobang to resign and student protesters were quietly suppressed.

On June 10, 1987 when the news that a Seoul National University student Park Jong-chul, who was tortured to death, was released it ignited demonstrations around the country. Eventually, Chun's party, the Democratic Justice Party, and its leader, Roh Tae-woo released the 6.29 Declaration which included the direct election of the president.

In 1987, elections of village chiefs were introduced in China.

During all those years, Taiwan's economy was doing well and Taiwan's politics began to open up in part because Taiwan needed to show convincingly that it deserved international and the US support. Chiang surrounded himself with some young, reform-minded people such as James Soong, Li Denghui, and Ma Yingjiu, and distanced himself from the old guards such as his stepmother Soong May-ling and his long-time comrade-in-arms Wang Sheng (王昇). He sought to come to terms with the advocates of democracy and responded to growing societal demands by sharing political power.

In contrast, China got out of its self-inflicted political mires existing before Mao's death in 1976 in a series of fits and starts. Its economy became less planned and more market-oriented. It became increasingly difficult to differentiate Taiwan from China economically as both adopted rapid economic development as a political instrument to win political legitimacy.

As a pragmatic person (Taylor 2000) and a driven man (Chao and Myers 1998), Chiang was sensitive to the circumstances of history that unfolded before his eyes. His reform was not precipitated by his humanistic urge to bring about democratic change, but rather reflected a pragmatic approach which maximized international support and which sought to sustain majority support for the GMD among the populace in Taiwan. His changes fit perfectly well with the tenets of "cognitive dissonance" theory (Festinger 1957), which proposes that people tend to minimize dissonance in thought experienced in life by modifying existing cognitions and adding new ones to generate a coherent belief system. Both domestic and international historical circumstances at once lured and cajoled him to behave democratically. The opposition pressure made democracy possible, and the political leadership made it real.

148 *Emerging challenges*

Chiang rode the tide of history and left two enduring legacies for Taiwan – namely, the Taiwanization of the GMD and a new identity for Taiwan. The first legacy resulted in the promotion of Li Denghui as his successor, ensuring that the GMD would remain in power during the democratic transition. Chiang's project of Taiwanization had its roots when he was appointed as the premier in 1971. This farsighted move prevented politics from becoming a straight ethnic clash between mainlanders in the GMD versus Taiwanese in the opposition.

The second legacy is the awakening of the "self" in Taiwan. Chiang Ching-Kuo, of course, in all likelihood, had no intention to carve out a distinct Taiwan identity. He was, however, interested in reconciling the claim of being the "free China" with the reality on the ground, establishing a new *political identity* that differentiated his regime from the oppressive regime in mainland China. It was this search for the reconciliation and a new political identity that unintentionally converged with the opposition's search for a distinctive Taiwanese identity.

Implication of Taiwan's democracy for China

In Chapter 1, we allude to the notion that Taiwan's democratic transition may serve as an example for China, which has also experienced rapid economic development over the past thirty plus years, becoming the second largest economy in the world in 2011. Despite the growth, the nation's political system remains decidedly authoritarian. One of the likely driving forces behind the democratic change for Chiang Ching-Kuo was to set up an example in Taiwan for people in China to think about. Indeed, as Lee (1999) and Chu (2012) proclaimed, the best model for social, economic, and political reforms in Chinese societies can be found in Taiwan.

Both the GMD and the CCP have used the existence of an outside threat to justify police state repression. While the threat of China overtaking Taiwan has been real, the idea that the forces of imperialism would invade or rob China of its riches is simply an imagined threat. Ironically, the ubiquitous and effective CCP's propaganda machine has succeeded in penetrating popular thought in regard to the belief that a militarily weak China would be bullied, while the ineffective propaganda of the GMD has made the actual threat nearly a joke.

Currently, there are some similarities between pre-martial law Taiwan and contemporary China: authoritarian leaders, a weak civil society, a suppressive political mechanism including the police, and the use of economic development as a political instrument to gain popular support (Kuo 1997; Tsang 1999). Specifically, the CCP has maintained a form of corporatist control over society (Hu 1993), which turns labor unions, educational institutions, civic organizations, village electoral processes, mass media, and the press into political rings of party-state control promoting the regime's legitimacy. The key differences, however, are that there is no commitment to democracy from the top leaders of the CCP, free religious institutions, and no local-level elections beyond those permitted in villages.

China and Taiwan also differ in the nature of the authoritarianism involved. China was a real Leninist party under Mao Zedong that had a far more invasive and brutal system than did Taiwan's GMD. The GMD followed the form of a Leninist party and had totalitarian aspirations. The carceral was a social reality under Mao (Dutton 1992), while in contrast a police state was more a matter of rhetoric than reality even under Chiang Kai-Shek. With the epic transition undertaken from totalitarianism to developmental authoritarianism under Deng Xiaoping, the CCP has gravitated closer to the GMD's political trajectory prior to the repeal of martial law. When the anti-corruption outcry reached the boiling point, however, Deng Xiaoping ordered troops to quell it ruthlessly in 1989. While China reassumed the use of economic development as a political instrument to maintain legitimacy, its political reform has by-and-large stalled ever since.

Some political scientists and politicians argue that the lack of progress toward democracy in China lies in the "Asian values" thesis (De Bary 1998; Pye 1968; 1985) – which holds that Chinese culture is fundamentally different from Western culture in ways that make it non-conducive to the protection of individual rights and social freedoms that undergird Western civil society, and by extension Western democracy.

The democratization of Taiwan suggests differently. A reform-minded leadership, aided by favorable international and domestic conditions, responded to growing societal demands by sharing political power (Dickson 1998). Both ex-presidents of Li Denghui and Chen Shuibian rejected the "Asian values" argument and embraced democracy, freedom, and human rights as universal values (see Cooney 2004). Unlike Japan, whose democracy was imposed upon the nation after its defeat in World War II, democracy in both South Korea and Taiwan can be considered as "homegrown." It originated primarily within repressive political atmospheres rather being imposed by outside forces. The idea of democracy had been introduced into Asia over a hundred years ago (Fung 2010), but both countries resisted it and chose instead the strong state and a government with a plan before finally adopting democracy. As in the case of South Korea, Taiwan lacked the background condition theorized by Rustow (1970) as essential – i.e., national unity. Both Taiwan and South Korea, however, transformed themselves into democracies while facing a legitimacy challenge from the other part of their divided nations. Rustow (1970), however, also posits that there are many likely roads to democracy.

Others (Lipset 1959; Peerenboom 2004; Sen 1999b; Welzel *et al.* 2003) believe that a developed economy in time will lead to democracy. While there indeed may be a correlation between economic development and democracy, it is likely that the relationship is not a causal one (Rustow 1970). High literacy rates and economic development are both requisites of democracy (Lipset 1959), not prerequisites (Rustow 1970). The diffusion of Western cultural and capitalist economy do not, ipso facto, guarantee that China will "grow" into a democracy.

Since Deng Xiaoping's repression of the massive student-led movement in 1989, China has walked down a different path toward modernity. China's road so far has proven to be eclectic. There is no mathematical modeling for it (for exceptions, see Inglehart and Welzel 2005 and Wang 2008). The repressive nature of the regime, however, makes the road highly contingent. The police are powerful and intrusive (Xu and Hua 2012). Progress toward the rule of law has stalled (Minzner 2013), and even worse the Chinese regime "treats western rule of law's promotion in China synonymously as imperialistic impulses" (He 2014: 160).

Beneath a general quiescence of the populace, public demand for democracy has continued to grow stronger in China (Li 2013; Nathan 2013; Wang 2008). Dissident voices have been suppressed, but have never been completely silenced. Some prominent dissidents are in jail (刘晓波, Liu Xiaobo; 许志永, Xu Zhiyong), or live in constant legal trouble and/or in limbo (艾未未, Ai Weiwei), or live in exile (陈光城, Chen Guangcheng). They are, collectively, however, like wild grass – "Wildfire never quite destroys them – they grow again in the spring wind" (Bai Juyi's poem (1957: 193)). Many new voices, such as those of Li Chengpeng (李承鹏) and Han Han (韩寒), are often warned or admonished by public security agents (also see Xu and Hua 2012). With another round of peaceful transition of top leadership, China may indeed be at a tipping point with respect to democratization in the coming years (see Minzner 2013; Nathan 2013; Pei 2012; Su *et al.* 2013).

The factional chasm between conservatives and reformists within the CCP leadership has become open over time. An editorial comment in *Yanhuang Chunqiu* (《炎黄春秋》) (2013b) – an out-spoken magazine of history – declares that Year 2013 is the Year of Constitutionalism for China in its initial issue of the new year. Democracy and rule of law are actually not alien ideas in China (Cao and Zhao 2009). A commitment to a form of democracy can be found in the 1982 Constitution, which has been primarily rhetorical and has had no practical consequences up to this point. The consensus among CCP reformists and scholars (He 2012; Qin 2013; Zhang 2011) is to implement what has been promised in the constitution instead of pushing for more unrealizable and meaningless paper commitments. Similar comments from another outspoken weekly journal – *Southern Weekend Journal* (《南方周末》) – were allegedly altered by the authorities, and that medication of opinion generated somewhat of a public outcry.

We believe that the CCP under Xi Jinping (习近平) will continue to evolve from a once *uninhibited* political center to an increasingly *inhibited* political center. An inhibited political center can be defined as institutions and people who allocate and exercise power, but who for various reasons feel the need to exert considerable self-restraint in the exercise of such power (Chao and Myers 1998; Tsang 1999). Instead of polarizing the two concepts, it is believed that the two concepts sit at two ends of a continuum. Viewed in this way, China was an uninhibited center state in the past, but has become increasingly an inhibited political center.

Viewing the US political scene in the 1830s, Tocqueville (2000) declared that the inexorable forces of history were on the side of democracy. He argued that rule from above would inevitably give way to the sovereignty of the people. Democracy represents both a borderless ideology and a working practice for reasons both historical and philosophical. The universal evolution in the development of science and technology points to a universal history of mankind. Both Hegel and Marx believed that the evolution of human societies was not open-ended, but would end when humankind had achieved a form of society that satisfied its deepest and most fundamental longings. Both thinkers thus posited an end of history, which simply meant that there would be no further progress in the development of underlying principles and institutions because all of the really big questions had been settled (see Fukuyama 1992).

More importantly, democracy has its intrinsic value: it is rooted in humanity's innate capacity for self-government (Fukuyama 1992; Rustow 1970; Welzel *et al.* 2003). Sen (1999b) argues that democracy is a universal value because of the *intrinsic* importance of political participation and freedom in human life; because of the *instrumental* importance of political incentives in keeping governments responsible and accountable; and because of the *constructive* role of democracy in the formation of values and in the understanding of needs, rights, and duties.

Among the main arguments raised against democracy as a universal value is the so-called "Chinese mentality" thesis (Pye 1968). This monolithic interpretation of Confucianism as hostile to democracy and political rights does not bear critical scrutiny. It is not hard, of course, to find authoritarian writings within Asian traditions. But neither is it hard to find them in Western classics; one has only to reflect on the writings of Plato or St. Thomas Aquinas to see that devotion to discipline is not a special Asian preference (Sen 1999b). To dismiss the plausibility of democracy as a universal value because of the presence of some Asian writings on discipline and order would be similar to rejecting the plausibility of democracy as a form of government in Europe or America today on the basis of the writings of Plato or Machiavelli or Hobbes.

Confucianism is an inclusive knowledge system. There are many different elements in that knowledge system. Confucius is the standard author quoted in attempts to articulate Asian values. As we noted in the previous chapter, when he was asked about which components of the state was the most important, Confucius answered unequivocally that trust in the government was the most imperative, followed by food supply, which in turn was more important than possession of weapons. Confucius is not the only intellectual influence worthy of note. The second sage in the Confucian school, Mencius, was even more straightforward in this regard. He states

> The people are of supreme importance in a state; the altars to the gods of land and grain come next; last comes the emperor. That is why he who can gain the confidence of the multitudinous people will be the Ruler (民为贵，社稷次之，君为轻。是故得乎丘民而为天子).
>
> (Mencius 1996)

Indeed, these should have been or should be the pillar of the imagined edifice of Asian values in the new century. They are resonant with President Lincoln's famous phrase "government of the people, by the people, and for the people." Moody (1988: 250) observes that "Confucianism taken in the abstract is probably as consistent with democracy as the mainstream of traditional western thought." The homogeneous worship of hierarch of emperor's order over freedom is only one of the possible interpretations of Confucianism which over two thousand years has overshadowed other possible – even more likely accurate – interpretations of Confucianism. Furthermore, political culture and ideology are not static, but rather continually evolve out of interactions between shared orientations, personalities, and formative episodes in concrete historical reality, a point stressed by eminent sociologists Robert Bellah *et al.* (1985) and by highly respected political scientist Ronald Inglehart (1997).

Historically, Max Weber (1951) argued that Confucian culture was a major obstacle to economic development; by the 1980s, however, many scholars (Berger and Hsiao 1988; Dore 1986; Morishima 1982) saw that same Confucianism as a major facilitator of the spectacular economic growth of East Asian societies. Modernization everywhere tends to erode the influence of traditional values, Confucianism and party dictatorship included. China has been changed by its rapid economic development, as even its critics agree (Liu 2011). The new cosmopolitan values of pro-emancipation, pro-equality, and pro-liberty are growing in influence (Wang 2008). Using data from the *Taiwan Social Change Survey 2004*, W. Chang (2012) showed that affiliations with Buddhism, Taoism, and folk religions were positively associated with democratic values. Similarly, Tsang (1999) did not find any conflicts between Confucian values and democracy. In fact, he argues that despite its Leninist organizational façade, the GMD was under the influence of Confucian values because both Chiangs were Confucian at heart.

While we believe that democracy is a universal ideal and that it can be a solution to the ills of authoritarian regimes, we hasten to admit that it is not an infallible nostrum for all social ills. In practice, democracy "may become a pack of shameless egomaniacs void of the least hint of honor pandering to our lowest desires and most small-minded envies in order to secure for themselves one of the limited number of places at the public trough" (Moody 1992: 179).

As for highly extolled Taiwan democratization experience, instead of being a positive factor, it actually has been serving as a somewhat negative lesson for conservative CCP leaders (Tsang 1999). The CCP leaders from Jiang Zemin to Hu Jintao continued to emphasize the Leninist principle of democratic centralism and saw their control of power being threatened by the ROC's democratic transition experience. Limited direct elections in villages were introduced as early as 1987 in China, but because of the experience of Taiwan it never "progressed" up to become township election, or city-wise election. The margin election process has been used for the selection of party central committee members since 1984, but it is limited to only 10 percent and has not been expanded into a full-scale multi-candidate competitive election where one position has two or more candidates (He 2013). All national-level top positions open up only for the single candidate election process.

There are signs of hope, however. Moody (1988) avers that in post-Confucian societies the state is so autonomous that democratization does not threaten it. Today's CCP top leaders do not show the "Red" tinge of years past when more ideologically socialist sentiments, held primarily by the influential seniors of the past generation, played a significant balancing role within the party. Instead, today's top leaders are generally driven by various identifiable interest groups within the party. If the current trend of transparency in governance continues, it is not out of bounds to predict that a constitutional challenge will grow stronger in the future. If successful, the change toward a democratic regime could be quite swift. In certain ways, but much less apparent than the constitution of ROC in 1946, the seeds of change toward the rule of law and democratic government have been buried in the current constitution.

In short, the democratization of Taiwan has great intrinsic value to all those who reside on the island. Although the peculiar concatenation of factors which gave rise to Taiwan's democracy in the 1980s and 1990s was unique, it is an invaluable reference point for the students of comparative politics. It provides a practical demonstration that this type of political regime can be made to work in a Chinese cultural setting – a demonstration with far-reaching implications for China and Singapore, and for those who theorize about supposed "Asian values" or "the clash of civilizations." Too many historically unique elements, however, have shaped Taiwan's experience to make it a viable model for widespread replication (Domes 1999; Gold 1986; Tsang 1999), but it is a highly effective if not entirely salubrious example of democracy in a post-Confucian cultural setting. The most important consequence is that the island's soft power of democracy serves as a better defense for its de facto independent status than all of the military resources at its command.

Democratic deficits of Taiwan's police

Liberal democracy is the best working ideal available for government. This does not mean that today's stable democracies are not without substantial injustice and serious social problems. Like everywhere else, there are serious challenges in every extant democracy. These "wicked" problems as some social scientists have labelled them, however, are most often matters of incomplete implementation of the twin principles of liberty and equality on which modern democracy is founded rather than representing flaws in the principles themselves. Democracy is much like the Buddha's palm: no matter how the problems change or become exacerbated over time, they remain within the limits of or under the watch of the Buddha's eyes.

According to Robert Dahl (1989), there are seven criteria of democracy (or seven "institutions of polyarchy"), including elected officials in control of government decision, free and fair elections, inclusive suffrage, the right to run for office, freedom of expression, alternative information, and associational autonomy. By 1997, Taiwan met all seven essential requirements of democracy, and it received the status of "free country" in the Freedom House publication of that year.

The drama of political life in Taiwan is different after the democratization miracle. The iron rectangle of the state, the ruling party, local factions, and conglomerates has gradually come to dominate Taiwan's political economy at the expense of distributional equality and economic efficiency (Kuo 2000). Democracy in Taiwan has been criticized as being "distorted" (Kuo 2000) or said to be best viewed as "devolution" during the Chen Shuibian era (Copper 2009).

The DPP continues to clutch their last straw of the ethnic divide by appealing to what Maier (1994) called "territorial populism." There is no doubt that there was an element of truth in this thesis. Taiwanese were underrepresented in the top political echelon during the martial law period. However, as Pye (1986: 622) observed, "Taiwanese dominate much of the economy, are among the richest people, and tend to discriminate against mainlanders in employing executives in the vast majority of enterprises on the island." The DPP, therefore, exaggerated their victim status under martial law; after all, Chen Shoushan (陳守山), a native Taiwanese, headed the Taiwan Garrison Command, the island's highest security force. Moreover, Li Denghui, a native Taiwanese, was a GMD-appointed president.

Civil liberties deteriorated to some degree owing to Chen Shuibian playing ethnic politics as well as his administration's lack of respect for democratic values (Copper 2009). Ethnic prejudice reached a new pitch under his watch. Aborigines, Hakka, and mainland Chinese all complained that the official and semi-official propagation of the use of Taiwanese (the dialect spoken by Fujian Taiwanese) discriminated against them since many did not speak or even understand it. Chen's regime, thus, was an outlier episode on the zigzag road to democracy in Taiwan, representing one of the inherent weaknesses of democracy – the "tyranny of the majority" in Tocqueville's words (Tocqueville 2000).

The identity of Taiwan's people likewise remains unsettled. This may be the case for a long time to come. Taiwan's frontier position during the Qing dynasty left an imprint on national identity, as did the Japanese colonial period and that of "sinicization" under the GMD government. More recently, democratization and "de-sinicization" under Chen Shuibian further complicated the process of nation-building and national identity formation (Hao 2010). The normally mild ethnic divisions have been highly politicized by the DPP. The divided and polarized Taiwan public cannot fully enjoy the fruit of democracy.

Democracy is also blamed for the paralysis of decision making at the top. Political gridlock is one of the problems that is currently bothering not only Taipei, but also Washington, DC. The issue of the fourth nuclear power station in Taiwan, for example, has been on the political agenda since Li Denghui's time. Millions and millions of hard-earned tax dollars have been spent on the project during both the DPP's two terms in office and under the GMD's prolonged rule. Hood (1996) believes that these problems will likely ameliorate as democratic institutions consolidate and people acquire an increasing attachment to democratic values.

Taiwan has not developed criminal justice institutions and practices fully consonant with the democratic ideals of equality, openness, fairness, and rule of law. Democracy certainly has not made Taiwan more peaceful or more moral in the conduct of its public officials, but it has certainly made it a more complex society. Among the various problems being dealt with in Taiwan, two key issues concern the police directly – namely, those of *inequality* and the *rule of law*. While the police force has little direct influence on social inequality, it can be a critical palliative force (Manning 2010) and it can most certainly do more to implement the rule of law.

Although the democratization process does not seem to help or hamper economic growth in Taiwan (Heo *et al.* 2012), market-induced inequality has been widening over years in the newly emergent Asian democracies of Taiwan and South Korea. Taiwan's inequality is more severe than that of South Korea (Chi and Kuo 2012). The issue of societal inequality is of great importance to the police. Studies have found that inequality is associated with social unrest and democratic instability, political corruption, and lower levels of social trust (Cao *et al.* 2012; Rothstein and Uslaner 2005).

To what extent can it reasonably be said that Taiwanese policing suffers from a persistent set of democratic deficits? After all, the most distinct feature of Taiwan's democratic transition is probably the smooth change accomplished at a low social cost (Tien and Cheng 1999). The whole process was characterized not by rupture or wholesale displacement of the elite, but rather by strategic interaction between the opposition and the GMD regime, attempting to steer the course of change. In crafting democratic institutions, the GMD did not clean the slate to redesign the whole thing from scratch. Instead, many pre-existing institutions were preserved and improved upon. This piecemeal approach turned out to be a mixed blessing: during the transition, it served as a force of stability and continuation. During the democratic consolidation, however, these residual authoritarian elements are preserved and serve as reminders of the past regime. Even though they are operational, they are potentially detrimental to a full functioning of democracy in Taiwan. The police represent one of those areas of Taiwan society where the democratization process is yet in mid-stream.

For example, the principle of civilian superiority has not been fully established in law enforcement. Both TPC and CPU represent the residues of the past regime. Its students enjoy the privilege of free tuition and seniority of civilian service once recruited. The professors there are mostly internally trained and they retire ridiculously young from the TPC and CPU and then find a teaching position at private universities earning one full pension and one salary. So far, none of the presidents at either TPC or CPU have been a civilian, and all of them have had extensive police backgrounds. The separate tracks for rank-and-file officers and for police management are questionable practices of the past (see Chapter 5).

In addition, the CPU is the only police university in the democratic world which grants PhD degrees. Only the authoritarian regime in China has a comparable university which also grants a PhD. When China's People's Public Security University began its PhD program in 2003, it justified the program as being a reflection of Chinese cultural characteristics and used the CPU as an example. Going through this entrenched system of police training, it is unlikely that the new cadets will be able to look at the world from a citizen's viewpoint. The strict patriarchal hierarchy and seniority in place at the university smothers creative research initiatives and prevents new thinking, making any reform extremely difficult. In talking with some MA and PhD students, we found that they are inclined to complain about the rigid atmosphere maintained in the graduate school. In addition, the recruitment system openly discriminates against female cadets by arbitrarily setting up a quota while refusing to give aboriginal applicants any form of special consideration for inclusion. Its existence also precludes an open and fair competition for students from two other criminology programs at National Taipei University and National Chung Cheng University.

Community policing has been embraced in Taiwan as a new philosophy for law enforcement and has been widely adopted as a new guiding principle (see Chapter 3), but it is largely rhetoric and has had few consequences for the character of police behavior. The police administration appears to be confused by the superficial similarities of community policing as a mechanism to better serve the community and the old community-outreach practices used as a mechanism to penetrate the community for a more effective control of the regime's enemies. The police continue to emphasize military drills in training and in their daily activities. Civilization of the police has yet to come to policing in Taiwan.

Many rank-and-file officers equate constraints on police power with the loss of police authority. The old culture of all-powerful police is fading away much too slowly. This sense of loss of authority has a big influence on police morale and is widely regarded as the most important source of police cynicism. In turn, cynicism ignites the shared nostalgia for the superficial efficacy and efficiency of policing during the authoritarian era (Y. Chang *et al.* 2011). After more than a decade of democratic consolidation, the police administration continues to struggle with these longstanding issues that should not persist in a well-functioning democracy.

Taiwan politics has been characterized by the phenomenon of *heijin* or "black gold" involving the infusion of money from gangster sources into elections. Although the connection between politics and underground societies antedates democracy, this particular form of malfeasance has become more overt. Gangster representatives control the Police Affairs Committees in many local assemblies, and gangsters have established many moles in the police system either through bribery or threat (Cai 1998). It is at these more concrete levels that the liberal democracy does not enjoy its proper discursive dominance. New reform measures must overcome the old cultural barriers – a complicated relationship network that blurs the legal and illegal. Admittedly, there is no quick fix to this particular wicked problem in local government affairs (Chapter 7).

The problem with a highly centralized structure has not been well understood in Taiwan. The highly centralized NPA tends to stifle creativity and the emergence of new initiatives from within law enforcement. Police officers sometimes "lose their bearings in the labyrinth of hierarchy," specialization, competitive examination, red tape, promotion based on seniority, and mass files (Niederhoffer 1969). Interference with scholars' independent investigations or academic freedom, such as the conducting of victimization surveys, has made it impossible to produce valid data. Research initiatives produced by scholars from the officially sanctioned CPU are prima facie questionable in their neutrality and objectivity (Chapter 5). Important questions about the similarities and differences in organizational culture across Taiwan's police agencies have never been raised, despite their importance for evidence-based practice (Chapter 6).

In Taiwan, the discrepancies between law and other social systems are greater than in the West. Morality and reputation continue to be more important than law, and the level of resistance to the intrusion of law into family activities seems to be stronger than is the case in the West. Female officers continue to face discrimination, both overt and covert (see Chapter 8). Disadvantaged groups too often do not get equal protection (see Chapter 9). With the instrument of law in their hands, lawsuits against quotas for women or sexual harassment are virtually unheard of. The general populace appears rather lukewarm in its support for liberal democracy, while political elites tend to pay more lip service to the idea of democracy than permit the principles of democracy to guide their actions. In this sense, Taiwanese are much less liberal in their protection of rights than they are democratic in their preferences for governance through popular elections.

In the eyes of much of the public, neither the police nor the judiciary have been able to establish themselves as credible guardians of social justice (see Chapter 10). Although homicide rates, which are the most consistent and reliable indicator of crime statistics, have in fact declined steadily since 1998 (Hebenton and Jou 2014), the perception of widespread disorder nonetheless looms large. In a low power distance society where the public expects to have input into decision making, this result is not particularly surprising. It is, however, rather consequential for an effective policing. Similarly, there is no convincing evidence that police misconduct has increased over the years, but the media exposures of police scandals have increased in frequency and the perception of corruption hovers over law enforcement (Chapter 7). Confidence in the police has not been used as one measure of police effectiveness, even though it was recommended by the Research Development and Evaluation commission.

Taiwan is dynamic, and Taiwan is changing. A state should be known not for being the greatest or the wealthiest, but as the most just (Durkheim 1992). Taiwan has been changing toward the direction of being most just. So too is the behavior of the police. An understanding of Taiwan's police, its practices, and its challenge illustrates why this small but vital island has become such a source of fascination. We explore the larger picture of Taiwan's politics and its international relationships, but our leitmotif has been the police and its reform – that is, how the police have changed after the democratic transition, what are the new challenges facing the police, and how are the police attempting to keep the delicate balance between the rule of law and prevailing local sentiments in a fresh democracy on ancient oriental soil. The most important conclusion is that the reform of the police is difficult, but nonetheless feasible. Democracy is the zeitgeist of today's world, but its application is context-sensitive. Taiwan remains a safe society under democracy. We are confident that the future of the police will follow its current trajectory set up during the democratic transition and that the old culture steeped in authoritarian practices will fade away sooner instead of later. Taiwan's police force is well educated and they are adaptive. If the pressures for change are large enough, the police will adapt like all police organizations have done in the democratic world (Zhao 1996).

Appendix: Chinese names and nouns with their romanization

Ai Weiwei 艾未未
Anti-Spiritual Pollution Campaign 清除精神污染
baidao 白道
baiping 攏平
baojia 保甲
bao-an 保安
bao-an jingcha 保安警察 (security police)
benshengren 本省人
Bo Yang 柏杨 (Po Yang)
Bureau of Entry and Exit Administration 入出境管理局
Cai Dehui 蔡德輝
Central Police Academy 中央警察学校
Central Police Officers' Academy 中央警官学校
Chen Bi 陈璧
Chen Cheng 陈诚
Chen Guangcheng 陈光城
Chen Hongshen 陳紅琛
Chen Lianzhen 陈连桢
Chen Quanmei 陳泉湄
Chen Shoushan 陳守山
Chen Shuibian 陈水扁
Chen Youhao 陈山豪
Chen Yuhui 陈玉辉
Chiang Ching-Kuo 蔣经国
Chiang Kai-Shek 蔣介石 (蔣中正)
dangguo 党国
dangwai 党外
Deng Ruwen 鄧如雯
Deng Xiaoping 邓小平
Even an upright judge finds it hard to settle a family quarrel (清官難斷家務事)
Examination Yuan 考试院
fan 番
Fang Lizhi 方励之
fenzusuo 分駐所 (FZS)
fengji 風紀 (disciplinary)
Formosa Incident 美麗島事件
gaoding 搞定
Gaoxiong 高雄
Gentarou Kodama 兒玉源太郎
guan 官
guanxi 關係
guoyu 国语
Han Han 韩寒
Hao Bocun 郝柏村
He Enting 何恩廷
heidao 黑道
heihan 黑函
heijin 黑金 ("black gold")
hongbao 紅包 (red envelopes)
Hou Youyi 候友宜
Hu Fuxiang 胡福相
Hu Yaobang 胡耀邦
Huang Fuxing Branch 黃復興黨部
Huang Shin-chieh 黃信介
inspector 警正
internal affairs officers 督察
Jiang Nan (江南, pen-name for Liu Yiliang, 劉宜良)
Jingqinqu 警勤区 (JQQ, police beats)
junzi 君子 (the gentry)
Kang Ningxiang 康宁祥

Kong Lingcheng 孔令晟
Kong Wenji 孔文吉
Law should be kept outside the door of a family (法不入家門)
Le Gan 樂幹
Lei Zhen 雷震
lifan 理蕃
Li Chengpeng 李承鵬
Li Denghui (Lee Teng-hui) 李登辉
Li Qian 李鶱
Li Shuangquan 李雙全
Li Tai-an 李泰安
Li Xingtang 李興唐
Lian Zhan 連戰
Lin A-qi 林阿祺
Lin Mucai 林木材
Lin Yishi 林益世
Liu Binyan 刘宾雁
Liu Xiaobo 刘晓波
Liu Zhongxing Branch 劉中興黨部
Luo Zhang 罗张
Ma Yingjiu 馬英九
Mei Kewang 梅可望
man 蠻
Miaoli Diubao Incident 苗栗丢包事件
officer 警佐
paichusuo 派出所 (PCS, field stations)
Peace Preservation Police Corps 保安警察
Police and Correction Officer Training Center of Taiwan Governor 台灣总督府警察及司狱官练习所
Police Torch 《警光杂志》
qing, li, fa 情理法 (sentiment, reason, and law)
Sakuma Samata 佐久間左馬太
shandiren 山地人 (the mountouneers)
Shimpei Goto 後藤新平
Soong May-ling 宋美齡
Southern Weekend Journal 《南方周末》
special examination students 特考生
Straightening Project 正風專案
Sun Yat-sen 孙中山（孙逸仙）
superintendent (警监)
Taiwan Provincial Police Training Center 台灣省警察訓練所

Tang Yingshen 湯英伸
the *Straightening Project* (正風專案)
Three Principles of the People 三民主義
waishengren 外省人
wandering cops 流浪警察
Wang Jin-wang 王進旺
Wang Minning 王民宁
Wang Ruowang 王若望
Wang Sheng 王昇
Wang Zhuojun 王卓鈞
wei-an 維安
Wei Desheng 魏德聖
Wei Jingsheng 魏京生
Weng Qinan 翁其楠
Wushe Incident 霧社事件
Wu Zhenji 吳振吉
Xi Jinping 习近平
xiaoren 小人 (the inferior)
Xie Fenfen 謝芬芬
Xie Ruizhi 謝瑞智
Xie Xiuneng 謝秀能
Xie Yindang 謝銀黨
xintaiwanren 新台灣人
xingzheng jingcha 行政警察 (administrative police)
Xu Zhiyong 许志永
Yan Shi-xi 颜世锡
Yanhuang Chunqiu 《炎黄春秋》
Yao Gaoqiao 姚高橋
yi 夷
yuanzhumin 原住民 (Aboriginal people)
Zhanghua 彰化
Zhang Tongrong 張通榮
Zhang Siliang 張四良
Zheng Chenggong 郑成功 (Koxinga)
zhi-an 治安
Zhao Longwen 趙龍文
Zhou Jucun 周菊村
Zhou Renshen 周人蔘
Zhou Shibin (周世斌)
Zhou Zhongfeng 周中锋
Zhu Zhenmin 朱拯民
Zhuang Heng-dai 莊亨岱

References

Adams, K. (1999) "What we know about police use of force," in *Use of Force by Police: Overview of National and Local Data*, Washington, DC: National Institute of Justice, pp. 1–14.
Alarid, L. F. and Wang, H.-M. (2000) "Cultural influences on Taiwanese police management and patrol practices," *International Journal of the Sociology of Law*, 28: 113–27.
Almond, G. A. and Verba, S. (1963) *The Civic Culture: Political Attitudes and Democracy in Five Nations*, Princeton, NJ: Princeton University Press.
Anonymous. (1995) "Taiwan fights illegal workers, increases foreign workers," *Migration News*, 2: 11, available at http://migration.ucdavis.edu/mn/more.php?id=799_0_3_0 [accessed January 12, 2014].
Armacost, B. (2004) "Organizational culture and police misconduct," *George Washington Law Review*, 72: 453–546.
Avakame, E. F. and Fyfe, J. J. (2001) "Differential police treatment of male-on-female spousal violence: Additional evidence on the leniency thesis," *Violence Against Women*, 7(1): 22–45.
Ayling, J. and Shearing, C. (2008) "Taking care of business: Public police as commercial security vendors," *Criminology and Criminal Justice*, 8(1): 27–50.
Bai, Juyi (1957) "Grass," in Shouzhen Yu (ed.), *An Analysis of 300 Poems of Tang Dynasty*, Beijing: China Book Press (白居易, "草", 《唐诗三百首详析》, 193页, 喻守真编注, 1957。北京: 中华书局).
Banton, M. (1964) *The Policeman in the Community*, New York: Basic Books.
Barefoot Angel (The) (1987) [Film] Wu Yiifeng (director), Taiwan: Anji Film Production.
Bayley, D. H. (1984) "Community policing in Japan and Singapore," in J. Morgan (ed.), *Community Policing: Proceedings*, Washington, DC: National Institute of Justice, pp. 19–35
Bayley, D. (1985) *Patterns of Policing*, New Brunswick, NJ: Rutgers University Press.
Bayley, D. (1969) *Police in the Political Development of India*, Princeton, NJ: Princeton University Press.
Bayley, D. H. (1991) *Forces of Order: Policing Modern Japan*, Berkeley, CA: University of California Press.
Bayley, D. (1994) *Police for the Future*, New York, NY: Oxford University Press.
Bayley, D. H. (1996) "Policing: The world stage," *Journal of Criminal Justice Education*, 7(2): 241–251.
Bayley, D. (1999) "Policing: The world stage," in R. Mawby (ed.), *Policing Across the World: Issue for the Twenty-first Century*, London, UK: University College London Press, pp. 3–12.

Bayley, D. and Mendelsohn, H. (1969) *Minorities and the Police: Confrontation in America*, New York, NY: Free Press.

Bellah, R., Madsen, R., Sullivan, W. M., Swidler, A., and Tipton, S. M. (1985) *Habits of the Heart*, Berkeley, CA: University of California Press.

Berger, P. L. and Hsiao, H. M. (ed.) (1988) *In Search of an East Asian Development Model*, New Brunswick, NJ: Transaction Books.

Berman, G. (2013) *Police Service Strength*, (SN00634). House of Commons Library.

Bian, Y. and Zhang, L. (2013) "Guanxi culture and guanxi social capital," *Journal of Humanities*, (1): 107–113 (边燕杰、张磊, 2013。论关系文化与关系社会资本,《人文杂志》第一期: 107–113页).

Bittner, E. (1980) *The Functions of the Police in Modern Society*, Cambridge, MA: Olgeschlager, Gunn, and Hain.

Bollen, K. A. (1993) "Liberal democracy: Validity and method factors in cross-national measures," *American Journal of Political Science*, 37: 1207–30.

Bordue, D. J. (1968) "The police," in *International Encyclopedia of Social Science*, New York: Free Press, pp. 171–81.

Bourdieu, P. (2001) *Masculine Domination*, Stanford, CA: Stanford University Press.

Bowling, B. and Philips, C. (2003) "Policing ethnic minority communities," in T. Newburn (ed.), *Handbook of Policing*, Cullompton, Devon: Willan Publishing, pp. 528–55.

Brodeur, J. (1983) "High policing and low policing: Remarks about the policing of political activities," *Social Problems*, 30(5): 507–20.

Brogden, M. (2005) "'Horses for courses' and 'thin blue lines': Community policing in transitional society," *Police Quarterly*, 8(1): 64–98.

Brogden, M. and Nijhar, P. (2013) *Community Policing: National and International Models and Approaches*, Cullompton, Devon: Willan.

Brown, J., Hegarty, P., and O'Neill, D. (2006) *Playing with numbers: A discussion paper on positive discrimination as means for achieving gender equality in the police service in England and Wales*. Review commissioned by British Association for Women in Policing.

Brown, J. M. (1998) "Aspects of discriminatory treatment of women police officers serving in forces in England and Wales," *British Journal of Criminology*, 38(2): 265–82.

Brown, M. (1988) *Working the Street: Police Discretion and the Dilemmas of Reform*, New York, NY: Russell Sage Foundation.

Cai, S. (1998) *Wanquan Heijin Dang-an* (*Complete File of the Black and the Gold*), Taipei: Congressional Workshop of Legislator Cai Shi-Yuan (蔡式渊, 1998。《完全黑金档案》。台北: 立法委员蔡式渊国会研究室).

Cai, Z. (2003) "The meaning and functions of police study," *The Newsletter of Association of Police Study* (蔡震荣, 2003, 警政学会之意义与功能,《中华警政研究学会第一期会讯》: http://www.pra.cpu.edu.tw/paper/1/1.pdf [accessed January 27, 2014].

Cao, L., (1999) "Security in Taiwan," in J. Zhang and Y. Yu (eds.), *Taiwan in the 21st Century: The Mainland Chinese Scholars Looking Ahead*, River Edge, NJ: Global Publishing Co. Inc., pp. 87–112 (曹立群, 1999。治安在台湾, 87–112页, 张杰、余燕敏编辑《大陆旅美学者之展望》。NJ: 八方文化企业公司).

Cao, L. (2007) "Returning to normality: Anomie and crime in China," *International Journal of Offender Therapy and Comparative Criminology*, 51(1): 40–51.

Cao, L. (2011) "Visible minorities and confidence in the police," *Canadian Journal of Criminology and Criminal Justice*, 53(1): 1–26.

Cao, L. and Dai, M. (2006) "Confidence in the police: Where does Taiwan rank in the world?" *Asian Journal of Criminology*, 1: 71–84.

Cao, L. and Hou, C. (2001) "A comparison of confidence in the police in China and in the United States," *Journal of Criminal Justice*, 29: 87–99.

Cao, L. and Huang, B. (2000) "Determinants of citizen complaints against police abuse of power," *Journal of Criminal Justice,* 28: 203–13.

Cao, L. and Stack, S. (2005) "Confidence in the police between America and Japan: Results from two waves of surveys," *Policing*, 28(1): 139–51.

Cao, L. and Zhao, S. (2009) "The great convergence? China and the United States in the new century," *Sociological Focus*, 42(3): 222–7.

Cao, L., Frank, J., and Cullen, F. T. (1996) "Race, community context, and confidence in the police," *American Journal of Police*, 15(1): 3–22.

Cao, L., Stack, S., and Sun, Y. (1998) "Public attitudes toward the police: A comparative study between Japan and America," *Journal of Criminal Justice*, 26(4): 279–89.

Cao, L., Deng, X., and Barton, S. M. (2000) "A test of Lundman's organizational product thesis with data on citizen complaints," *Policing* 23: 356–73.

Cao, L., Lai, Y. L., and Zhao, R. (2012) "Shades of blue: Confidence in the police in the world," *Journal of Criminal Justice*, 40(1): 40–9.

Chan, J. (1997) *Changing Police Culture: Policing in a Multicultural Society*, New York: Cambridge University Press.

Chan, J., Doran, S., and Marel, C. (2010) "Doing and undoing gender in policing," *Theoretical Criminology*, 14(4): 425–46.

Chang, C. (2000a) "An evaluation of community policing: A case study of Taipei City," *Theory and Policy*, 14: 87–116 (章光明, 2000, 社區警政方案評估研究-臺北市個案分析, 《理論與政策》, 第14卷3期, 第87–116頁).

Chang, C. (2000b) "The police and politics," *Police Science Quarterly*, 30: 177–202 (章光明, 2000, 警察與政治, 《警學叢刊》, 第30卷6期, 第177–202頁).

Chang, C. (2002) "The worldwide localization of community policing," *Police Science Quarterly*, 32: 15–31 (章光明, 2002, 社區警政的全球在地化, 《警學叢刊》, 第32卷5期, 第15–31頁).

Chang, C. (2003) "The lament of the foreign brides," *Taiwan Panorama*, August 11.

Chang, C. (2004) "The police and human rights: A moving line in between," *Journal of Central Police University*, 41: 1–14 (章光明, 2004, 警察與人權:一條流動期間的界限, 《中央警察大學學報》, 第41期, 第1–14頁).

Chang, C. (2010) "A review and prospect of the parade and assembly system in Taiwan," *Journal of the Central Police University*, 47: 23–45 (章光明,2010, 我國集會遊行制度的回顧與前瞻, 《中央警察大學學報》, 第47期, 第23–45頁).

Chang, C. (2012) *Police Administration*, Taoyuan: Central Police University Press (章光明, 2012。《警察政策》。桃园龟山: 中央警察大学出版社).

Chang, C., Lee, Y., and Hwang, C. (2008) "An evaluation research of ISO 9001 quality management system as in National Police Administration," *Bimonthly Journal of Research, Development and Evaluation*, 32: 6–10 (章光明、李湧清、黃啟賓, 2008, 警察機關導入ISO 9001品質管理系統成效評估, 《研考雙月刊》, 第32卷1期, 第6–10頁).

Chang, C., Qiu, J., and Sang, W. (2011) "The 100-year evolution of Taiwan policing policy and future prospect," in *Taiwan 100-Year Anniversary, Police Reforms, and Future Developments Conference Proceedings*, Taoyuan, Taiwan: Central Police University, pp. 1–19 (章光明、邱俊誠、桑維明,2011,台灣百年警察政策之變遷與展望, 《建國百年治安警政變革與展望學術研討會論文集》, 第1–19頁).

Chang, J. (2011) "Aboriginal movement," *Encyclopedia of Taiwan*, available online: http://taiwanpedia.culture.tw/en/content?ID=5063&Keyword=Aborigine [accessed August 17, 2013].

Chang, R. (2006) "Court orders arrest of Lee Tai-an," *Taipei Times,* available online: http://www.taipeitimes.com/News/taiwan/archives/2006/06/03/2003311466 [accessed January 17, 2014].

Chang, R. (2010) "Police detain 'mastermind' of mob boss assassination," *Taipei Times*, available online: http://www.taipeitimes.com/News/taiwan/archives/2010/06/28/2003476529 [accessed January 17, 2014].

Chang, W. (2012) "Eastern religions and attitude toward direct democracy in Taiwan," *Politics and Religion*, 5: 55–583.

Chang, Y. T., Chu, Y. H., and Huang, M. H. (2011) "Procedural quality only? Taiwanese democracy reconsidered," *International Police Science Review*, 32(5): 598–619.

Chao, L. and Myers, R. H. (1998) *The First Chinese Democracy: Political Life in the Republic of China on Taiwan*, Baltimore, MD: The Johns Hopkins University Press.

Chapman, B. (1970) *Police State*, New York, NY: Praeger.

Chen, C. (1992) "Civil servants political behavior regulation and police political neutrality," *Police Science Quarterly*, 23(1): 31–8 (陳春林, 1992, 公務員政治行為規範與警察政治中立,《警學叢刊》, 第23卷1期, 第31–38頁).

Chen, C. (1997) "Exploring the establishment and development of policewomen in Taiwan," *Research on Women in Modern Chinese History*, 5: 17–54 (陳純瑩, 1997, 臺灣女警的創建與發展初探,《近代中國婦女史研究》, 第5期, 第17–54頁).

Chen, F. (2005) *The Impact of Organizational Culture and ISO on Internal Service Quality and Organizational Performance*, MA Thesis, Jiayi, Taiwan: Nanhua University (陳富祥, 2005,《組織文化與ISO品質制度對內部服務品質與組織績效影響之研究:以台灣區各縣市警察局為例》, 碩士論文,南華大學管理科學研究所).

Chen, J. (2001) "This is the election that police officers have strictly followed administrative Neutrality," *China Times*, available online: http://forums.chinatimes.com/report/corrupt/htm/forums/news/901204f3.htm [accessed July 20, 2013]. (陳俊雄, 這是警察最守行政中立的選舉,中國時報,2001年12月3日).

Chen, L. (1988) *A Study of the Occupational Capability and Utilization by Police Supervisors with Four Years of Education*, MA Thesis. Central Police University, Taiwan (陳隆裕, 1988,《我國四年警官教育養成之職業能力及運用之研究》, 碩士論文, 中央警察大學警政研究所).

Chen, L. (2012) "Introduction to 'Essential translation of 'The model speech patterns of police officers in Taiwanese'," *Police Forum*, 3: 37–8 (陈连桢, 2012。简介,《警专论坛》, 3期: 37–38頁).

Chen, M. (1981) *The Analysis of Taiwanese Police Agencies' Inspiring Management*, MA Thesis, Central Police University, Taiwan (陳明傳, 1981,《我國警察機關激勵管理之研究》, 碩士論文, 中央警察大學警政研究所).

Chen, M. (2004) "New police management strategies," *Police Science Quarterly*, 34(6): 1–22 (陳明傳, 2004, 警政管理新策略,《警學叢刊》, 第34卷6期, 第1–22頁).

Chen, M. (2011) "The new developments of global policing and initiatives in Taiwan policing at the century anniversary: The reform of local level police agencies," in *Taiwan 100-year Anniversary, Police Reforms, and Future Developments Conference Proceedings*, Taoyuan, Taiwan: Central Police University, pp. 43–59 (陳明傳, 2011, 全球警政策略之新發展與我國建國百年警政之新嘗試,《建國百年治安警政變革與展望學術研討會論文集》, 第43–59頁).

Chen, Q. (1994) *The Analysis of Police Organizational Recognition*, MA Thesis, Central Police University, Taiwan (陳其鋒, 1994,《警察組織認同之研究》, 碩士論文, 中央警察大學警政研究所).

Chen, Q. (2005) *Foreign Workers Crime and Regulations*, MA Thesis, Taiwan: National Cheng Kung University (陳啟杰, 2005,《外籍勞工犯罪與規範之研究》, 碩士論文, 成功大學法律學研究所).

Chen, R. (2011) "Historical development of official police magazines," *Changes and Prospects of One Hundred Years' Security and Police Development*, a conference organized by Central Police University on May 24, 2011 (陈瑞南, 2011。警察官方刊物历史演进与发展之研究。《建国百年治安、警政变革与展望》, 中央警察大学主办, 中华民国100年5月24日).

Chen, S. (1998) "State, media and democracy in Taiwan," *Median, Culture & Society*, 20: 11–29.

Chen, S. (2007) "Is the NPA gender ratio of recruitement illegal?," *United Evening News*, p. 3, August 29 (陳素玲, 2007。警署招考女生錄取超少, 不違法?,《聯合晚報》2007年8月29日第3版).

Chen, T. (2010) *History of Taiwan's Security System*, Taipei: Lan-Tai Press (陈添寿, 2010。《台湾治安制度史》。台北: 兰台出版社).

Chen, Y., Hsieh, W., and Tsai, T. (2003) *The Characteristics of Marriage Violence with Marriage Immigrant Female and Their Help Seeking and Response Strategy*, Taipei: Domestic Violence and Sexual Assault Prevention Committee, Ministry of Justice (陳玉書、謝文彥、蔡田木, 2003,《外籍新娘親密關係暴力特性、求助行為及其保護措施之研究》, 內政部家庭暴力及性侵害防治委員會委託研究報告).

Cheng, L. (2008) *The Development of the Taiwan Policewoman During the Postwar Years (1947–2000)*, Executive Master Dissertation, National Central University, Chung Li, Taiwan (鄭麗君, 2007。《戰後台灣女警的發展—以台北市為例》, 國立中央大學碩士論文).

Cheng, R. (1993) *Police Officers' Perceptions of Work Values*, MA Thesis, Taiwan: Central Police University (陳稔惠, 1993,《警察人員工作價值觀之研究》, 碩士論文, 中央警察大學警政研究所).

Cheng, T. J. (1989) "Democratizing the quasi-Leninist regime in Taiwan," *World Politics*, 41(4): 471–99.

Cheng, Y. and Sun, Y. (2013) "The history and development of cross-strait police cooperation," in *Annual Asian Association of Police Studies Conference Proceedings*, Taoyuan, Taiwan: Central Police University, pp. 186–97.

Chi, E. and Kuo, H. Y. (2012) "Unequal new democracies in East Asia: Rising inequality and government responses in South Korea and Taiwan," *Asian Survey*, 52(5): 900–23.

Chin, K. (2003) *Heijin: Organized Crime, Business, and Politics in Taiwan*, Armonk, NY: M. E. Sharpe.

China Statistical Yearbook (2008). Available online: http://www.stats.gov.cn/tjsj/ndsj/2008/indexeh.htm [accessed October 25, 2009].

Chinese Women's Research Network (2013) "Taiwan sees more female police officers," available online: http://en.wsic.ac.cn/academicnews/4412.htm [accessed July 13, 2013].

Chiu, H. (2013) "Taiwan's malevolent, mafia-like subculture," *Taipei Times*, available online: http://www.taipeitimes.com/News/editorials/archives/2013/07/23/2003567933, [accessed January 17, 2014].

Chiu, H. Y. (Producer) (1993, November 1) "From anti-trafficking to social discipline," *The Argument of the Number of Underage Prostitutes*. [Political comments] Available online: http://www.ios.sinica.edu.tw/hyc/index.php?p=columnID&id=496 [accessed January 17, 2014].

Chu, C. (2004) *Police Misconduct Case Study*, MA Thesis, Yaoyuan: Central Police University (朱正倫, 2004。《警察人員違反風紀案件之研究》, 中央警察大學碩士論文).
Chu, D. and Sun, I. (2006) "Female police officers' job-related attitudes," *Women & Criminal Justice*, 18(1–2): 107–30.
Chu, D. and Sun, I. (2007) "A comparison of Taiwanese and American police supervisors' attitudes," *Police Quarterly*, 10: 63-86.
Chu, D. and Sun, I. Y. (2010) "Reactive versus proactive attitudes toward domestic violence: A comparison of Taiwanese male and female police officers," *Crime & Delinquency*, 56: 1–22.
Chu, H. Y. (2012) "The Taiwan factor," *Journal of Democracy*, 23(1): 42–56.
Chu, P. (2013) "Democratic reform is being stifled by 'old boys'," *Taipei Times*, available online: http://www.taipeitimes.com/News/editorials/archives/2013/08/07/2003569095 [accessed January 20, 2014].
Chuang, J. (2010, August 11) "Police announce plans to recruit more aborigines," *Taipei Times*, available online: http://www.taipeitimes.com/News/taiwan/archives/2010/08/11/2003480109 [accessed 20 January, 2014].
Chung, O. (2008) "Fair society for the fair sex," *Taiwan Review*, 58(4), available online: http://taiwanreview.nat.gov.tw/ct.asp?xItem=30733&CtNode=1337&mp=1 [accessed January 27, 2014].
Clark, C. (2001) "Successful democratization in the ROC: Creating a security challenge," in A.C. Tan, S. Chan, and C. Jillson (eds.), *Taiwan's National Security: Dilemmas and Opportunities*, Aldershot: Ashgate, pp. 18–59.
CNA (2004, November 15) "Taiwan police clash with 1000 aboriginal protesters in Taipei," *Central News Agency*, available online: http://www.accessmylibrary.com/coms2/summary_0286-14477711_ITM [accessed 17 December, 2013].
CNA (2008) "Police reaffirm respect for aboriginal hunters," *The China Post*, January 23, available online: http://www.chinapost.com.tw/taiwan/2008/01/23/140209/Police-reaffirm.htm [accessed January 27, 2014].
CNA (2013) "Keelung's mayor escapes Control Yuan impeachment," *Taipei Times*, available online: http://www.taipeitimes.com/News/taiwan/archives/2013/07/07/2003566540 [accessed January 27, 2014].
Cohen, M. (1988) *Taiwan at the Crossroad: Human Rights, Political Development, and Social Change on the Beautiful Island*, Washington, DC: Asian Resource Center.
Coleman, J. S. (1990 *Foundations of Social Theory*, Cambridge, MA: Harvard University Press.
Collins, S. C. (2004) "Sexual harassment and police discipline: Who's policing the police?" *Policing: An International Journal of Police Strategies & Management*, 27(4): 512–38.
Confucius (2003) *Confucius Analects*, translated by Edward Slingerland, Indianapolis, IN: Hackett Pub. Co.
Cooney, S. (2004) "The effects of rule of law principles in Taiwan," in R. Peerenboom (ed.), *Asian Discourse of Rule of Law*, London: Routledge, pp. 417–45.
Copper, J. F. (1997) *The Taiwan Political Miracle: Essays on Political Development, Elections and Foreign Relations*, Lanham, MD: University Press of America.
Copper, J. F. (2005) *Consolidating Taiwan's Democracy*, Boulder, CO: University Press of America.

Copper, J. F. (2009) "The devolution of Taiwan's democracy during the Chen Shui-bian era," *Journal of Contemporary China*, 18(60): 463–78.
Council of Labor Affairs. (2009) "Hot line 1955 supports foreign workers," available online: http://www.cla.gov.tw/cgi-bin/Message/MM_msg_control?mode=viewnews&ts=4a4adab8:73cf&theme=/.theme/default [accessed July 29, 2013] (行政院勞工委員會網站,專線1955挺外籍勞工).
Council of Labor Affairs (2010) "Foreign worker statistics," available online: http://www.cla.gov.tw/cgi-bin/siteMaker/SM_theme?page=41761dc1 [accessed October 26, 2010] (行政院勞工委員會, 外籍勞工統計).
Crank, J. (1998, 2004) *Understanding Police Culture*, Cincinnati, OH: Anderson.
Crank, J. and Langworhty, R. (1992) "An institutional perspective of policing," *Journal of Criminal Law and Criminology*, 83: 338–363.
Da Guang, G. F. (2011) "New Taiwanese," *Encyclopedia of Taiwan*, available online: http://taiwanpedia.culture.tw/web/content?ID=26712# [accessed August 17, 2013].
Dahl, R. (1989) *Democracy and its Critics*, New Haven, CT: Yale University Press.
Davis, R. C., Ortiz, C. W., Gilinskiy, Y., Ylesseva, I., and Briller, V. (2004) "A cross-national comparison of citizen perceptions of the police in New York City and St. Petersburg, Russia," *Policing*, 27(1): 22–36.
De Bary, W. T. (1998) *Asian Values and Human Rights: A Confucian Communitarian Perspective*, Cambridge, MA: Havard University Press.
Deming, E. (1986) *Out of the Crisis*, Cambridge, MA: MIT Center for Advanced Engineering Study.
Dickson, B. J. (1998) *Democratization in China and Taiwan: The Adaptability of Leninist Parties*, Oxford: Oxford University Press.
Domes, J. (1999) "Electoral and party politics in democratization," in S. Tsang and H. M. Tien (eds.), *Democratization in Taiwan*, Hong Kong: Hong Kong University Press, pp. 49–66.
Dore, R. (1986) *Flexible Rigidity*, Stanford, CA: Stanford University Press.
Du, J. (2011) "Chiang Chingkuo: from a strong man to a great man" (杜君立, 2011。蔣经国: 从强人到伟人), available online: http://www.21ccom.net/articles/rwcq/article_2011011328074.html [accessed March 31, 2013].
Durkheim, E. (1992) *Professional Ethics and Civil Morals*, translated by C. Bookfield, London: Routledge.
Dutton, M. R. (1992) *Policing and Punishment in China: From Patriarchy to "the People"*, New York: Cambridge University Press.
Eastern Survey Center (2001) *Public Satisfaction with Police Work: A Survey Report*, Taipei: Eastern Survey Center (東森民調中心, 2001。《九十年警察滿意度調查報告》, 台北: 東森民調中心).
Executive Yuan (2012) *Social Indicators 2011*, Taipei: Directorate General of Budget, Accounting and Statistics, Executive Yuan, available online: http://ebook.dgbas.gov.tw/public/Data/331311353471.pdf [accessed January 27, 2014].
Farrell, A., McDevitt, J., and Fahy, S. (2010) "Where are all the victims? Understanding the determinants of official identification of human trafficking incidents," *Criminology & Public Policy*, 9(2): 201–33.
Ferreira, B. R. (1996) "The use and effectiveness of community policing in a democracy," *Policing in Central and Eastern Europe: Comparing Firsthand Knowledge with Experience from the West*, College of Police and Security Studies, Slovenia, available online: https://www.ncjrs.gov/policing/use139.htm [accessed January 27, 2014].

Festinger, L. (1957) *A Theory of Cognitive Dissonance*, Stanford, CA: Stanford University Press.
Fetzer, J. S. and Soper, J. C. (2011) "The determinants of public attitudes toward the rights of indigenous peoples in Taiwan," *Taiwan Journal of Democracy*, 7(1): 95–114.
French, W. and Bell, C. (1995) *Organization Development: Behavioral Science Interventions for Organization Improvement*, Upper Saddle River, NJ: Prentice Hall.
Fu, J. (1992) *Taiwan and Geopolitics of the Asian American Dilemma*, New York: Praeger.
Fuchs, R. (2011) *Human Trafficking of Legal and Illegal Migrant Workers in Taiwan*, Taiwan: Hope Worker' Center.
Fukuyama, F. (1992) *The End of History and the Last Man*, New York, NY: Free Press.
Fulda, A. M. (2002) "Reevaluating the Taiwanese democracy movement," *Critical Asian Studies*, 34(3): 357–94.
Fung, E. S. K. (2010) *The Intellectual Foundations of Chinese Modernity*, Cambridge, UK: Cambridge University Press.
Fyfe, J. J., Klinger, D. A., and Flavin, J. M. (1997) "Differential police treatment of male-on-female spousal violence," *Crimiology*, 35(3): 455–73.
Gao, P. (1999) "Police Officer Chen Hsiu-feng," *Free China Review*, 49(5), available online: http://taiwanreview.nat.gov.tw/ct.asp?xItem=1397&ctNode=1342&mp=1 [accessed January 27, 2014].
Garcia, V. and Cao, L. (2005) "Race and satisfaction with the police in a small city," *Journal of Criminal Justice*, 33: 191–9.
Gardner, B. and Reece, J. (2012) "Revolutionizing policing through servant-leadership and quality management," *FBI Law Enforcement Bulletin*, 81(6): 25–32.
Gastil, R. D. (1987) *Freedom in the World: Political Rights and Civil Liberties, 1985–1986*, New York: Greenwood Press.
Giddens, A. (1991) *Modernity and Self-Identity: Self and Society in the Late Modern Age*, Cambridge, UK: Polity Press.
Gold, T. B. (1986) *State and Society in the Taiwan Miracle*, New York: M. E. Sharpe, Inc.
Goldsmith, A. (1990) "Taking police culture seriously: Police discretion and the limits of law," *Policing and Society*, 1: 91–114.
Goldstein, H. (1975) *Police Corruption: A Perspective on its Nature and Control*, Washington, DC: The Police Foundation.
Goldstein, H. (1977) *Policing a Free Society*, Cambridge, MA: Ballinger Publishing.
Grabosky, P. (2008) "Democratic Policing" (in Chinese), *Crime and Criminal Justice International* 11, 1–25.
Grabosky, P. and Ayling, J. (2007) "Ambiguous exchanges and the police," *International Journal of the Sociology of Law*, 35: 18–28.
Grigor'ev, L. and Ovchinnikov, M. (2009) "Corruption as an obstacle to modernization," *Problems of Economic Transition*, 51(11): 40–61.
Guo, S. (1999) *Kong Ling-cheng and Modernization of Policing*, MA Thesis, Taoyuan: Central Police University (郭世雅, 1999: 孔令晟与警政现代化。硕士论文。桃园: 中央警察大学).
Hajek, C., Giles, H., Barker, V., Lin, M., Zhang, Y., and Hummert, M. (2008) "Expressed trust and compliance in police-civilian encounters: The role of communication accommodation in Chinese and American settings," *Chinese Journal of Communication*, 1(2): 168–80.
Hao, Z. (2010) *Whither Taiwan and Mainland China: National Identity, the State, and Intellectuals*, Hong Kong: Hong Kong University Press.

Harty, H. and Greiner, J. (1984) *How Can Police Departments Better Apply Management-by-objectives and Quality Circle Programs?* Washington, DC: Urban Institute.

Hassell, K. (2006) *Police Organizational Cultures and Patrol Practices*, New York, NY: LFB Scholarly Book.

He, B. (2013) "Political participation," in C. Ogden (ed.), *Handbook of China's Governance and Domestic Politics*, London: Routledge, pp. 120–30.

He, N. (2014) *Chinese Criminal Trials: A Comprehensive Empirical Inquiry*, New York: Springer.

He, N. and Marshall, I. H. (1997) "Social production of crime data: A critical examination of Chinese crime statistics," *International Criminal Justice Review*, 7: 46–64.

He, W. (2012) *In the Name of Justice: Striving for the Rule of Law in China*, New York: Brookings Institution.

Hebenton, B. and Jou, S. (2008) "Conceptual approaches to the study of 'national' traditions in criminology," *International Journal of Law, Crime and Justice*, 36: 115–30.

Hebenton, B. and Jou, S. (2014) "Unmasking crime and criminology in Taiwan," in L. Cao, I. Y. Sun, and B. Hebenton (eds.), *The Routledge Handbook of Chinese Criminology*, London: Routledge, pp. 253–67.

Hebenton, B., Jou, S., and Chang, Y (2010) "Developing public safety and crime indicators in Taiwan," *Asian Journal of Criminology*, 5: 45–67.

Heidensohn, F. (2003) "Gender and policing," in T. Newburn (ed.), *Handbook of Policing*, Cullompton: Willan Publishing, pp. 556–77.

Heo, U., Hahm, S. D., and Kim, D. (2012) "The impact of democratization on economic growth in Asia: An interrupted time-series analysis," *Korea Observer*, 43(1) 21–45

Ho, J. (Producer) "From Anti-Trafficking to Social Discipline." *Emerging Challenges to Feminist Gender/Sexuality Theories and Politics in East Asia* [The 13th IGS Evening Seminar Series (2003, June 27)], available online: http://sex.ncu.edu.tw/members/Ho/tokyo2/lecture04.html [accessed January 27, 2014].

Hofstede, G. (2001) *Culture's Consequences: Comparing Values, Behaviours, Institutions, and Organizations Across Nations*, Thousand Oaks, CA: Sage.

Holdaway, S. and Parker, S. K. (1998) "Policing women police: Uniform patrol, promotion and representation in the CID," *The British Journal of Criminology*, 38(1): 40–60.

Hood, S. (1996) "Political change in Taiwan: The rise of KMT factions," *Asian Survey*, 36(5): 468–820.

Hou, C. (2007) "A study on police working attitudes: The case of the support of the performance measures among Taiwanese police officers," *Journal of Taiwan Studies*, 3: 61–85. (侯崇文, 2007, 警察工作態度之研究：以績效支持度為例,《研究臺灣》, 第三期, 第61–85頁).

Hou, C., Miracle, A., Poole, E., and Regoli, R. (1983) "Assessing determinants of police cynicism in Taiwan," *Police Studies*, 5: 3–7.

Hsieh, H. (2000) "On the service orientation of the police in Taiwan: An empirical research of Taoyuan County Police Bureau," *Taiwan Police College Bulletin*, 2(8): 1–22 (谢秀能, 2000年。我国警察机关为民服务理念刍议—桃园县警察局实证研究。《警专学报》第二卷第八期: 1–22頁).

Hsieh, M. (2007) *An Empirical Study on Sexual Harassment Experience of Policewomen in Taipei City*, MA Thesis, Taipei: National Taipei University (謝孟璇, 2007。《我國女警遭遇工作場所性騷擾經驗之研究—以台北市為例》, 國立台北大學碩士論文).

Hu, C. (2005) "Taiwan's geopolitics and Chiang Ching-kuo's decision to democratize Taiwan," *Stanford Journal of East Asian Affairs*, 5: 26–44.

Hu, F. (1993) "The electoral mechanism and political change in Taiwan," in S. Tsang (ed.), *In the Shadow of China*, Honolulu, HI: University of Hawaii Press, pp. 134–168.

Huang, C. (2002) "Public satisfaction with the police: The digest from the first survey in 2001," *Journal of the Central Police University*, 49(2): 1–32 (黃翠紋, 2002年。警政民意滿意度調查研究--中華民國九十二年度調查報告摘要。《中央警察大學學報》, 39期: 1–32頁).

Huang, C. (2003) "Public satisfaction with the police: The digest from the second survey in 2001," *Journal of Central Police University*, 40: 29–58 (黃翠紋, 2003年。警政民意滿意度調查研究--中華民國九十二年度調查報告摘要。《中央警察大學學報》, 40期: 29–58頁).

Huang, C. (2004) "Research on public satisfaction with the police: The digest from the 2003 Survey," *Journal of the Central Police University*, 41: 75–106 (黃翠紋, 2004年。警政民意滿意度調查研究--中華民國九十二年度調查報告摘要。《中央警察大學學報》, 41期: 75–106頁).

Huang, C. (2006) *Taiwan in Transformation 1895–2005: The Challenge of a New Democracy to an Old Civilization*, New Brunswick: Transaction Publishers.

Huang, F. (2010) "The meaning of two-stream police recruitment system," *National Elite*, 6: 1–16 (黃富源, 2010。警察特考雙軌進用考選分流制的意義與再精進。《國家菁英專論》, 6卷3期, 1–16頁).

Huang, J. and Li, X. (2010) *Inseparable Separations: The Making of China's Taiwan Policy*, Singapore: World Scientific Publishing Company.

Huang, L. (2003) *Reducing Repeat Victimisation in England and Wales: An Inspiration for Taiwan (Republic of China)?* PhD Dissertation, Manchester: University of Manchester.

Huang, L. (2005) *A Survey on the Work Environment for Policewomen in Taipei*, Taipei: Bureau of Social Security (黃蘭媖, 2005。《警察機關建構對女警友善之職場空間及需求調查》, 台北市政府社會局).

Huang, L. and Cao, L. (2008) "Exploring sexual harassment in a police department in Taiwan," *Policing*, 31(2): 324–40.

Huang, L. and Sun, I. Y. (2014) "Official reaction to crime in Taiwan," in L. Cao, I. Y. Sun, and B. Hebenton (eds.), *The Routledge Handbook of Chinese Criminology*, London: Routledge, pp. 268–83.

Huang, L., Lin, Y., and Wei, A. (2010) "An exploratory analysis on police-registered IPV incidents of female immigrant victims," *Crime and Criminal Justice International*, 15: 75–115 (黃蘭媖、林育聖、韋愛梅, 2010。警察機關受理之新移民女性遭受親密關係暴力案件探索性分析。《犯罪與刑事司法研究》, 15期, 75–116頁).

Huang, L., Lin, Y., Wei, A., Shiou, L., and Lu, C. (2010b) "Ten years of domestic violence prevention law in Taiwan," paper presented at the Academy of Criminal Justice Sciences Annual Meeting, CA: San Diego.

Huang, L., Chang, Y., Chang, C., and Tsai, M. (2013) *Access to Justice for Victims of Human Trafficking in Taiwan*. Paper presented at the Asian Criminological Society 5th Annual Conference on Access to Justice for the Marginalised in Asia: A Human Rights Perspective, Mumbai, India.

Huang, S. (2002) "Councillors allege police in cahoots with weigh stations," *Taipei Times*, available online: http://www.taipeitimes.com/News/taiwan/archives/2002/08/31/0000166252 [accessed January 27, 2014].

Huang, S. (2008) "An analysis of security mechanism for mainland Chinese entering Taiwan," in *The Second Annual Conference on Border Security and Population*

Mobility Proceedings, Taoyuan, Taiwan: Central Police University, pp. 21–43 (黃紹祥, 2008, 大陸人民來臺安全機制探討,《第二屆「國境安全與人口移動」學術研討會論文集》, 第21–43頁).

Huang, Y. (2012). *The Media, Political Party Orientation, and Attitudes toward the Police*, MA Thesis, Taipei: National Taipei University (黃玉秀, 2012,《民眾媒體、閱聽政黨傾向與警察滿意度》, 碩士論文, 臺北大學犯罪學研究所).

Huang, Z. R. (2012) "Police officer punished for passing information to certain funeral service at crime scene" (殯葬業搶屍風波, 員警記申誡), *The Liberty Times*, available online: http://www.libertytimes.com.tw/2012/new/may/10/today-so13.htm [accessed January 27, 2014].

Huntington, S. P. (1991) *The Third Wave: Democratization in the Later Twentieth Century*, Norman, OK: The University of Oklahoma Press.

Huntington, S. P. and Moore, C. H. (1970) *Authoritarian Politics in Modern Society*, New York: Basic Books.

Inglehart, R. (1997) *Modernization and Postmodernization: Cultural, Economic and Political Change in 41 Societies*, Princeton, NJ: Princeton University Press.

Inglehart, R. and Welzel, C. (2005) *Modernization, Cultural Change, and Democracy: The Human Development Sequence*, New York: Cambridge University Press.

Jackson, J. and Bradford, B. (2010) "What is trust and confidence in the police?" *Policing*, 4: 241–8.

Jiang, J. (2011) "The adaption of Taiwan policing to social development and future prospect," in *Taiwan 100-year Anniversary, Police Reforms, and Future Developments Conference Proceedings*, Taoyuan: Central Police University, pp. 207–17 (蔣基萍, 2011, 警政因應台灣社會變遷的調適與前瞻,《建國百年治安警政變革與展望學術研討會論文集》, 第207–217頁).

Jou, S., Hou, C., and Cao, L. (2010) "Value dimension in civil society: Public attitudes towards sex workers across countries," *Journal of Criminology*, 13(2): 109–40 (周愫嫻、侯崇文、曹立群, 2010。公民社會的價值維度: 以各國對性工作者民意取向為例。《犯罪學》, 13: 109–140頁).

Jou, S., Sun, I., and Hou, C. (2011) *A Study of Police Images and Public Satisfaction with Law and Order*, Grant report submitted to Ministry of the Interior (周愫嫻、孫懿賢、侯崇文, 2011,《警察形象與治安滿意度之研究》, 內政部委託研究報告)。

Jou, Y. (1994) "Exploring the social support of abused women in Taiwan," *Journal of Women and Gender Studies*, 5: 69–108.

Kelling, G., and Moore, M. (1988) "From political to reform to community: The evolving strategy of police," in J. Greene and S. Mastrofski (eds.), *Community Policing: Rhetoric or Reality*, New York, NY: Praeger, pp. 3–25.

Kennedy, B. L. (2003) "Taiwan's criminal-justice system: clash of cultures," *Taiwan Review*, 53 (4), available online: http://taiwanreview.nat.gov.tw/fp.asp?xItem=833&CtNode=128 [accessed on August 26, 2013].

Kingshott, B. (2009) "Women in policing: Changing the organizational culture by adopting a feminist perspective on leadership," *Criminal Justice Studies*, 22: 49–72.

Klockars, C. (1985) *The Idea of Police*, Newbury Park, CA: Sage.

Klockars, C. B., Ivkovic, S. K., and Haberfeld, M.R. (2004) *The Contours of Police integrity*, Thousand Oaks, CA: Sage.

Knapp Commission. (1972) "New York City Commission to investigate allegations of police corruption and the city's anti-corruption procedures," *The Knapp Commission Report*. New York: George Braziller.

Kuo, C. (2000) "Taiwan's distorted democracy in comparative perspective," *Journal of Asian and African Studies,* 35(1): 85–111.
Kuo, P. (1994) Deadly gravel trucks create fear on Taiwan's roads, village streets, *The Seattle Times,* available online: http://community.seattletimes.nwsource.com/archive/?date=19940320&slug=1901098 [accessed January 27, 2014].
Kuo, W. H. (1997) "Democratization and the political economy of Taiwan," *International Journal of Politics, Culture, and Society,* 11(1): 5–24.
LaFree, G. (2003) "Criminology and democracy," *The Criminologist,* 28(1): 1–5.
LaFree, G. (2007) "Expanding criminology's domain," *Criminology,* 45: 1–31.
Lai, C. (2010) *A Research on Suitable Duty by Male and Female Police Officers of Taipei City Police Stations,* MA Thesis, Taipei: National Taipei University (賴俊堯, 2010。《警勤區男、女警執勤合適性之研究－以臺北市派出所為例》，國立台北大學碩士論文).
Lai, C. (2012) "Comfort women," *Encyclopedia of Taiwan,* available online: http://taiwanpedia.culture.tw/web/content?ID=100130 [accessed August 17, 2013].
Lai, M. (2010) *A Research on Working Problems of Female Police: In Cases of Miaoli County Police Stations,* MA Thesis, Taipei: National Taipei University (賴銘助, 2010。《分駐派出所女警工作問題之研究－以苗栗縣警察局為例》，國立台北大學碩士論文).
Lai, Y., Cao, L., and Zhao, J. S. (2010) "The impact of political regime on confidence in legal authorities: A comparison between China and Taiwan," *Journal of Criminal Justice,* 38(5): 934–41.
Laio, F. (1991) *Policing in Taiwan: Contemporary Observations and Comparative Implications,* PhD Dissertation, Knoxville, TN: The University of Tennessee.
Langton, L. (2010) "Women in law enforcement, 1987–2008," *NCJ 230521,* available online: http://www.bjs.gov/content/pub/pdf/wle8708.pdf [accessed August 21, 2013].
Lee, J. (2005) "Human trafficking in East Asia: Current trends, data collection, and knowledge gaps," *International Migration,* 43(1–2): 165–201.
Lee, L., Cheurprakobkit, S., and Denq, F. (1998) "Neighborhood watch programmes in Taiwan," *International Journal of Police Science and Management,* 2: 57–77.
Lee, T. (1999) *The Road to Democracy: Taiwan's Pursuit of Identity,* Kyoto: PHP Institute.
Lee, Y. (1994) "Theories of police tasks: Macro and micro observations and reflections," *Police Science Quarterly,* 24: 3–48 (李湧清,1994,有關警察勤務之理論-宏觀與微觀之觀察與省思,《警學叢刊》,第24卷4期,第3–48頁).
Lee, Y. (2000) "Strategies and the establishment of positive police culture," *Police Science Quarterly,* 31: 1–14 (李湧清,2000,優質警察文化的建立與策略,《警學叢刊》,第31卷1期,第1–11頁).
Li, C. (2013) "Top-level reform or bottom-up revolution?" *Journal of Democracy,* 24(1): 41–8.
Li, Y. F. (1987) *Forty Years' Democratic Movement in Taiwan,* Taipei: Zili Wanbao (李筱峰, 1987年。《台湾民主运动四十年》。台北: 自立晚報).
Liang, H. H. (1992) *The Rise of the European State System from Metternich to the Second World War,* Cambridge, UK: Cambridge University Press.
Lin, C. (1978) "A Study on the police discipline in the Taiwan," *Police Science Quarterly,* 8(3): 69–73 (林崇陽, 1978。警察風紀問題抽樣研究。《警學叢刊》, 8期3卷, 69–73頁).

Lin, J. (1999) *An Analysis of the Execution of Community Policing in Taipei City*, MA Thesis, Taoyuan: The Central Police University (林炯棋, 1999,《臺北市社區警政政策執行之研究: 組織文化之觀點》, 碩士論文, 中央警察大學警政研究所).

Lin Mu-Tsai (林木材) (2010) "Tang Ying-Shen Event" (湯英伸事件) *Encyclopedia of Taiwan*, available online: http://taiwanpedia.culture.tw/web/content?ID=22021 [accessed August 17, 2013].

Lin, T., Deng, H., and Mao, Q. (2000) "Community-based and problem-oriented policing in the strategy of crime prevention," *Journal of the Central Police University*, 37: 1–36 (林燦璋、鄧煌發、毛昆益, 2000, 社區問題導向警政在犯罪預防上的實證研究,《中央警察大學學報》, 第37期, 第1–36頁).

Lin, X. (2004) *The Introduction of the ISO System into Police Field Stations*, MA Thesis, Taipei: Shih-Hsin University (林祥明, 2004,《ISO品質管理系統導入警察派出所之研究》, 碩士論文, 世新大學行政管理學研究所).

Lin, Y. (1997) *The Problems of Policewomen in Taiwan*, MA Thesis, Taipei: National Taiwan University (林幼琦, 1997.《台灣女警的工作處境與困境》, 國立臺灣大學碩士論文).

Linz, J. and Stepan, A. (1996) "Toward consolidated democracies," *Journal of Democracy*, 7(2): 14–33.

Lipset, S. M. (1959) "Some social requisites of democracy: Economic development and political legitimacy," *American Political Science Review*, 53: 69–105.

Liu, J. (2003) *A Study of Policewomen's Work Pressure, Social Support, and Working Satisfaction Relationship*, MA Thesis, Kaohsiung: National Kaohsiung Normal University (劉榮哲, 2003.《女警工作壓力、社會支持與工作滿意關係之研究》, 高雄師範大學大學碩士論文).

Liu, J. (2004) "Police office political neutrality during election," *Journal of Central Police University*, 41: 55–74 (劉嘉發,2004,論選舉期間警察人員行政中立之分際,《中央警察大學學報》, 第41期, 第55–74頁).

Liu, J. (2010) "An analysis of the issue of police administrative neutrality," *Journal of Policing*, 10: 121–44 (劉嘉發, 2010, 警察行政中立問題之研究,《中央警察大學警政論叢》, 第10期, 第121–44頁).

Liu, X. (2011) "Changing the regime by changing society," *Journal of Democracy*, 22(1): 160–6.

Loa, L. (2012, June 15) "Police to rally against overwork," *Taipei Times*, available online: http://www.taipeitimes.com/News/taiwan/archives/2012/06/15/2003535388 [accessed January 27, 2014].

Loader, I. and Mulcahy, A. (2003) *Policing and the Condition of England*, Oxford, UK: Oxford University Press.

Lovrich, N. P. (1978) "Reducing crime through police-community relations," *Policy Study Journal*, 7(s1): 505–12.

Lu, C. (2000) "Politics of foreign labor policy in Taiwan," *Journal of Asian and African Studies*, 35: 113–31.

Lundman, R. J. (1980) *Police and Policing: An Introduction*, New York: Halt, Rinehart and Winston.

Luo, Z. (1980) *An Investigation of Service Attitudes of Taiwanese Police Officers*, MA Thesis, Taoyuan: The Central Police University (羅傳賢, 1980,《臺灣地區警察人員服務態度問題之調查研究》, 碩士論文, 中央警察大學警政研究所).

McBeath, G. (1979) "Political training and attitudes of Taiwan's police recruits," *International Journal of Comparative and Applied Criminal Justice*, 3: 157–166.

McFarlane, J., Malecha, A., Gist, J., Watson, K., Batten, E., Hall, I., and Smith, S. (2002) "Intimate partner violence against immigrant women: measuring the effectiveness of protection orders," *American Journal of Family Law*, 16: 244–52.
MacKinnon, C. (1979) *Sexual Harassment of Working Women*, New Haven, CN: Yale University Press.
Maguire, K. (1997) "Modernization and clean government," *Crime, Law and Social Change*, 28: 73–88.
Maier, C. S. (1994) "Democracy and its discontents," *Foreign Affairs*, 74(3): 48–64.
Manning, P. K. (1997) *Police Work* (2nd ed.), Prospect Heights, IL: Waveland Press.
Manning, P. K. (2005) "The study of policing," *Policing Quarterly*, 8(1): 23–43.
Manning, P. K. (2010) *Democratic Policing in a Changing World*, Boulder: Paradigm Publishers.
Marks, D. and Sun, I. (2007) "The impact of 9/11 on organizational development among state and local law enforcement agencies," *Journal of Contemporary Criminal Justice*, 23: 159–73.
Marsh, R. M. (2005) "Tolerance of civil liberties in a new democracy," *Comparative Sociology*, 4: 313–33.
Martin, J. (2006) *Keeping the Peace in a Changing Regime: Police Work in Taiwan*, PhD Dissertation, Chicago: University of Chicago.
Martin, J. (2007) "A reasonable balance of law and sentiment," *Law and Society Review*, 41(3): 665–97.
Martin, S. E. (1980) *Breaking and Entering: Policewomen on Patrol*, Berkeley, CA: University of California Press.
Martin, S. E. (1989) *Women on the Move? A Report on the Status of Women in Policing*, Washington, DC: Police Foundation.
Mencius (1996) "Chapter 14 of Jinxin (ii), *Mencius*," in *The Contemporary Interpretation of Four Books*, interpreted by Z. Xia, M. Tang, and F. Liu. Nanchang: Jiangxi People's Press (《孟子/第七篇/尽心章句/第14章》,《四书今译》, 南昌: 江西人民出版社 1996年, 第581页), p. 581.
Mencius (1997) "Excerpts from Jin-xin 2, Chapter 14, Mencius," in *New Interpretation of Four Books* by Xia Yanzhang, Tang Manxian and Liu Fangyuan, Nanchang: Jiangxi People's Press, p. 581 (孟子, 第七篇, 尽心章句下, 十四章,《四书今译》, 译注夏延章、唐满先、刘方元, 南昌: 江西人民出版社, 1997年).
Ministry of Foreign Affairs (1976) "Police women playing vital roles in ROC life," *Free China Review*, 26(3). Available online: http://taiwanreview.nat.gov.tw/ct.asp?xItem=142191&CtNode=103 [accessed January 27, 2014].
Ministry of Foreign Affairs (1998) "Behind the statistics," *Free China Review*, 48(5). Available online: http://taiwanreview.nat.gov.tw/ct.asp?xItem=1275&ctNode=1342&mp=1 [accessed January 27, 2014].
Ministry of Foreign Affairs (2012) *The Republic of China at a Glance 2012*, Taipei.
Ministry of Interior (2010) "Analysis of gender statistics on interior affairs." Available online: http://www.moi.gov.tw/stat/gender.aspx (內政部, 99年內政性別統計分析專輯, 2010年) [accessed August, 2013].
Minzner, C. (2013) "The turn against legal reform," *Journal of Democracy*, 24(1): 65–72.
Mishler, W. and Rose, R. (2001) "What are the origins of political trust?" *Comparative Political Studies*, 34(1): 30–62.
Mo, Y. C. (2011) "Foreign workers to be targeted," *Taipei Times*, October 8, available online: http://www.taipeitimes.com/News/taiwan/archives/2011/10/08/2003515221 [accessed January 27, 2014].

Mon, W. and Liang, X. (2011) "A century of evolution in policing in Taiwan," *Police Science Quarterly*, 41(6): 1–28 (孟維德、梁欣丞, 2011。我國百年來的警政變遷。《中央警察大学警學叢刊》, 第41卷第6期, 頁1–28).

Mon, W. (2003) "The police and democratic society: An empirical study on police role," *The Chinese Public Administration Review*, 12(4): 1–42 (孟維德, 2003, 警察與民主社會: 警察角色定位之實證研究, 《中國行政評論》, 第12卷4期, 第1–42頁).

Moody, P. R. Jr. (1988) *Political Opposition in Post-Confucian Society*, New York: Praeger.

Moody, P. R. Jr. (1992) *Political Change on Taiwan: A Study of Ruling Party Adaptability*, New York: Praeger.

Monthly Bulletin of Interior Statistics (2013) Available online: sowf.moi.gov.tw/stat/month/list.htm [accessed August, 2013].

Morishima, M. (1982) *Why has Japan "Succeeded"?* New York: Cambridge University.

Muir, W. (1977) *Police: Streetcorner Politicians*, Chicago, IL: University of Chicago Press.

Munro, J. L. (1995) "Personal reflections: Three transitions of the Taiwan police," *Journal of Police College*, 8: 321–6 (Munro, J. L.,1995, 中華民國警察的三項轉變—個人的看法, 《警專學報》, 第8期, 第321–326頁).

Myhill, A. and Bradford, B. (2013) "Overcoming cop culture? Organizational justice and police officers' attitudes toward the public," *Policing*, 36: 338–56.

Nalla, M., Rydberg, J., and Mesko, G. (2011) "Organizational factors, environmental climate, and job satisfaction among police in Slovenia," *European Journal of Criminology*, 8: 144–56.

Nathan, A. (2013) "Foreseeing the unforeseeable," *Journal of Democracy*, 24(1): 20–5.

National Immigration Agency (2013a) "Immigrant spouse (Foreign and People's Republic of China) by Nationality in Counties and Cities" (各縣市外籍配偶人數按國籍分與大陸配偶人數), available online: http://www.immigration.gov.tw/ct.asp?xItem=1216276&ctNode=29699&mp=1 [assessed August, 2013].

National Immigration Agency (2013b), "Statistics of human trafficking cases investigated by law enforcement agencies" (各司法警察機關查緝人口販運案件統計表), available online: http://www.immigration.gov.tw/ct.asp?xItem=1212472&ctNode=29699&mp=1 [accessed August 27, 2013].

National Police Agency (NPA), Republic of China (1988) *Crime Statistics: 1988*, Taipei, Taiwan: Criminal Investigation Bureau, National Police Agency (警政署, 刑事警察局1988年刑案統計).

National Police Agency (NPA), Republic of China (1998) *Crime Statistics: 1998*, Taipei, Taiwan: Criminal Investigation Bureau, National Police Agency (警政署, 刑事警察局1998年刑案統計).

National Police Agency (NPA), Republic of China (2002) *Police White Paper, 2001*, Taipei, Taiwan: National Police Agency (警政署, 2001年警政白皮書).

National Police Agency (NPA), Republic of China (2012a) *The Enforcement of Contemporary Police Gender Policy* (警政署, 現行警察性別政策推動情形, 2012年12月31日).

National Police Agency (NPA), Republic of China (2012b) *Crime Statistics* (刑案統計). Available online: http://www.npa.gov.tw/NPAGip/wSite/mp?mp=1 [accessed April, 2013].

National Police Agency (NPA), Republic of China (2013) "Important indicators of policing statistics," available online: http://www.npa.gov.tw/NPAGip/wSite/lp?ctNode=12596&CtUnit=1741&BaseDSD=7&mp=1 [accessed July 29, 2013] (警政署, 警政統計重要參考指標, 內政部警政署全球資訊網).

National Statistics, R.O.C. (Taiwan) (2009) Available online: http://www.stat.gov.tw/mp.asp?mp=4 [accessed October 4, 2009].

National Statistics (2013) Available online: http://ebas1.ebas.gov.tw/pxweb/Dialog/..%5CDialog%5Cvarval.asp?ma=PS0204A1M&ti=%C4%B5%EF%BF%BD%EF%BF%BD%EF%BF%BD%EF%BF%BD%EF%BF%BDB%EF%BF%BDz%EF%BF%BD%EF%BF%BD%EF%BF%BD%7C%EF%BF%BDC%EF%BF%BD%EF%BF%BDo%EF%BF%BD%CD%BC%EF%BF%BD-%EF%BF%BD%EF%BF%BD&path=../PXfile/PublicSafety/&lang=9&strList=L [accessed April, 2013].

Niederhoffer, A. (1969) *Behind the Shield: The Police in Urban Society*, New York: Anchor Books.

Novak, K. J., Brown, R. A., and Frank, J. (2011) "Women on patrol: an analysis of differences in officer arrest behavior," *Policing*, 34(4): 566–87.

O'Leary, V. and Sheu, C. (1992) "Thinking about policing in Taiwan in the 21st century," *Police Studies*, 15: 118–23.

Ong, T. (2004) "A preliminary analysis of police officers' work values," *Police Science Quarterly*, 33: 107–38 (翁萃芳, 2004, 警察人員工作價值觀:一個初步調查,《警學叢刊》, 第33卷4期, 第107–138頁).

Paoline, E. (2001) *Rethinking Police Culture: Officers' Occupational Attitudes*, New York: LFB Scholarly Publication.

Paoline, E. A. and Terrill, W. (2004) "Women police officers and the use of coercion," *Women and Criminal Justice*, 15(3–4): 97–119.

Paolino, P. and Meernik, J. (ed.) (2008) *Democratization in Taiwan: Challenges in Transformation*, Aldershot, UK: Ashgate Publishing.

Parsons, D. and Jesilow, P. (2001) *In the Same Voice*, Santa Ana, CA: Seven Locks Press.

Peerenboom, R. (2004) "Preface," in R. Peerenboom (ed.), *Asian Discourses of Rule of Law*, London: Routledge, pp. x–xxiii.

Pei, M. (2012) "Is CCP rule fragile or resilient?" *Journal of Democracy*, 23(1): 27–41.

Peng, Y. (2008) "An implementation research on how the street level police curb prostitution: The use of a critical interpretative approach," *Journal of Public Administration*, 28: 115–51 (彭渰雯, 2008。基層員警取締性交易的執行研究: 批判性詮釋途徑之應用。《公共行政學報》, 28期, 115–51頁).

Perilla, J. L., Bakeman, R., and Norris, F. H. (1994) "Culture and domestic violence: The ecology of abused Latinas," *Violence and Victims*, 9(4), 325–39.

Poll Center of TVBS (1998) Available online: http://www1.tvbs.com.tw/tvbs2011/pch/tvbs_poll_center.aspx [accessed January 27, 2014].

Poll Center of TVBS (2004) Available online: http://www1.tvbs.com.tw/tvbs2011/pch/tvbs_poll_center.aspx [accessed January 27, 2014].

Poteyeva, M. and Sun, I. (2009) "Gender differences in police officers' attitudes: Assessing current empirical evidence," *Journal of Criminal Justice*, 37(5): 512–22.

Prenzler, T. and Sinclair, G. (2013) "The status of women police officers: An international review," *International Journal of Law, Crime and Justice*, 41(2): 115–31.

Punch, M. (2000) "Police currption and its prevention," *European Journal on Criminal Policy and Research*, 8(3): 301–24.

Pye, L. (1968) *The Spirit of Chinese Politics*, Cambridge, MA: Harvard University Press.

Pye, L. (1986) "Taiwan's development and its implications for Beijing and Washington," *Asian Survey*, 26(6): 611–29.

Pye, L. (1990) "Political science and the crisis of authoritarianism," *American Political Science Review*, 84(1): 3–19.

Pye, L. W. (1985) *Asian Power and Politics: The Cultural Dimensions of Authority*, Cambridge, MA: Harvard University Press.
Qin, H. (2013) *The Common Denominator*, Nanjing: Literary and Artistic Press of Jiangsu (秦晖, 2013。共同的底线, 南京: 江苏文艺出版社).
Qiu, J. (2005) "A study on satisfaction of Taiwan police," *Newsletter of Police Association of ROC*, 3 (邱俊誠, 2005年: 台灣警察工作滿意度与不滿意度之研究.《中华警政研究学会第三期会讯》, 民國94年9月: available online: http://www.pra.cpu.edu.tw/paper/3paper.html [accessed 27 January, 2014].
Qiu, Z. (1991) *Police Officers' Satisfaction with the Evaluation System*, MA Thesis, Taoyuan: Central Police University (邱子珍, 1991,《我國警察人員對現行考核制度滿意程度之調查研究》, 碩士論文, 中央警察大學警政研究所).
Rawnsley, G. D. and Rawnsley, M. T. (1998) "Regime transition and the media in Taiwan," in Vicky Randall (ed.), *Democratization and the Media*, London: Frank Cass, pp. 106–24.
Rawls, J. (1999) *The Laws of Peoples, with "The Idea of Public Reason Revisited,"* Cambridge, MA: Harvard University Press.
Reiss, A. (1971) *The Police and the Public*, New Heaven, CT: Yale University Press.
Ren, L., Cao, L., Lovrich, N., and Gaffney, M. (2005) "Linking confidence in the police with the performance of the police," *Journal of Criminal Justice*, 33: 55–66.
Reuss-Ianni, E. and Ianni, F. (1983). "Street cops and management cops: Two cultures of policing," in M. Punch (ed.), *Control in the Police Organization*, Cambridge, MA: MIT Press, pp. 251–74.
Rigger, S. (1999) *Politics in Taiwan: Voting for Democracy*, London: Routledge.
Riksheim, E. and Chermak, S. (1993) "Causes of police behavior revisited," *Journal of Criminal Justice*, 21: 353–82.
Rothstein, B. and Uslaner, E. (2005) "All for all: equality, corruption, and social trust," *World Politics*, 58: 41–72.
Rustow, D. A. (1970) "Transition to democracy: Toward a dynamic model," *Comparative Politics*, 2(3): 337–63.
Seediq Bale (2011) [Film] Wei Desheng (director). Taiwan: Art Film Production.
Sellin, T. (1938) "Culture conflict and crime," *American Journal of Sociology*, 44(1): 97–103.
Sen, A. (1999a) *Development as Freedom*, New York: Anchor Books.
Sen, A. (1999b) "Democracy as a universal value," *Journal of Democracy*, 10(3): 3–17.
Sever, M. (2008) "Effects of organizational culture on police decision making," TELEMASP Bulletin, 15(1): 1–11.
Shang, H. H. (2003) *A Study of the Policewomen's Work and Role in Taiwan*, MA Thesis, Huanlien: National Dong Hwa University (商綉慧, 2003。《台灣地區女警工作與角色之研究》, 國立東華大學大學碩士論文).
Shaw, B. (1989) "Quality circles and British police service," *Police Journal*, 61: 87–104.
Shelley, L. (2011) "Human trafficking: why is it such an important women's issue?" in D. Bergoffen, P. R. Gilbert, T. Harvey, and C. L. McNeely (eds.), *Confronting Global Gender Justice: Women's Lives, Human Rights*, London: Routledge, pp. 35–49.
Shen, C. H. (2003) "Abused women's experiences of applying protection order in Taipei City," *The Journal of Guidance and Counseling*, 24: 169–206 (沈慶鴻, 2003。婚姻暴力受虐婦女保護令聲請經驗之探討－以臺北市為例.《彰化師大輔導學報》24期, 169–206頁).
Sherman, L. (1975) "Evaluation of policewomen on patrol in a suburban police department," *Journal of Police Science and Administration*, 3: 434–8.
Sherman, L. (1980) "Causes of police behavior: The current state of quantitative research," *Journal of Research in Crime and Delinquency*, 17: 69–100.

Sherman, L. (2005) "Trust and confidence in criminal justice," *Annual Editions of Criminal Justice*, 05/06: 43–50.

Sherman, L. W. (1978) *Scandal and Reform: Controlling Police Corruption*, Berkeley, CA: University of California Press.

Sheu, C. J. (2010) *Criminology*, Taipei: Shanmin Publishing (許春金, 2010。《犯罪學》, 台北: 三民書局).

Shi, Y. (2009) "A study of the state's accountability for using police weapon," *Journal of Central Police University*, 29(4): 23–47 (施源欽, 2009, 警械使用國家責任之研究,《警學叢刊》, 第39卷4期, 第23–47頁).

Shieu, C. (2007) *Police Misconduct and Accountability in Miaoli County Police Department*, MA Thesis, Taoyuan: Central Police University (謝志敏, 2007。《警察風紀課責之研究－以苗栗縣警察局為例》, 中央警察大學碩士論文).

Shih, C. (2010) *The Research of Police Corruption*, MA Thesis, Sanshia: National Taipei University (施嘉文, 2010。《警察人員貪污犯罪之研究》, 國立台北大學碩士論文).

Silvestri, M. (2007) "'Doing' police leadership: Enter the 'new smart macho'," *Policing and Society*, 17(1): 38–58.

Skogan, W. G. (2009) "Concern about crime and confidence about the police: Reassurance or accountability?" *Police Quarterly*, 12(3): 301–18.

Skolnick, J. (1966) *Justice without Trial: Law Enforcement in Democratic Society*, New York, NY: John Wiley.

Skolnick, J. (1994) *Justice Without Trial*, New York, NY: Macmillan.

Sparrow, M., Moore, M., and Kennedy, D. (1990) *Beyond 911: A New Era for Policing*, New York: Basic Books.

Stack, S. and Cao, L. (1998) "Political conservatism and confidence in the police: A comparative analysis," *Journal of Crime and Justice*, 21(1): 71–6.

Statistical Yearbook of Interior (2012) Available online: sowf.moi.gov.tw/stat/year/list.htm [accessed August 2013].

Stevens, D. (2001) "Community policing and managerial techniques: Total Quality Management Techniques," *Police Journal*, 74: 26–41.

Stoddard, E. (1979) "Organizational norms and police discretion: An observational study of police work with traffic violators," *Criminology*, 17(2): 159–71.

Stoutland S. (2001) "The multiple dimensions of trust in resident/police relations in Boston," *Journal of Research in Crime and Delinquency*, 38: 226–56.

Su, Z., Zhao, H., and He, J. (2013) "Authoritarianism and contestation," *Journal of Democracy*, 24(1): 26–40.

Sun, I. (2003) "A comparison of police field training officers' and non-training officers' resolution styles: Controlling versus supportive strategies," *Police Quarterly*, 6: 22–50.

Sun, I. (2007) "Policing domestic violence: Does officer gender matter?" *Journal of Criminal Justice*, 35(6): 581–95.

Sun, I. Y. and Chu, D. (2006) "Attitudinal differences between Taiwanese and American police officers," *Policing*, 29(2): 190–210.

Sun, I. and Chu, D. (2008a) "Gender differences in policing: An analysis of Taiwanese officers" attitudes," *Police Practice and Research: An International Journal*, 9: 431–43.

Sun, I. and Chu, D. (2008b) "A comparison of occupational attitudes between Taiwanese and American police officers," *International Journal of Police Science and Management*, 10: 36–50.

Sun, I. and Chu, D. (2008c) "A cross-national analysis of female police officers' attitudes in the United States and Taiwan," *International Criminal Justice Review*, 18: 5–23.

Sun, I. and Chu, D. (2009) "Rural v. urban policing: A study of Taiwanese officers' occupational attitudes," *The Police Journal*, 82: 222–46.

Sun, I. and Chu, D. (2010) "Who is better suited for handling domestic violence: A comparison between Taiwanese female and male officers," *Journal of Criminal Justice*, 38: 453–9.

Sun, I. and Payne, B. (2004) "Racial differences in resolving conflicts: A comparison between black and white police officers," *Crime and Delinquency*, 50: 516–41.

Sun, I., Jou, S., Hou, C., and Chang, Y. (2013a) "Public trust in the police in Taiwan: A test of instrumental and expressive models," *Australia and New Zealand Journal of Criminology*, available online: http://anj.sagepub.com/content/early/recent [accessed january 27, 2014].

Sun, I., Wu, Y., and Hu, R. (2013b) "Public assessments of the police in rural and urban China: A theoretical elaboration and empirical investigation," *British Journal of Criminology*, 53: 643–64.

Sun, I. Y., Wu, Y., Huang, L., Lin, Y., Li, J. C. M., and Su, M. (2012) "Preferences for police response to domestic violence: A comparison of college students in three Chinese societies," *Journal of Family Violence*, 27: 133–44.

Sung, H. E. (2006) "Police effectiveness and democracy: Shape and direction of the relationship," *Policing*, 29: 347–67.

Sung, H. E. (2009) "Transnational corruption in weapons procurement in East Asia: A case analysis," *Sociological Focus*, 42(3): 254–75.

Tao, J. (2010) "Trust within democracy: A reconstructed Confucian perspective," in Kampor Yu, Julia Tao, and Philip J. Ivanhoe (eds.), *Taking Confucian Ethics Seriously*, Albany, NY: SUNY Press, pp. 99–122.

Tarng, M. Y., Hsieh, C. H., and Deng, T. J. (2001) "Personal background and reasons for choosing a career in policing: An empirical study of police students in Taiwan," *Journal of Criminal Justice*, 29(1): 45–56.

Taylor, J. (2000) *The Generalissimo's Son*, Cambridge, MA: Harvard University Press.

The China Post (2012, April 27) "Police accused of foreign worker assault cover-up," available online: http://www.chinapost.com.tw/taiwan/national/national-news/2012/04/27/339212/Police-accused.htm [accessed January 27, 2014].

The Control Yuan (2009) *The Official Report of Control Yuan* (2663). Taipei: The Control Yuan, available online: www.cy.gov.tw [accessed January 27, 2014] (監察院, 2009。《監察院公報》, 2663期, 12頁).

Tien, H. (1975) "Taiwan in transition: Prospects for social-political change," *China Quarterly*, 64 (December): 615–44.

Tien, H. (1989) *The Great Transition: Political and Social Change in the Republic of China*, Stanford, CA: Stanford University Press.

Tien, H. M. and Cheng, T. J. (1999) "Crafting democratic institutions," in S. Tsang and H. M. Tien (eds.), *Democratization in Taiwan*, Hong Kong: Hong Kong University Press, pp. 23–48.

Tocqueville, A. (2000) *Democracy in America*, edited and translated by H. C. Mansfield and D. Winthrop, Chicago: The University of Chicago Press.

TPC (2014) *Educational Goals and Perspectives*, available online: http://www.tpa.edu.tw/eng/03_egp.htm [accessed January 9, 2014].

Tsai, D. and Yang, S. (1999) "The public's demands on community policing," *Journal of Criminology*, 4: 1–52 (蔡德輝、楊士隆, 1999年。社區警察因應民眾對治安需求之研究。《犯罪學期刊》, 4期: 1–52頁).

Tsai, S. (2011) *Research on the Adaptability of Field Female Police Officers*, MA Thesis, Taipei: National Taipei University (蔡淑琳, 2011。《外勤女警執行警察勤務適應問題之研究》, 國立台北大學碩士論文).

Tsai, T. (1982) "A study of police corruption," *National Taiwan University Law Journal*, 12(1): 1–48 (蔡墩銘, 1982。警察貪瀆問題之研究。《台大法學論叢》, 12期1卷, 1–48頁).

Tsang, S. (1999) "Transforming a party state into a democracy," in S. Tsang and H. Tien (eds.), *Democratization in Taiwan*, Hong Kong: Hong Kong University Press, pp. 1–21.

Tsao, E. (1983) *A Study of Work Pressure of Taiwanese Rank-and-File Officers*, MA Thesis, Taoyuan: The Central Police University (曹爾忠, 1983,《臺灣地區基層警(隊)員工作壓力之研究》, 碩士論文, 中央警察大學警政研究所).

Tyler, T. (2002) "A national survey for monitoring police legitimacy," *Justice Research and Policy*, 4: 71–86.

Tyler, T. and Huo, Y. (2002) *Trust in the Law: Encouraging Public Cooperation with the Police and Courts*, New York: Russell Sage Foundation.

Unger, R. M. (1998) *Democracy Realized: The Progressive Alternative*, London: Verso.

US Department of State (2006) *Trafficking in Person Report: 2006 Report Taiwan*, Washington, DC: US Department of State.

Van Maanen, J. (1974) "Working the street: A developmental view of police behavior," in H. Jacob (ed.), *The Potential of Reform of Criminal Justice*, Beverly Hills, CA: Sage, pp. 88–130.

Vanstone, A. (2001) "No longer 'lady policemen': The changing role of women in law enforcement in Australia," *Forum on Crime and Society*, 1(2): 119–28.

Walker, S. (1999) *The Police in America: An Introduction*, Boston: McGraw-Hill.

Walker, S. and Katz, C. M. (2002) *The Police in America: An Introduction*, New York, NY: McGraw-Hill.

Wang, A. (2008) "Modern women, traditional men," *Taiwan Review*, 58(4). Available online: http://taiwanreview.nat.gov.tw/ct.asp?xItem=30734&CtNode=1337&mp=1 [accessed January 27, 2014].

Wang, J. (2012a) "Essential translation of 'The model speech patterns of police officers in Taiwanese'," *Police Forum*, 3: 37–42 (王建成, 2012a。"警察官对民众台语训话要范" 译粹,《警专论坛》, 3期: 37–42頁).

Wang, J. (2012b) "Records of police speech in Taiwanese during the Japanese occupation," *Police Forum*, 5: 34–42 (王建成, 2012b。日治时期警察官对民众"台语训话要范"实纪,《警专论坛》, 5期: 34–42頁).

Wang, K. (2011) "A survey study on judicial police's anti-human trafficking in Taiwan," *Journal of Homeland Security and Border Management*, 15: 163–210 (王寬弘, 2011。我國司法警察防制人口販運執行意見實證調查。《國土安全與國境管理學報》15期, 163–210頁).

Wang, K. H. (2010) "A survey study on police's anti-trafficking action in Taiwan," *Journal of Homeland Security and Border Management*, 14: 69–110 (王寬弘, 2010。我國警察機關防制人口販執行作為意見之實證調查－以女性被性剝削案件為例。《國境警察學報》14期, 69–110頁).

Wang, T. Y. and Chang, G. A. (2006) "External treats and political tolerance in Taiwan," *Political Research Quarterly*, 59(3): 377–88.

Wang, Y. (2005) "An analysis on poverty of families with foreign/Chinese spouses in Taiwan," *NTU Social Work Review*, 4: 1–32 (王永慈, 2005。外籍與大陸配偶家庭之貧窮分析。《臺灣社會學刊》4期, 1–32頁).

Wang, Z. (2000) "The police system in the People's Republic of China," in O. N. I. Ebbe (ed.), *Comparative and International Criminal Justice Systems: Policing, Judiciary, and Corrections* (2nd ed.), Boston, MA: Butterworth-Heinemann, pp. 171–82.

Wang, Z. (2008) *Democratization in Confucian East Asia*, New York: Cambria Press.
Weber, M. (1947) [1922] *Theory of Social and Economic Organization*, translated by A. R. Anderson and Talcott Parsons, New York: Free Press of Glencoe.
Weber, M. (1951) *The Religion of China: Confucianism and Taoism*, translated and edited by Hans H. Gerth, Glencoe, IL: Free Press.
Wei, A. M. (2010) *Criminal Justice Responses to Domestic Violence Incidents*, PhD Dissertation, Central Police University, Taiwan: Taoyuan.
Weller, R. P. (1999) *Alternate Civilities: Democracy and Culture in China and Taiwan*, Boulder: Westview Press.
Welzel, C., Inglehart, R., Klingemann, H. (2003) "The theory of human development," *European Journal of Political Research*, 42(2): 341–80.
Weng, T. (2003) "The drinking behavior of police in Taiwan," *Research in Applied Psychology,* 18: 227–48 (翁萃芳, 2003。台灣員警人員的飲酒行為。《應用心理研究》, 18期, 227–48頁)
Wesley, W. (1970) *Violence and the Police*, Cambridge, MA: The MIT Press.
Whaley, G. L. and Tucker, S. H. (1998) "A theoretical integration of sexual harassment models," *Equal Opportunities International*, 17(1): 21–9.
White, S. (1972) "A perspective on police professionalization," *Law and Society Review*, 7: 61–85.
Wiatrowski, M. D. and Goldstone, J. A. (2010) "The ballot and the badge: Democratic policing," *Journal of Democracy*, 21(2): 79–92.
Williams, L. and Yu, M. K. (2006) "Domestic violence in cross-border marriage: A case study from Taiwan," *International Journal of Migration, Health and Social Care*, 2(3–4): 58–69.
Wilson, J. Q. (1968) *Varieties of Police Behavior*, Cambridge, MA: Harvard University Press.
Winckler, E. A. (1984) "Institutionalization and participation on Taiwan: From hard to soft authoritarianism?" *China Quarterly*, 99: 481–99.
Winterdyk, J. and Cao, L. (ed.) (2004) *Lessons of International/Comparative Criminology/Criminal Justice*, Toronto: de Sitter Publications.
Wong, K. (2005) "Law of assembly in China: People's Republic of China vs. Republic of China," *International Journal of the Sociology of Law*, 33: 215–45.
Worden, R. (1995a) "The causes of police brutality: Theory and evidence on police use of force," in A. William and H. Toch (eds.), *And Justice for All: Understanding and Controlling Police Abuse of Force*, Washington DC: Police Executive Research Forum, pp. 31–60.
Worden, R. (1995b) "Police officers' belief system: A framework for analysis," *American Journal of Police*, 14: 49–81.
Worrall, J. L., Ross, J. W., and McCord, E. S. (2006) "Modeling prosecutors" charging decisions in domestic violence cases," *Crime & Delinquency*, 52(3): 472–503.
Wu, K. (1999) "An exploratory empirical study of police ethics in the Republic of China," *Journal of Police Science,* 34: 55–104 (吳國清, 1999。我國警察倫理之探索與其實證之研究。《中央警察大學學報》, 34期, 55–104頁).
Wu, M. (2011a) "Aborigine governing," *Encyclopedia of Taiwan*, available online: http://taiwanpedia.culture.tw/en/content?ID=3719 [accessed August 17, 2013].
Wu, M. (2011b) "Five-year plan for governing Aborigines," *Encyclopedia of Taiwan*, available online: http://taiwanpedia.culture.tw/en/content?ID=3720 [accessed August 17, 2013].
Wu, M. (2011c) "Wushe Incident," *Encyclopedia of Taiwan*, available online: http://taiwanpedia.culture.tw/en/content?ID=3722 [accessed August 17, 2013].

Wu, T. (2010) "The impact of work stress and work value on Taiwanese police job satisfaction," *Journal of Police College*, 4: 127–42 (伍姿蓉, 2010, 警察人員工作壓力與工作價值觀影響職業滿意度之研究,《警專學報》, 第4卷8期, 第127–142頁).

Wu, X. (1985) "An analysis of special police culture," *Journal of Police Sciences*, 8: 43–55 (吳學燕, 1985, 警察特殊文化之研究,《警政學報》, 第8期, 第43–55頁).

Wu, X. (1990) "A discussion of police culture," *Journal of Police Science*, 17: 105–18 (吳學燕, 1985, 論警察文化,《警政學報》, 第17期, 第105–118頁).

Wu, X. (2002) *The Analysis of the Promotion of the ISP System in Police Departments*, MA Thesis, Taipei: National Taipei University (吳思陸, 2002,《警察機關推動ISO國際品質管理系統之研究》, 碩士論文, 台北大學公共行政暨政策學系).

Wu, Y. (1993) *The Study on the Influence of Police Organizational Culture on Decision-making Process in the R.O.C*, MA Thesis, Taoyuan: The Central Police University (吳耀南, 1993,《我國警察組織文化對其決策影響之研究》, 碩士論文, 中央警察大學警政研究所).

Wu, Y., Sun, I., and Smith, B. (2011) "Race, immigration and policing: Chinese immigrants' satisfaction with police," *Justice Quarterly*, 28: 745–74.

Wu, Y., Poteyeva, M., and Sun, I. (2012) "Public trust in police: A comparison between China and Taiwan," *International Journal of Comparative and Applied Criminal Justice*, 36: 189–210.

Wu, Z. and Cao, L. (2014) "Historical themes of crime and causation in China," in L. Cao, I. Sun, and B. Hebenton (eds.), *The Routledge Handbook of Chinese Criminology*, London: Routledge, pp. 3–15.

Wycoff, M. and Skogan, W. (1994) "The effect of a community policing management style on officers' attitudes," *Crime and Delinquency*, 40: 371–83.

Xi, X. (2012) *The Police and 2/28 Incidence*, Taipei: Shiying Press (习贤德, 2012:《警察与二二八事件》, 台北: 时英出版社).

Xia, Y., Tang, M., and Liu, F. (1996) "Zilu 13," in *The Interpretation of Four Books*, Nanchang: Jiangxi People's Press, pp. 208–20 (夏延章、唐满先、刘方元, 1996年。子路第十三,《四书今译》, 208–220页。南昌: 江西人民出版社).

Xu, Y., and Hua, Z. (2012) *Close Encounter with the Police Officers* (in Chinese), Hong Kong: Kaifang Press (徐友渔、华泽 (编), 2012年。《遭遇警察》。香港: 开放出版社).

Yan, S. (2012) "Some suggestions for police education and police services," *Police Forum*, 2: 2–7 (颜世锡, 2012年: 对于警察教育及勤务的一些建议。《警专论坛》, 2期: 2–7页).

Yang, G. (1995) *An Investigation of Police Work Pressure and Adaptation*, MA Thesis, Taoyuan: The Central Police University (楊國展, 1995,《警察工作壓力與適應之調查研究》, 碩士論文, 中央警察大學警政研究所).

Yang, L. R., Yen, H. F., and Chiang, Y. F. (2012) "A framework for assessing impacts of leadership competency on police project performance: Mediating role of job satisfaction and moderating role of project type," *Policing*, 35(3): 528–50.

Yang, S., Cheng, J., and Lou, W. (2010) *The Investigation of Victimization and Public Satisfaction with Government Efforts in Maintaining Law and Order for the First Half of 2010*. Chiayi, Taiwan: Crime Research Centre, National Chung Cheng University (楊士隆、鄭瑞隆、樓文達, 2010, 九十九年上半年度全國民眾犯罪被害暨政府維護治安施政滿意度調查, 國立中正大學犯罪研究中心).

Yang, Y. (1999) *An Analysis of Police Organization*, Taoyuan: Central Police University Press (杨永年, 1999。《警察组织剖析》, 桃园: 中央警察大学).

Yang, Y. (2000) "Taiwan's police force should be apolitical," *Taipei Times*, available online: http://www.taipeitimes.com/News/editorials/archives/2000/02/19/0000024726 [accessed July 29, 2013].

Yanhuang Chunqiu (2013a) "New Year's message" (新年贺词,《炎黄春秋》2013年, 第1期).

Yanhuang Chunqiu (2013b) "Constitutionalism is the consensus of political reform," 1: 1 (本刊编辑部, 2013. "宪法是政治体制改革的共识",《炎黄春秋》, 第一期).

Yeh, Y. (1999) "Policing by consent and partnership: A model of community policing in Taiwan," *Police Science Quarterly*, 30: 27–48 (葉毓蘭,1999, 以共識與同夥關係為基礎的新警政:臺灣的社區警政模式,《警學叢刊》, 第30卷1期, 第27–48頁).

Yeh, Y. (2004) "The evaluation of policewomen policy and its perspective," *Journal of Central Police University*, 41: 107–32 (葉毓蘭, 2004。女警政策回顧與前瞻。《中央警察大學學報》, 41期, 107–32頁).

Yeh, Y. and Li, Z. (2003) "The myths and reflections of 'one station, two systems': A review of specialized operation beat experiment in Taiwan," *Police Science Quarterly*, 33: 37–62 (葉毓蘭、李政峰, 2003,「一所兩制」的迷思與省思–臺灣地區試辦專責勤務區制度回顧,《警學叢刊》, 第33卷5期, 第37–62頁).

Yu, C., Chen, C., Juang, W., and Hu, L (2008) "Does democracy breed integrity? Corruption in Taiwan during the democratic transformation period," *Crime, Law and Social Change*, 49: 167–84.

Zhang, Q. (2011) "Chinese mission: Transiting toward constitutionality and remaking Chinese characters," *Leaders*, 42 (张千帆, 2011, "宪政转型与人格再造的中国使命",《领导者》, 总第42期).

Zhang, Y., Cao, L., and Vaughn, M. S. (2009) "Social support and corruption: Structural determinants of corruption in the world," *Australian and New Zealand Journal of Criminology*, 42(2): 204–17.

Zhao, J. (1996) *Why Police Organizations Change: A Study of Community-Oriented Policing*, Washington, DC: Police Executive Research Forum.

Zhao, J., Lovrich, N., and Thurman, Q. (1999) "The status of community policing in American cities," *Policing*, 22: 74–92.

Zhao, J., Herbst, L., and Lovrich, N. (2001) "Race, ethnicity and the female cop," *Journal of Urban Affairs*, 23: 243–57.

Zhao, J., He, N., and Lovrich, N. P. (2006) "The effect of local political culture on policing behaviors in the 1990s," *Journal of Criminal Justice*, 34: 569–78.

Zhao, J., Ren, L., and Lovrich, N.P. (2010) "Wilson's theory of local political culture revisited in today's police organizations," *Policing*, 33(2): 287–304.

Zhao, J., Ren, L., and Lovrich, N.P. (2013) "Political culture versus socioeconomic approaches to predicting police strength in US police agencies," *Crime & Delinquency*, 58(2): 67–95.

Zhao, R. and Cao, L. (2010) "Social change and anomie: A cross-national study," *Social Forces*, 88(3): 1209–29.

Zhu, J. (2001) "On police structural change," in K. Huang *et al.* (eds.), *Jingcha Xingzheng*, Taipei: Wu-nan (警察組織變革之研究).

Zhuang, D. (2001) "The police and public relationship," *Journal of the Central Police University*, 31(4): 111–36 (莊德森, 2001年。警察公共關係。《警學叢刊》, 31卷4期: 111–136頁).

Zimring, F. E., Hawkins, G., and Kamin, S. (2001) *Punishment and Democracy: Three Strikes and You're Out in California*, Oxford, Oxford University Press.

Index

Figures and tables are given in italics.

Aboriginal Control Principles 122
aboriginal peoples 118–25, 130–1, 154
Accord on Anti-crime Collaboration and Mutual Legal Assistance across the Strait 53–4
Act of Gender Equality in Employment (AGEE) 2002 106–7
airline hijackings 38
Ai Weiwei 150
Almond, G. A. 133, 139
Anti-Child-Prostitution Jog (November 1993) 123
Anti-hoodlum Law 1985 28
Anti-Spiritual Pollution Campaign 146
Aquino, Benigno Jr 146
"Arab Spring" 12
Article 100 (ROC Criminal Law) 32
Asian values 149, 151, 153
assemblies 36, *37*
Assembly Law 1988 32
Assembly Law 1992 34, 36
Associations of Police Friends 93

Banton, Michael xiv
baojia organization 27, 90
Barefoot Angel, The (film) 122
Barker, V. 142–3
Bayley, David xiv, 26, 61, 71, 78
Beitou Police Bureau 45
Bellah, R. 152
Bittner, E. 97
"black gold" 89
Black Gold Politics 93
Bo Yang 16
Brown, M. 79
Brown, R. A. 110
Bureau of Aboriginal Affairs 122
Business Process Re-engineering (BPR) 47

C3I Management Theory 27–8
Cai Dehui 24
Cai, S. 92
Cairo Declaration (1943) 5, 15
Cao, L. 115, 139–43
Central Police Academy 66, 69–70, 106; *see also* Central Police University
Central Police College 24; *see also* Central Police University
Central Police Officers' Academy 66
Central Police University (CPU): close relationship with NPA 98; cultivation of police supervisors 64–71; and females 107–8, *108*, 113–14; founding of 24–6, *24*; PCS commanding position essential 85; purpose of xvi, 61–2; represents residues of past regime 155; survey projects 137
certificate of indigenous culture and language examination 123–4
Chang, C. 22, 26, 36, 39, 40, 41, 47, 49, 50, 51, 124
Chang, W. 152
Chang, Y. 134, 138–9, 143
Chao, L. 17
Chen Guangcheng 150
Chen Hongshen 125
Chen Lianzhen 62
Chen Quanmei 105
Chen Shoushan 154
Chen Shuibian: criminal charges against 16, 99; democracy as "devolution" 153–4; elected leader in 2000 6, 11, 43; increased number of female officers 106; and interaction with China 53; leader of new ruling party 138; and meeting with Wu Zhenji 45; "new Taiwanese" slogan 119; rejected "Asian values" 149

Chen Youhao 54
Chiang Ching-Kuo: appointment as Minister of Defense 22; became premier in 1972 27; began process of democratic change 2, 6–7, 28; Confucian at heart 152; death of in 1988 30; enlightened, era-breaking leader 20–1; and Jiang Nan's biography 18; and the Korean War 27; legacy 119, 145–8; lifting of martial law 29, 30; slogan of "new Taiwanese" 119
Chiang Kai-Shek: Confucian at heart 152; considered police extension of military 23–4, 59; death of 2, 19; and dream of reunification 17; founder of PRC xv, 6, 15; police state a matter of rhetoric 149; political survival depended on military strength 22
Child Welfare Law 1993 32–3, 41
China: and "Asian values" thesis 149–50; and the CCP 148; changed by rapid economic development 152; cooperation in crime fighting 53–4; Democracy Wall Movement 146; and the DPP 44; and human trafficking 96–7; indicators of public safety and crime 134; lack of domestic violence prevention law 130; policing issues 8, 139, 140–2; relationship with Taiwan xvi, 2, 5–6, 37; wage gap with Taiwan 38
Chinese Communist Party (CCP) 6, 147–50, 152
"Chinese mentality" 151
Chinese People's Public Security University 66
Chu, C. 95
Chu, D. 77, 112–13
Chun Doo-hwan 146
Civil Organization Law 1991 32
Civil Service Administrative Neutrality Law 2009 46, 54
Cobb, Gail 81
coercive behavior 79–80
community policing 31, 38–41, 47–8, 75–6, 82, 110, 134, 156
Computer-Processed Personal Data Protection Law (1995) 94
Confucianism xvi, 10, 67, 103, 118, 134, 138, 151–2
Confucius 8, 135, 151
consumer scam crime 52
Control Yuan 60
Cooney, S. 46
Council of Grand Justices 15, 32, 34

Crank, J. 78, 81
Crime Investigation Police 124
crime rates 34–5, *35*
cultural exceptionalism 2
cultural theories 135

Dahl, Robert 153
Dai, M. 139–42
dangguo 15
dangwai movement 16, 19, 21, 30
democratic consolidation period 44
democratic policing xv, 3, 7, 26, 141–2
Democratic Progressive Party (DPP): attitudes toward unification 53; and Chen Youhao 54; election in 1991 6; exploiting pre-and post-1949 division 119; founding of 19–20, 30; gender equality agenda in police organizations 106; and nuclear power 154; political party orientation 138–9; in power 2000–8 2, 43, 46; and prostitution 95; and "territorial populism" 154
Deng Ruwen 127
Deng Xiaoping 20, 146–7, 149
domestic violence: and the 1998 Act 32, 34; and female officers 77, 110, 112–13, 117; and the police in a democracy 12; and socially disadvantaged groups 119, 121, 127–9, 131
Domestic Violence Prevention and Control Act 1998 32–3, 34, 41, 121
Dutton, M. R. 17, 149
DVPA 1998 127

Electronic Game Arcade Business Regulation Act 95
England and Wales 104
European Union 134
Examination Yuan 25, 46, 60, 63, 109, 114
Executive Yuan 46–7

Fahy, S. 127
fan (barbarians) 121
Fang Lizhi 147
Farrell, A. 127
FBI Academy 60
female officers 69–70, 77, 83, 103–17, *104*, 157
fengji (disciplinary problems) 88, 98
fenzusuo (FZS) 39
field training officers (FTO) 73
Finland 139
"Five Year Plan for Police Administration" 28

foreign brides 124
Forest and Nature Conservation Police Unit 123
Formosa Incident 1979 17–19, *18*, 146
Formosa Magazine 17–18
Frank, J. 110
Frankpledge system *see baojia* organization
free China 148

gambling 95–6
Gaoping Bridge collapse (2000) 96
gender equality 106–17; *see also* female officers
Gentarou Kodama 26–7
Giddens, Anthony 19
Giles, H. 142–3
globalization 125
GMD branches: Huang Fuxing 44; Liu Zhong-shin 41; Liu Zhongxing 44–5
Goldstein, H. 97
Gorbachev, Mikhail 147
Grabosky, P. 88, 90, 133
"grass eaters" 92
gravel truck industry 96
guanxi 99
Guomindang (GMD): and aboriginal peoples 122; arrival in Taiwan in 1945 xv, 27; and Chen Youhao 54; and Chiang Ching-Kuo 148; and controlled flow of news 29; and equal rights in political participation 119–20; establishment of Central Police Academy 65; and the Formosa Incident 18–19; and gender equality 105; and influence of Confucian values 152; its part in democratic transition 155; lifting of emergency decrees 20–1; loosening of press grip 19; and martial-law era 6–7, 44–5, 76; monopolization of power 15–17; and nuclear power 154; out of power in 2000 43; and the police 1–2, 21–2, 31, 41, 59, 148; political party orientation 138–9; and prostitution 95; recruitment of women police officers 69; relocation of criminal gangs 89; and the The Sunnist doctrine 25; totalitarian aspirations 149; withdrawal from police agencies 46; won presidential election in 2008 44
guoyu 16
Gwangju Democratization Movement 146

Hajek, C. 142–3
Hakka 154
Han 117–21: *benshengren* 119; *waishengren* 119

Han Han 141, 150
Hao Bochun 38, 114
He Enting 24
He, W. 150
Hebenton, B. 134, 143, 157
Hegel, Georg Wilhelm 150–1
heijin (black gold) 156
hoko system 26–7
homicide 53, 143, 157
Hong Kong 130
hongbao (red envelopes) 87
Hood, S. 154
Hou, C. 77, 87, 138–9, 142–3
Hou Youyi 51
Hsieh, M. 115
Hu Fuxiang 27, 62
Hu Jintao 152
Hu Yaobang 147
Huang, C. 137, 143
Huang, L. 111, 115, 129
Huang Shin-chieh 17
Huang, Y. 138–9
human trafficking 95–6, 124–7, 130
Hummert, M. 142–3
Huntington, S. P. 11

immigration 31, 38, 45, 120, 125–6
Immigration Act 1999 125
Immigration Bureau 125
Incident of Jiang Nan (1984) 89
inequality 104, 106–7, 116, 154–5
Inglehart, Ronald 152
inhibited political center 17, 150
institution-centered approaches 136
Investigation Bureau 98
ISO quality management certificate 49–50

Japan 4–5, 6–7, 39, 65, 121–2, 142, 149
Jesilow, P. 110
Jiang Nan 18, 146
Jiang Nan Incident (1984) 21
Jiang Zemin 152
Jiayi City Police Department 49–50
Jilong Police Bureau 45
Jingqinqu (JQQ) 39–40, 90
Jinmen Accord 38, 53
Jou, S. 87, 134, 138–9, 143
Judicial Yuan 15, 31
Juvenile Welfare Law 1989 32–3, 41

Kang Ningxiang 19
Kaohsiung Incident *see* Formosa Incident
Kennedy, B. L. 97
Knapp Commission (US) 92
koban system 6–7, 39, 84

Kong Lingcheng 24, 27
Kong Wenji 123

Lai, Y. 139–43
Law for Punishment of Police Offenses 1953 90
Lee, Y. 83
Legislative Yuan 7, 31, 34, 43, 127
Lei Zhen 16
Li Chengpeng 141, 150
Li Denghui 6, 16, 20, 30, 53, 149, 154
Li Shuangquan 125
Li Tai-an 125
Lian Zhan 43
Liberal democracy 7, 9, 153
lifan (aboriginal governance) 121
Lin A-qi 127
Lin, M. 122, 142–3
Lin Yishi 99, 112, 129
Lincoln, Abraham 151
Lipset, S. M. 133, 139
Liu, J. 111
Liu Binyan 147
Liu Xiaobo 141, 150, 152
Local Autonomy Statute 1999 34, 52, 71
Local Government Act 2010 98
Lovrich, N. P. 39
Lundman, R. J. 97
Luo Zhang 24, 28

Ma Yingjiu 11, 44–5, 107, 119–20
McBeath, G. 76
McDevitt, J. 127
Madison, Wisconsin, Police Department 48
Madsen, R. 152
Maier, C. S. 154
management-by-objectives (MBO) 48
Manning, P. K. 9–10, 25, 60, 81, 134
Mao Zedong 17, 146, 148–9
marriage 120–1, 124, 127, 129–31
martial law xv, 6, 11, 15–29, 30–1, 34, 41, 44, 106
Martin, Jeffery T. xvi, 7, 25, 28, 32, 81, 90, 91, 94, 97, 99, 136
Marx, Karl 150–1
"meat eaters" 92
Mencius 150
Miaoli Diubao Incident 124
Ministry of the Interior (MOI) 34, 114
Minnan 16
Mishler, W. 142
Mon, W. 45, 51, 54
Moody, P. R. Jr 151–2
Muir, W. 79

Municipal City Self Governance Statute 1994–9 98
Munro, J. L. 41
Myers, R. H. 17

National Anthem 26
National Chung Cheng University 67, 71, 156
National Immigration Agency (NIA) 125
National Police Agency (NPA): and community policing 39–40, 42; control of Taiwan Police College 62; dealing with specific types of crime 52; and domestic violence 34; and field stations 84; focus on law and order 44–5; functions within Ministry of Interior 59; funding of survey projects 137; and immigration 125; Kong Lingcheng appointed as Director-General 27; meeting with China's Minister of Public Security 54; and the military 24; one of two in Taiwan 21; and performance indicators 98; and "Police Gender Policy" 107, 109; and police misconduct 99; and promotion 71–2; quick leadership turnover ramifications 51, 55; recruitment of female officers 115; regulating extra-marital affairs 88; repressing snake/anti-slavery projects 124–5; supplemental funds for quality management plans 49; tendency to stifle creativity 156; tracking/recording police use of weapons 81; transfer of powers to in 1987 32; vehicle parts engraving program 52–3
National Security Council 15
National Security Law (NSL) 1987 31–2
National Taipei University 67, 70–1, 156
New York City Police Department (NYPD) 61–2, 92
Novak, K. J. 110

"obscurity" 81
Office of Foreign Affairs Police 124
Okinawa 4

paichusuo (PCS): basic unit of police organization 39, 90; culture of 84–5; and female officers 106, 109, 112–13, 116; main tactics of 42; and martial law 27–9; and police misconduct 99; police officers living in 78; training in 63; unique culture of 11
Paoline, E. A. 110
parades 36, *37*
Park Chung-hee 146

Park Jong-chul 147
Parsons, D. 110
patrol and watch system 39
Peace Preservation Police Corps (PPPC), Fourth and Fifth 34, 36
Peel model xiv
Peel, Sir Robert 9
Peng, Y. 93
People's Public Security University (China) 155
People's Republic of China (PRC) 6, 124
"performance first" 98
Pi-Ya Lew 116
"pink-ghettos" 106–7
Pinuyumayan tribesmen 123
Police Affairs Committees 156
police field stations (PCS) 49
Police Law 1953 27
"Police Modernization Movement" 27–8
Policing: administrative police 90; challenges 145–8; civil-police relations 23; community 38–42, 48, 82, 90, 156; confidence in 132–44; during democratic transition 30–8; female officers 69–70, 77, 83, 103–17, 104; high (undemocratic) 8–9, 44, 59, 81, 139–40; integration of female officers 12; low (democratic) 8–9, 44, 59, 81, 139–40, 157; misconduct/corruption 87–99; in the new century 44–55; operational culture of 73–82; organizational culture of 82–6; promotion 68–72; security police 90; socially disadvantaged groups 118–31; training 11, 59–68, 69–72; under martial law 15–29
Political Donations Act 99
polls 137–8
Poteyeva, M. 110, 139, 141–3
Potsdam Conference (1945) 5, 15
Property Declaration by Public Servants Act 99
prostitution 95–6, 122–3, 130
protection orders 128–9
Province and County Self Governance Statute 1994–9 98
Punch, M. 92, 99
Punishment of Police Offences Law 25, 31–2
Pye, L. W. 2, 149, 154

Quality Circles (QCs) 47–8
Quality Control Circle (QCC) 49
Qin, H. 150
Qing dynasty 4, 154

racism 74, 118
Rainbow Project (Presbyterian Church) 122
Rawls, John 9
Reiss, A. 97
Relations between the People of the Taiwan Area and the Mainland Area Act 38
Republic of China (ROC) 6, 60, 152–3
Research Development and Evaluation Commission 134
Rose, R. 142
Rustow, D. A. 149

SAFE project (2004) 51
St. Louis County Police Department (US) 110
Sakuma Samata 122
Sam Houston State University (US) 67
San-min Doctrine 25
security: agencies 89; agents 150; apparatus 1
Seediq Bale (film) 121
Seediq people 121
Sellin, T. 121
Sen, A. 3
sexual exploitation 125–6
sexual harassment 115, 117, 157
Shang, H. H. 111
Shelley, L. 130
Sherman, L. 97, 110, 138
Shi, Y. 82
Shimpei Goto 27
Sino-British Joint Declaration on Future of Hong Kong (1984) 146
slavery 124
snakeheads 124–5
Social Order Maintenance Act 1991 32, 90
South Korea 142, 146, 149, 155
Southern Weekend Journal 150
Soviet Union 1, 7, 9
Special Police Fourth and Fifth Headquarters *see* Peace Preservation Police Corps (PPPC), Fourth and Fifth
Stack, S. 138, 142, 143
Straightening Project 122
Sullivan, W. M. 152
Sun, I. Y. 77, 87, 110, 112–13, 138–9, 141–3
Sun Yat-sen 7, 21–2, 25, 60
Sung, H. E. 139, 144
Swidler, A. 152

Taidong County Police Department 49–50
Taipei City Police Department 69, 111, 123

Taipei Women's Police Squad 106
Taiwan: challenges 145–8; confidence in the police 137–42; cross-national public opinions 135; deep-seated national traditions in policing 61; and democracy 44, 153; dominant social forces in 132–3; history of 4–8, 11; "homegrown" democracy 149; international/regional cooperation in crime fighting 53; large wage gap with China 38; and liberal democracy 153–7; low power distance society 138; map of 5; never a fully Leninist society 17; perception of police misconduct widespread in 98–9; police organizational culture 81–3; post-Confucian society 10, 29, 45–6, 54, 60, 88, 91, 99, 103; strained relationship with China 44; trafficking in 124; transformed into new democracy 28; ubiquitous clientele networks 91; underground businesses 95–6
Taiwan Garrison Command (TGC) 15, 32, 154
Taiwan Investigation Bureau 68
Taiwan Police Academy 62
Taiwan Police College (TPC) xvi, 25, 61–5, 62, 68, 70–1, 107–8, 113–14, 155
Taiwan Provincial Police Academy 62
Taiwan Provincial Police Training Center 27, 62, *see also* Taiwan Police College
Taiwan Social Change Survey 2004 152
Taizhong County Police Department 49–50
Tang Yingshen 122
telephone fraud 52
Temporary Provisions 1948 15, 25
Terrill, W. 110
theft 44, 51–2, 55, 123
"thin blue line" 7–8
third wave of democratization 1, 10
Three Anti-Violence Act 106
Tipton, S. M. 152
Tocqueville, A. 150, 154
Total Quality Management (TQM) 47–8
Trafficking in Persons Report 2006 124
Treaty of Shimonoseki (1895) 5

United Kingdom 114–15, 143
United Nations 17
United States: cross-national public opinions 135; highest police ranking 142–3; and misconduct/corruption 92, 97–8; no unified policing system 59–60; police culture 77–9, 81–5; police promotion 71–2; police training in 67;

replacement of police weight/height requirements 63; team policing 50; and trafficking in Taiwan 124; women police officers 104, 110–11, 114

Vanstone, A. 116–17
Verba, S. 133, 139

Wang Jin-wang 45–6, 51
Wang, K. 126
Wang Minning 24
Wang Ruowang 147
Wang Zhuojun 51, 54
Weber, Max 2, 152
Wei, A. 128
Wei Desheng 121
Wei Jingsheng 141, 146
Weng Qinan 91
"White Terror" 7, 16, 20, 26
Wilson, J. Q. 74, 82, 98
Women and Children's Squad 106, 109
Women's Police Squad *see* Women and Children's Squad
Wong, K. 32
World Values Surveys 1995 138, 141–2
World Values Surveys 2005 142
Wu, X. 75–6, 78, 80
Wu, Y. 139, 141–3
Wu Zhenji 45
Wushe Incident 121

Xi Jinping 150
Xie Fen-Fen 113
Xie Yindang 51
Xu Zhiyong 150

Yan Shi-xi 24, 66
Yang, S. 132
Yanhuang Chunqiu (magazine) 150
Yeh, Y. 111
Yi-lan County Police Department 113
yuanzhumin see aboriginal peoples

Zhang, Q. 150
Zhang Siliang 51
Zhang Tongrong 91
Zhang, Y. 142–3
Zhao, J. S. 3, 7, 52, 74, 117, 134, 139–43, 157
Zheng Chenggong 4
Zhou Jucun 24
Zhou Renshen 95
Zhou Zhongfeng 24, 27
Zhuang Heng-dai 33